The Rise of Protestant
Evangelism in Ecuador,
1895–1990

Alvin M. Goffin

University Press of Florida
Gainesville · Tallahassee · Tampa · Boca Raton
Pensacola · Orlando · Miami · Jacksonville

Copyright 1994 by the Board of Regents of the State of Florida

Printed in the United States of America on acid-free paper

99 98 97 96 95 94 6 5 4 3 2 1

The words and music to "Waiting for a Miracle" were written by Bruce Cockburn. Copyright 1987 by Golden Mountain Music Corp. Taken from the album *Waiting for a Miracle*. Used by permission.

Library of Congress Cataloging-in-Publication Data

Goffin, Alvin Matthew.
    The rise of Protestant evangelism in Ecuador, 1895–1990/Alvin Matthew Goffin.
        p.   cm.
    Includes bibliographical references and index.
    ISBN 0-8130-1260-0 (cloth: alk. paper)
    1. Missions, American—Ecuador—Controversial literature.
    2. Evangelistic work—Ecuador—Controversial literature.
    3. Protestant churches—Ecuador—Controversial literature.   4. World Radio Missionary Fellowship.   5. Summer Institute of Linguistics.
    6. World Vision International.   7. Ecuador—Church history—19th century.   8. Ecuador—Church history—20th century.   I. Title.
    BV2853.E2G64   1994
    266'.023708—dc20   93-36886

The University Press of Florida is the scholarly publishing agency for the State University System of Florida, comprised of Florida A & M University, Florida Atlantic University, Florida International University, Florida State University, University of Central Florida, University of Florida, University of North Florida, University of South Florida, and University of West Florida.

University Press of Florida
15 Northwest 15th Street
Gainesville, FL 32611

To my mother,
in loving memory

———————————

CONTENTS

Contents

PREFACE

I FIRST EXPERIENCED Ecuador in August 1972, arriving with my wife to visit her family. I returned on summer vacations in 1974 and 1976 and to live in 1978. My initial view of Ecuador was one of overwhelming wonder. As a product of the urban confines of New York City, I never had seen anything to compare to it in natural beauty. In Quito, where we stayed, the panoramas are magnificent. The region has majestic snow-capped volcanoes, lush green valleys, a deep-blue sky, crystal-clear air, and billowing white clouds.

On that first trip, I traveled throughout the country and learned much about the Ecuadorean people and culture. Among the places I visited was the city of Esmeraldas on the Pacific coast. An important port inhabited mostly by descendants of ex-slaves, Esmeraldas is home to a vibrant brand of marimba music and an oil refinery that serves as the terminal of the pipeline crossing the Andes from the eastern jungle to the Pacific. This pipeline is an important achievement and the vein through which the lifeblood of Ecuador flows. On a tour of the refinery, an engineer-guide explained how petroleum would help develop Ecuador. This new boom, like the earlier cacao and banana booms, was expected to transform the country. The guide's words were inspiring, and in that moment of hope, no one present doubted that what he suggested would fail to come about.

As the history of Ecuador since 1972 demonstrates, however, the country's development has been a long, difficult process that is far from complete. It was slowed by the external-debt problems of the 1980s. As it turned out, petroleum was a blessing, but it was also a curse that sapped the traditional spirit of the Ecuadorean people. It gave the pretense of development, not the reality. The material wealth produced by black gold never touched the lives of the overwhelming majority of Ecuadoreans.

Preface

The idea for this book came during the years that I lived in Ecuador. Its conception was linked to my observation that Protestant churches and tent revivals were conspicuous wherever I traveled. At that time the general reaction of the Ecuadorean people to this phenomenon was surprise and curiosity; how could Protestantism make inroads in Ecuador, a country where people were traditionally Catholic? In the view of many people, Quito's San Diego Cemetery, which I saw on All Souls' Day, provided an accurate metaphorical representation of the country's socioeconomic structure. On that holiday thousands of Ecuadoreans, very traditional Catholics, came to spend the day picnicking near their departed loved ones. San Diego Cemetery could be said to represent the conservatism of Ecuador and its semifeudal class system, which prevailed in death as in life. The poor were buried in the ground, the middle class in high-rise wall tombs, and the rich in lavishly decorated mausoleums. On the surface it seemed impossible that this conservative, multitiered society could ever truly accept new religious doctrines. Viewed another way, however, San Diego Cemetery made it clear why the society was ripe for religious change. From the perspective of the harsh economic realities of the Ecuadorean people, amply shown in the graves at San Diego, the growth of Protestantism was easier to understand.

On another level, the conception of this book was connected to the author's personal relationships. Because of my marriage to an Ecuadorean, I witnessed firsthand the nature of Ecuadorean religiosity and the contradictions it fostered. My mother-in-law is a strong believer in Catholicism; there is no other religion that she can faithfully follow. Her faith, however, was not instilled in her children. When I first met them, in the early 1970s, they, like most of the youth in Latin America, believed more in Che Guevara and Fidel Castro than in Jesus Christ. For them, Catholicism represented superstition and the injustices of the past. Their generation espoused revolutionary notions that frightened the dominant elite classes, who wanted to curb the radical wave. Part of their answer was to use North American fundamentalist Protestantism increasingly as a means to abort revolutionary undercurrents. From the 1960s to the 1980s, Protestant groups entered the country and heeded the call to battle against the leftist fringe.

This book, the result of much contemplation, research, writing, and experience, is my attempt to put the history of Protestant evangelism in Ecuador in perspective. Behind this objective is the desire to educate readers on the timeliness and importance of the book's complex theme. It is an attempt also to furnish historical insights on Ecuador, a country that in the past has been neglected by historians of Latin America. While I make no pretense that the findings I have elaborated here represent a definitive analysis, I have tried to impart new knowledge and to contribute to recent literature on the issue of Protestant growth in Latin America.

Acknowledgments are in order for all those who assisted in this endeavor. In the United States, my deepest appreciation goes first to those at Florida State University who gave their time, constructive criticism, and moral support. Most important, thank-yous go to Darrell E. Levi, Rodney D. Anderson, Morton D. Winsberg, and Neil Betten. The same goes to Ralph Della Cava and Ron Schneider of the City University of New York, who furthered my interest in Latin America through their excellent teaching and scholarship. Also, I thank Ray Mohl of Florida Atlantic University, who gave me the opportunity to teach Latin American history when I returned to the United States in 1985. Finally, an expression of gratitude is in order to Frank MacDonald Spindler and John D. Martz for reading the manuscript and making pertinent suggestions for its improvement. Likewise, thanks to Dick Crepeau of the University of Central Florida for assisting with technical details.

In Ecuador, my appreciation goes to Polibio Cordova of the Centro de Estudios y Datos (CEDATOS) for his counsel and direction; to the late Washington Padilla for his kindness in granting an interview; to Irwin Zapater of the Banco Central for arranging the use of the bank's archives and periodical collection; to friends and acquaintances including Simón Espinosa, José Pereira, José Zurita, Joe Brenner, and Moritz Thomsen; and to the many centers of investigation that opened their doors to me. Among them must be mentioned: the Centro de Estudios y Difusión Social (CEDIS), the Centro de Planificación y Estudios Sociales (CEPLAES), the Centro Internacional de Estudios Superiores de Comunicación para América Latina (CIESPAL), and the Centro de Investigaciones y Estudios Socio-Económicos (CIESE).

Also, a special thank-you to those closest to me: Gerry, María Luisa, Nelson, Alba, Maggie, Bolívar, Edgar, Vicente, Jonathan, Ana, and Erik. In the traditional sense of Latin America and its people, they are my extended family. Finally, and most importantly of all, my deepest appreciation goes to my wife Olivia who, true to her Ecuadorean nature, provided tranquillity, understanding, and love. Without her, this book never would have been written.

ABBREVIATIONS

AID   Agency for International Development

AIECH   Asociación Indígena Evangélica de Chimborazo (Association of Indigenous Evangelicals of Chimborazo)

BPC   Brazil para Cristo (Brazil for Christ)

CAM   Central American Mission

CARE   Cooperative American Relief Everywhere

CBN   Christian Broadcasting Network

CCC   Christian Center of Communications

CCI   Confraternidad Cristiana de Iglesias (Christian Brotherhood of Churches)

CEB   Ecclesial Base Community

CED   Center for Evangelism and Discipleship

CEDEN   Comité Evangélico de Desarrollo y Emergencia Nacional (Evangelical Committee of Development and National Emergency)

CEDHU   Comisión Ecuménica de Derechos Humanos (Ecumenical Human Rights Commission of Ecuador)

CEDOC   Confederación Ecuatoriana de Obreros Católicos (Ecuadorean Confederation of Catholic Workers)

CEE   Confraternidad Evangélica Ecuatoriana (Ecuadorean Protestant Brotherhood)

CELAM   Consejo Episcopal Latinoamericano (Latin American Episcopal Conference)

CEPE   Corporación Estatal Petrolera Ecuatoriana (Ecuadorean State Petroleum Corporation)

CIA   Central Intelligence Agency

CLAI   Consejo Latinoamericano de Iglesias (Latin American Council of Churches)

CMA	Christian and Missionary Alliance
CMS	Christian Medical Society
CONAIE	Confederación de Nacionalidades Indígenas del Ecuador (Confederation of Indigenous Nations of Ecuador)
CONFENIAE	Confederación de Nacionalidades Indígenas de la Amazonia Ecuatoriana (Confederation of Indigenous Nations of the Ecuadorean Amazon)
DRI	Secretaria de Desarrollo Rural Integral (Office of the Secretary of Integrated Rural Development)
ECUARUNARI	Runacunapac Riccharimi (Indigenous Masses Awake)
ELN	Army of the National Liberation
FEPP	Fondo Ecuatoriano Populorum Progresso (Ecuardorean "Populorum Progressio" Foundation)
FGBMFI	Full Gospel Businessmen's Fellowship International
FICI	Federación Indígena y Campesina de Imbabura (Indigenous Peasant Federation of Imbabura)
FODERUMA	Fondo de Desarrollo Rural Marginal (Rural Development Fund)
GMU	Gospel Missionary Union
HCJB	Heralding Christ Jesus' Blessings
IBEC	International Basic Economy Corporation
ILV	Instituto Lingüístico de Verano (Summer Institute of Linguistics)
IPC	International Petroleum Corporation
JAARS	Jungle Aviation and Radio Services
LTI	Leadership Training Institute
MAF	Missionary Aviation Fellowship
MAP	Medical Assistance Program
MARC	Missions Advanced Research Communications Center
MIC	Movimiento Indígena de Cotopaxi (Indigenous Movement of Cotopaxi)
NACLA	North American Congress on Latin America
NBC	National Broadcasting Company
OPEC	Organization of Petroleum Exporting Countries
PACS	Program Automatic Control System
SDA	Seventh-Day Adventists

SERPAJ	Servicio Paz y Justicia (Peace and Justice Service)
SIL	Summer Institute of Linguistics
SVM	Student Volunteer Movement
UFCO	United Fruit Company
UNAE	Unión de la Amazonía Ecuatoriana (Ecuadorean Amazon Native Union)
UNELAM	Movimiento Pro-Unidad Evangélica Latinoamericana (Provisional Commission for Latin American Evangelical Unity)
WBT	Wycliffe Bible Translators
WCC	World Council of Churches
WJBT	Where Jesus Blesses Thousands
WRMF	World Radio Missionary Fellowship
YFC	Youth For Christ
YMCA	Young Men's Christian Association

INTRODUCTION

THE YEAR 1990 brought an important development in Protestantism in Ecuador. In April a Protestant relief and development agency, the Christian Medical Society (CMS), entered the Sierra province of Chimborazo with a contingent of eighty North Americans, offering health care to indigenous people in exchange for religious conversion. Chimborazo, historically a battleground between North American–backed fundamentalist Protestants and Catholics subscribing to neo-Marxian liberation theology, had been witness to many such comings since Protestantism first officially entered Ecuador in 1896. Ecuadorean critics of Protestantism in their country called the CMS health and evangelization campaign one more example of general long-term Protestant invasion.

The CMS, a fundamentalist group with offices in the United States and the Dominican Republic, professed to be a nondenominational, professional, ecumenical, and evangelical organization of doctors, dentists, and students. It came into Chimborazo with the approval of the Ecuadorean government, the provincial office of public health, and the regional military command. Before its arrival local indigenous church leaders told their congregations that North American Protestant doctors and specialists would be coming to give them medical attention free of charge. During the health campaign, known as "La Campaña de Atención de Salud," the CMS lavishly dispensed medicine, which led to general overconsumption and the intoxication of recipients. In one community an old woman died as a result of treatment by a CMS "specialist."[1]

The CMS health and evangelization campaign, apart from emphasizing rapid medical checkups and doling out medicine, brought with it the millennial message that the end of the world was at hand. The intent was to pacify the indigenous population, especially those involved in ongoing land conflicts with local hacienda owners. As evidence of the political aims of

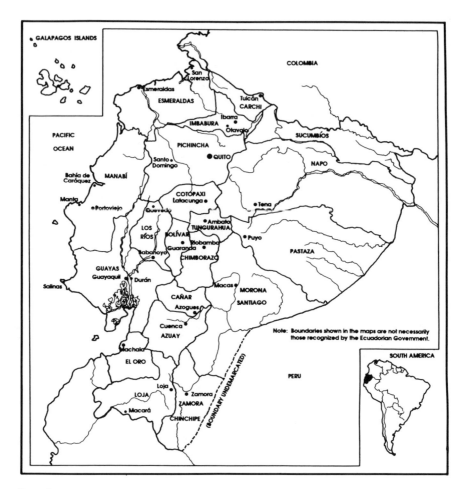

Ecuador

CMS and their ties to the hacienda owners, the North American Protestants took hundreds of photos and interviewed community leaders in an attempt to gather data on how they were organized politically and to ascertain what landholdings they possessed.[2]

The work carried on by the CMS alarmed many indigenous people in Chimborazo, who complained to the Ministry of Health. They asked why no national doctors were trained to confront health problems in the rural areas; whether or not it was legal for the state to delegate to foreigners the control and treatment of health problems in the country; and what agency of the government or the Ministry of Health verified and evaluated the Protestant health campaign. The indigenous people of Chimborazo and their representatives called on the Federación Nacional Médica (National Medical Federation) and the Federación de Médicos Rurales (Federation of Rural Doctors) to speak out against the Protestant intrusion.

Since the 1950s, North American fundamentalist Protestants of all denominations and categories have increasingly invaded Latin America to proselytize and convert its people. They have been successful; because of their efforts, Protestantism has grown markedly throughout Central America, the Caribbean, and most of South America. In 1949 the number of Protestants in Latin America totaled only 3,172,000. By 1961 the number had increased to 7,710,000 and, by 1980, to 28 million. In 1989 the Latin American Protestant population was estimated at 48 million out of a total of 480 million. They made up 20 percent of the population in Chile and Panama, 28 percent in El Salvador, and 33 percent in Guatemala. Two-thirds to three-fourths of these estimated 48 million Protestants adhered to Pentecostalism, a relatively new faith. In Brazil, the Pentecostal Assemblies of God alone claimed 6 million followers, and one locally rooted charismatic church had more than 20,000 members. It was also estimated that if current growth rates continued, Latin America would have a Protestant majority by the early twenty-first century.[3]

In Latin America the growth of Protestantism, especially Pentecostalism, has been viewed by many as a response to political, economic, and social turmoil in the region. Foreign debt, civil war in some countries, rapid urbanization, industrialization, and poverty have forced Latin Americans to turn to new forms of spirituality for comfort. The Protestant movement has attracted primarily the poor, and it competes, for the most part, with the traditional Catholic church and liberation theology. Liberation theologians have attempted to ward off the Protestant "threat" by establishing ecclesial base communities (CEBs), the political, economic, social, and educational units of the progressive church at the grass-roots levels. Liberation theology clergy and lay people hope to find options to the miserable conditions that characterize the daily life of the poor in Latin America. Protestants and Catholics are not always in conflict, however. In many Latin American countries, ecumenical Protestants adhere to the principles and practices of liberation theology while Pentecostal or Charismatic Catholics organize faith-healing crusades.[4]

Ecuador, like the rest of Latin America, has witnessed Protestant growth since the 1950s. In 1962 the Protestant community numbered only 13,000 followers out of a total population of 4.5 million. By 1986 that figure had increased to 250,000 out of a total population of more than 8 million. Forty percent of the Protestant population belonging to the Gospel Missionary Union (GMU) and the Christian and Missionary Alliance (CMA), both off-shoots of the United States fundamentalist movement of the late nineteenth and early twentieth centuries. Thirty percent adhered to Pentecostalism, which encompassed the Church of the Foursquare Gospel, the Assemblies of God, the United Pentecostal Church of Ecuador, and the many indepen-dent churches in the major urban and rural areas. The remaining 30 percent formed homegrown evangelical associations such as the GMU-inspired AIECH, the *Asociación Indígena Evangélica de Chimborazo* (Association of Indigenous Evangelicals of Chimborazo).[5] According to David Stoll, an anthropologist who has written extensively on Protestantism in Latin America, based on 1960–85 growth rates, evangelicals or conservative Protestants will make up 15.7 percent of Ecuador's total population by the year 2010.[6]

Protestant growth in Ecuador has affected important sectors of society. Throughout the 1980s the Catholic church, indigenous people, and nation-alists perceived Protestantism as a grave threat to Ecuadorean culture, tra-dition, and life. The Catholic church felt the loss of its dominion over religious matters and found itself in a struggle it thought it had won long ago. The Ecuadorean Catholic church's view corresponded to that ex-pressed in 1979 at Puebla, Mexico, at the Third General Latin American Bishops Conference. Participants in that conference spoke of an invasion of anti-Catholic sects that had come to Latin America to criticize the church and attempt to occupy its traditional role by evangelizing the least educated Catholics. Indigenous people worried about the North American funda-mentalist Protestant incursion, not so much out of fear of their own reli-gious conversion, but because they perceived it as a threat to their cultural and physical survival. For the three out of four indigenous people in Ecua-dor who were not Protestant, the intrusion represented a new wave in a five-hundred-year history of conquest and domination.

Nationalists were divided in their perceptions of the Protestant incur-sion. Some, including journalists, historians, and anthropologists, viewed it in the context of the Cold War in Latin America, a conspiracy sponsored by the United States Central Intelligence Agency (CIA) and Agency for International Development (AID) to rid the country of so-called subversive or Communist elements and to further an exploitative capitalist system.[7] They believed the Protestant surge was part of an anti-Communist crusade, a reaction to the Cuban Revolution of 1959, elaborated after the publication of the *Rockefeller Report on the Americas* in 1969. That official report of a U.S. presidential mission to Latin America, under the direction of Nelson A. Rockefeller, warned President Richard M. Nixon and the United States that the Alliance for Progress development program initiated during the administration of John F. Kennedy had failed to bring stability to the region and that the hemisphere was once again in the throes of violent political, economic, and social convulsions that threatened to produce "more Castros" in Latin America. Rockefeller called for the United States to take a fresh view of the region, and he put forth a list of specific recommendations for improving U.S.–Latin American relations. He proposed preferential trade treatment for Latin America and other underdeveloped regions; refinancing the foreign debt; and developing education, health, and housing. He also proposed the resumption of personal relationships between North and South Americans and called upon multilateral institutions and child-rearing programs to assist the U.S. government in subduing radical political doctrines in Latin America. While the *Rockefeller Report* did not mention any group by name, many Protestant relief agencies were involved in providing assistance.[8]

The visit of the Rockefeller mission met with a violent and profound nationalistic reaction throughout Latin America. It touched the sensibilities of many Ecuadoreans because Nelson Rockefeller and his family had long held economic interests in their country, notable among them Standard Oil of New Jersey and its subsidiary the Leonard Drilling Company, which initiated the search for oil in the Ecuadorean Oriente, the eastern rain forest, in 1920.[9] Furthermore, the report summoned unhappy memories of an earlier Rockefeller report, issued in 1949 during the "Banana Boom" presidency of Galo Plaza Lasso, who had ties to the United Fruit Company (UFCO). At that time Rockefeller's International Basic Economy Corporation (IBEC) drew up a blueprint that contained recommendations for development based on the continued fostering of UFCO's interests.[10]

Against the background of the Rockefeller reports, Ecuadorean nationalists cited CIA and AID links to specialized Protestant groups as evidence of a conspiracy in which they also implicated CARE, the Peace Corps, the Fulbright Commission, the University of Wisconsin's Land Tenure Center, and the universities of Pittsburgh, Texas, and Florida. The nationalists believed that the U.S. government and some Protestant groups compelled Ecuador to adopt agrarian reform laws in 1964 and 1974 that turned over to indigenous people and campesinos land that did not produce enough for their survival. As a result, these Andean peasants were forced to find work for wages on large haciendas, where they also could not survive. Ultimately they migrated to the Coast and the Oriente, where they caused a colonization crisis and experienced conflict with the people of those lowland regions.[11]

For other nationalists, however, the problem was not Protestantism itself but the North Americans who were its principal proponents. These nationalists regarded North American Protestants as cultural imperialists. The late Washington Padilla, a noted theologian, historian, and leader of the national Protestant church, thought that the recent Protestant influx from the United States and North American movies, television, music, and violence were aspects of cultural imperialism. He was less harsh than the conspiracy theorists, however, because he also believed that North American Protestantism provided much that was good, including help in health care, nutrition, and communications. However, his firsthand experience indicated that North American Protestants were closed-minded and preferred to live apart from Ecuadorean society. Padilla related that during his years as the director of Spanish programming at the evangelical HCJB radio station, North American Protestants kept him subordinate. Their prevailing view was that North Americans were managers and Ecuadoreans laborers. In sum, Padilla believed that the North American variety of Protestantism damaged Ecuadorean values related to family, education, and love of country.[12]

As recent history has demonstrated, the issue of Protestant evangelism in Ecuador is important for all of Latin America. First, because of its diminutive size and its distinct ecological zones of Coast, Sierra, and Oriente, Ecuador serves as a laboratory from which to study Protestant growth elsewhere. Ecuador's Coast offers insights into littoral areas throughout Latin America; its Sierra parallels the highland reaches of Central America and Mexico; and its Oriente compares to tropical rain forests in Brazil, Peru, Colombia, and Venezuela. In Ecuador, all the historical, sociopolitical, and economical effects of climate and environment on people and their religious practices in Latin America can be viewed in one country.

A second reason Ecuador is an important country in which to examine Protestant evangelism is its multiethnic nature. Indigenous people make up approximately 40 percent of the population, and all aspects of society—food, music, dress, attitudes toward family and community—are drawn largely from native culture. It therefore provides an opportunity to investigate the cultural clash between Protestant evangelists from what is generally regarded as a highly developed society and the so-called primitive people of an underdeveloped, predominantly indigenous one. In such a setting, the success or failure of Protestant evangelism becomes the ultimate test of will for both societies.

Chapter 1 of this book presents the historical setting into which Protestantism arrived in Ecuador. It examines the colonial period, the Liberal-Conservative struggles of the nineteenth century, and the Revolution of 1895. Chapter 2 describes the early Protestant groups, traces their roots, and determines where and how they progressed. Chapters 3 to 6 analyze the specialized Protestant groups that entered between the 1930s and 1990, assess their importance, and consider the issues that surrounded them. Chapter 3 is a discussion of radio station HCJB and its parent organization, the World Radio Missionary Fellowship (WRMF). It posits that HCJB is significant because its transmission of Protestant doctrine by radio helped pave the way for the spread of Protestantism throughout Latin America. Chapters 4 and 5 study the Summer Institute of Linguistics (SIL), an organization that is world renowned because of its proselytizing under the guise of such scholarly endeavors as Bible translation and linguistic studies. In Ecuador, the SIL was controversial because of the help it gave to the Ecuadorean government and petroleum companies in removing the Huaorani Indians from lands rich in oil. Chapter 6 describes the fundamentalist world development organization World Vision and its projects in the Ecuadorean Sierra provinces of Imbabura and Chimborazo. World Vision had links to the CIA and AID; in the 1980s, however, it claimed to have almost completely disassociated itself from any U.S. government agency.

Chapter 7 surveys the dramatic growth of Pentecostalism in what has been termed a mother-daughter pattern from 1950 to 1990. This growth alarmed those who saw themselves as the targets of the latest Protestant move, principally the Catholic church and indigenous people. Chapter 8 studies the responses of the Catholic church and demonstrates how many in the church turned toward liberation theology as a means to repel the Protestant invasion. Chapter 9 deals with the ways indigenous people responded and how they organized themselves into a confederation that worked to ensure their cultural and physical survival. The conclusion considers, in general terms, the significance of Protestant evangelism for Ecuador, Latin America, and the international community.

This book is a history of Protestant evangelism in Ecuador from 1895 to 1990. It recounts the factors behind Protestantism's growth and its overall effects on Ecuadorean society and tradition. It is structured chronologically and thematically and focuses on the most important Protestant groups: their histories, accomplishments, failures, and motivations. In addition, it analyzes the responses of Ecuador's Catholic church, indigenous people, and nationalists and attempts to answer some pertinent questions. For example, did the entrance of Protestantism signify real change? If so, what kind? Which sectors of society were most receptive to Protestant ideology? Were the Protestants sincere missionaries, imperialists, or both?

Because of the broad nature of the topic, this discussion also treats a number of important related issues: imperialism, nationalism, ecology, cultural survival, external debt, and U.S.–Latin American relations. In some measure it deals with the facts and controversies surrounding these issues in Ecuador and Latin America. Protestantism brought not only a religious intrusion but also a vast change that touched all aspects of culture and life. Because of this, the reader must gain a thorough historical foundation in order to understand how that change came about and what it portends for the future. If this book furthers such an understanding, it will have accomplished its mission.

WAITING FOR A MIRACLE

Look at them working in the hot sun
the pilloried saints and the fallen ones
working and waiting for the night to come
and waiting for a miracle

Somewhere out there is a place that's cool
where peace and balance are the rule
working toward the future like some kind of mystic jewel
and waiting for a miracle

You rub your palm
on the grimy pane
in the hope that you can see
You stand up proud
you pretend you're strong
in the hope that you can see
like the ones who've cried
like the ones who've died
trying to set the angel in us free
while they're still waiting for a miracle

Struggle for a dollar, scuffle for a dime
step out from the past and try to hold the line
so how come history takes such a long, long time
When you're waiting for a miracle.

Bruce Cockburn
Managua, January 1986

CHAPTER 1

The Historical Setting

OFFICIALLY, PROTESTANTISM CAME to Ecuador in the wake of the Liberal Revolution of 1895. It entered a world in which religion had played an important role in history since Spain first began its conquest of the region in 1526. The earliest Spaniards to arrive were part of an expedition sponsored by Diego de Almagro and Francisco Pizarro. Under the command of Bartolomé Ruiz, these conquistadors disembarked at the Bay of Esmeraldas, where they encountered natives who showered them with gold and emeralds. Inspired by this generous reception, they continued their journey further south, where they captured an Incan vessel. Ruiz's reports to Pizarro of the riches he found encouraged the later conquest of Peru.[1]

During the 369 years that passed from the arrival of the first Spaniards to the Liberal Revolution, the basis of Ecuadorean society was the relationship between the Catholic church and the state. Throughout that period religion and history were inseparable. Simón Bolívar portrayed by Eurocentric history as the liberator of South America from Spanish rule, observed while witnessing the dissolution of the Confederation of the Gran Colombia in 1830 that Venezuela would always be a country of the military, Colombia a country of intellectuals, and Ecuador "a convent."[2] Aurelio Espinosa Polit, an Ecuadorean Jesuit and former rector of the Catholic University of Ecuador, added, "The basic element of the Ecuadorean tradition is religion. On what page of the annals of our country is there not something to be said about religion?"[3]

Simón Bolívar and Espinosa Polit both understood Ecuadorean history very well. In their view, Ecuador had been and would always be a country in which religion dominated events. In the 1980s Marie Danielle Demelas and Yves Saint-Geours, in a study on religion and politics, underscored that theme by pointing out Ecuador's importance for Latin American history in general. For these scholars, Ecuador represented a laboratory from which to investigate South American political culture—Ecuador was richer, more classical, and less secular than previously thought.[4]

During the colonial period, religion manifested itself in all aspects of Ecuadorean society. Priests came with the conquistadors; they helped write history; they ministered to the sick, the wounded, and the dying; they influenced the legal system; they evangelized, educated, and collected tribute from the indigenous population; they built churches; with the help of the Indian, they determined the styles of colonial art and architecture; and they fought with and against the revolutionary struggles of the Independence Era. Throughout the colonial period, the Catholic church possessed power, prestige, and wealth.

The strong influence of the Roman Catholic church in Ecuador had its roots in Spain prior to the conquest and colonization of the New World. The political and ecclesiastical consolidation of Spain culminated in 1492, the year of the "discovery" of the New World, when the Spanish crown completed the *reconquista,* the securing of Christian control over the Iberian peninsula from the Muslims, with the liberation of Granada and the expulsion of the Spanish Moors and Jews. The Spanish monarchs Ferdinand and Isabella saw themselves as secular defenders of the faith. They revived the Inquisition, united the powers of church and state, and, with the assistance of conquistadors and clergy, expanded both the Spanish Empire and Christendom.

In 1534, under the leadership of Sebastián de Benalcázar, this coalition of church and state effected the conquest of the Inca kingdom of Quito. One thousand Canari warriors resentful of Inca rule and a volcanic eruption that frightened the Incas and their commander Rumiñahui aided Benalcázar and the Spaniards at the decisive battle of Liripamba, near present-day Riobamba in Chimborazo. With that rout, Rumiñahui and his forces retreated northward to Quito, which they burned to the ground. Benalcázar, in pursuit, entered the smoldering ruins, proclaimed himself lieutenant governor, and set up a municipal administration over approximately 250 inhabitants.[5]

From Quito the Spanish conquerors sent out expeditions to colonize the remotest regions of the Inca kingdom. In 1537 they founded Guayaquil on the third attempt; Indian tribes had destroyed two earlier Spanish settlements. In that same year Benalcázar grew weary of his administrative post and set out northward seeking treasure and land in the vicinity of Popayán in southern Colombia. There he claimed administrative control and governed until his death in 1551. In 1538 Gonzalo Díaz de Pineda explored the Oriente unsuccessfully, and in 1541 Gonzalo Pizarro trekked into its deepest reaches, where he surveyed the Napo River, one of the main headwaters of the Amazon. Pizarro found the Napo navigable, and after his band had diminished its supplies and manpower, he ordered the construction of a ship to search for friendly Indians and food. He placed Francisco de Orellana in command. Orellana sailed down the Napo but never returned to Pizarro and his men; he discovered and sailed down the Amazon, crossed the Atlantic, and arrived in Spain to a hero's welcome and the governorship of the Amazonian territory he had found. Some time later, Orellana returned to the New World, but he died as his ship entered the mouth of the great river he had discovered. In the interim, Gonzalo Pizarro had returned to Quito, where, in June 1542, he learned that his brother Francisco had been killed and the power of the Pizarro family in Peru destroyed forever.[6]

Throughout this early period of the conquest and exploration of Quito and its surroundings, Catholic priests were present. In 1534 Juan Rodriguez said the first mass. In 1541 the Dominican Gaspar de Carvajal and the Mercedarian Gonzalo de Vera explored the Amazon with Orellana. In 1546 Bishop Garcia Díaz Arias established the diocese of Quito, which in 1564 gained a measure of independence from Peru after the founding of the Royal Audiencia of Quito, the administrative and judicial subdivision of the Viceroyalty of Peru.[7]

In the late sixteenth and early seventeenth centuries, increasing numbers of clergy traveled to Quito, and churches and monasteries proliferated. Quito became known as the city of convents, and from there the newly arrived clergy set out through the Sierra and into the Oriente to evangelize indigenous people. To assist in this evangelization process, the Spanish crown set up *encomiendas* and *reducciones* where Indians could be brought together for indoctrination and labor. The encomienda, a system of land grants to individuals, used indigenous labor in return for protection and moral education in the form of Christianity. It was supposedly a civilizing arrangement beneficial to both the indigenous people and the Spaniards. As the system actually functioned, cheap labor and the payment of tribute in the form of precious metals by indigenous people became the primary motivation for the *encomendero,* for whom it supported a life of leisure and provided insurance for the future. Reducciones, missions employed primarily by Jesuit missionaries, consolidated Indians and their families into compounds that purported to be protective, where priests forced them to work while receiving a Christian education. This clerical institution led to the abuse, exploitation, and indebtedness of the indigenous people. From the initial reducciones, close to Quito, the Jesuits ultimately moved deep into the Oriente to establish others. Of importance was the settlement they founded at Mainas in Peru.[8]

Throughout Ecuadorean and Latin American history, indigenous people were a prime source of labor, working in the fields, mines, and factories under often inhuman conditions and subject to exploitation, punishment, and death. They provided the foundation upon which the affluent classes thrived. In the colonial period they were generally viewed by the Spanish crown and the Catholic church as in need of Christianization and salvation. They were also defended by the likes of Bartolomé de Las Casas, who tried to instill some sense of justice in the Spanish colonial mentality. The efforts of Las Casas had little long-term effect, however, and ultimately the indigenous people of Latin America were victimized by a system that decimated them. While they were Christianized by the church on the one hand, on the other they were robbed of their land by the political and economic institutions of the Spanish crown and settlers.[9]

Although recent research has attempted to show that some indigenous groups collaborated with the Spaniards and were in that sense agents of their own history, generally the taking of indigenous peoples' land destroyed ancient communities.[10] Upon the ruins the Spaniards built cities, new homes, churches, and haciendas. The dispossessed and displaced indigenous people were forced into a new way of life in which they became exploited laborers on the encomiendas and reducciones and in the *obrajes,* the small-scale textile factories of the colonial period. Furthermore, the Spaniards employed institutions like the *mita,* or conscripted labor, and the *corregimiento,* a system of dividing the countryside into administrative districts, to exploit, disperse, and annihilate indigenous people. The mita imposed upon the *mitayos,* laborers taken from nearby encomiendas or reducciones, the personal obligation to work in the mines of the Spanish crown. They were removed for indefinite periods of time and forced to work in unfavorable climatic conditions and without proper nutrition. In most cases they died without returning home. The enslavement of the Indians contributed greatly to the decline in their numbers. Deaths occurred because the labor systems employed by the Spaniards concentrated workers in places where they were susceptible to such European diseases as small-pox, typhus, measles, and influenza. One estimate of this decimation of in-digenous people between 1519 and 1650 shows that about six-sevenths of the indigenous population of Middle America was wiped out, and other ar-eas suffered proportionately similar decreases.[11] In 1535 the Indian popu-lation in the Ecuadorean mining district of Zamora was 20,000; by 1592 it was only five hundred.[12]

The corregimiento, established in the Spanish colonies in 1531, initially attempted to provide administrative justice in small communities. It was used to protect indigenous people from the sins of alcoholism and idleness. It evolved into a system of extortion and abuse. Twice a year the *corregidor* (administrator) would collect tribute from the indigenous population. Ac-cording to the law, tribute could be collected only from people between the ages of eighteen and fifty-five. The corregidor, however, rarely knew or checked the age of any contributor; he collected from the very young and old as from the rest of the population. Each contributor was required to present a receipt for the last payment made. The indigenous people usually lost their receipts and were forced to repeat the payment. If there was no money, the corregidor would take the family pig or cow. After a while the corregidor was given license to sell articles of necessity to the indigenous people at exorbitant profits: the markup on these goods was 500 percent.[13]

During the colonial period in Ecuador, violent indigenous uprisings often occurred because of Spanish attempts at evangelization and colonization. The first of these rebellions took place in 1578 in the Oriente when indig-enous tribes rebelled and burned the towns of Avila and Archidona. In 1599 a second insurrection caused the destruction of Logroño and Sevilla de Oro. In these cases and later ones, the indigenous people temporarily drove the Spanish colonists out, with the result that much of the Oriente was liberated from the white man. According to Oswaldo Hurtado,

> the consequences of the liberation of the Oriente from white domination can
> be appreciated today in the sharp contrast between the manifest cultural pride
> and libertarian character of the Indians of the Oriente—the case of the Shua-
> ras is illustrative—and the submissive resignation of the highland Indians, the
> result of four centuries of exploitation and systematic persecution of the val-
> ues and autochthonous expression of native culture in the area.[14]

In the Sierra, most colonial-period indigenous rebellions took place dur-ing the eighteenth century. One Ecuadorean historian documented twelve such movements between 1730 and 1803.[15] They occurred in the provinces with large indigenous populations and the worst conditions of exploitation. The most important uprising, which took place in the vicinity of Riobamba in 1764, and was linked to others in the region, had a strong millenarian component. According to Hurtado, "the war cries of these groups seemed to reflect an implicit desire to resurrect ancient gods and kings, and simultaneously to reject the values and institutions imposed by the whites."[16]

These early indigenous responses to the conquest left a legacy that carried over into the nineteenth and twentieth centuries. The independence era, the result of the Latin American wars of liberation from Spain, merely brought a change of masters for the indigenous people. Newly created Ecuador, originally part of the Confederation of Gran Colombia, entered a period of internal colonization. In place of the Spanish crown, the indigenous people faced governments run by creoles, descendants of Spaniards born in the New World, who owned the land and continued the application of labor systems that exploited them. The new governments also saw fit to try to mold the cultural identity of the indigenous people by Europeanizing them and integrating them into the dominant society. This was a way of obstructing indigenous responses and ultimately destroying Indians as a people.

Indian uprisings continued. They were caused by harsh taxation, exploitation, and the struggle to defend or win back communal lands. In 1871 a rebellion broke out in Chimborazo against the abuses and taxation of the government of Gabriel García Moreno. Fernando Daquilema, the leader of the rebellion, was successful in setting up political and military control over much of Chimborazo for a short while. Eventually, however, he was captured and sentenced to death by a military tribunal; as one writer notes, he "has been banished from Ecuadorean 'history' by its historians."[17]

As the creole elite attempted to implant an official dominant culture, indigenous resistance took on new forms based on increased appreciation of indigenous culture and history. Implicit within this resistance was the idea of the importance of land as the foundation of indigenous identity, autonomy, and religion. Without land, the Indian did not exist; it was his source of heritage, wealth, and well-being. As expressed by the Peruvian José Carlos Mariátegui, the "problem of the Indian" was really "the problem of land." Mariátegui categorically asserted that the Indian had a right to possess it.[18]

During the colonial period in Latin America, the evangelical and prose-lytizing work of the church was based on the *Patronato Real* (Royal Patronage), which linked the church and the crown in an arrangement that strengthened royal authority by guaranteeing its rights over the church in the New World. Papal bulls published between 1493 and 1508 provided the legality for this agreement. They were issued because of the Spanish monarchy's desire to obtain title to the New World and to extend the dominion of the Roman Catholic faith.[19]

Pope Alexander VI published two bulls on May 4, 1493. The first, Inter Caetera, gave the Spanish sovereigns title to lands discovered or to be discovered to the west of a line drawn from pole to pole one hundred leagues west of the Azores and Cape Verde Islands. Part of this grant set aside the obligation of the Catholic rulers to evangelize the inhabitants of newfound lands. The second bull, Eximae Devotionis, granted "all of the concessions, privileges, exemptions, rights, liberties, immunities and indults" that had been previously granted by other pontiffs to the kings of Portugal as a result of Portuguese expansion in the Atlantic and Africa. A third bull, also called Eximae Devotionis, published on November 19, 1501, increased the patronal concession of the Spanish monarchs by giving them the use of the tithes in the New World. In return for this grant, the Spanish crown assumed the cost of the propagation and maintenance of the faith. This meant that in America all revenues would go to the crown, and the church, in theory, would be supported by royal outlays. A fourth bull, Universalis Ecclesiae, published by Pope Julius II on July 28, 1508, ended a conflict with Ferdinand in the king's favor by granting patronage in perpetuity to the sovereigns of Castile and Aragon. This bull once and for all established universal patronage in the Indies for the Spanish crown.[20]

In the Audiencia de Quito, with the establishment of the Patronato Real, both the Spanish crown and the Catholic church grew wealthy, in part from the human and natural resources of the region. The church received the moral and financial support of the crown and acted as the chief agent for the introduction of Spanish culture. It became the custodian of education, establishing schools and universities. Artistic and intellectual endeavors also depended on the church. Priests wrote and collected manuscripts and established convent and university libraries. Hispano-American baroque art and architecture began to flower in the middle of the sixteenth century. With the priests from the Old World came a handful of Flemish, Spanish, and Italian master artisans who helped build the churches and monasteries of Quito, using Indian labor and craftsmen. In 1552 two Flemish friars, Jodoko Ricke and Pedro Gosseal, founded the first New World school of arts and crafts. These craftsmen taught native artisans their skills; together they created a style combining European and indigenous forms that was followed from the 1550s to the nineteenth century. Among the important native artisans of the Quito School were Pampite, a creator of dramatic Christs; Menacho, a great maker of retables; and Caspicara, the most famous Ecuadorean sculptor of the eighteenth century. Many other unnamed Indians and mestizos painted the masterpieces that still hang in the churches of Quito. These churches are monuments to the indigenous and European blend of colonial Quito art and architecture. Examples abound: the Monastery of San Francisco, La Compañía, La Merced, and La Catedral Metropolitana are particularly notable among them. The Indian artists, reluctant collaborators with the crown and the church, were left with no other recourse than to work. Many Indians and mestizos became the teachers of succeeding generations and thus left their imprint for all time. For many people, Quito became a renaissance city; in time it grew to possess "the largest and most privileged architectural and artistic ensemble in Hispanic America."[21] In 1979, as a tribute to its artistic and cultural tradition, the United Nations designated Quito one of the cities in the world that had made a unique cultural contribution to humanity.

As demonstrated by its art and architecture, Quito was the center of religious activity in colonial Ecuador. The emphasis on religion, however, had negative effects on the economy of the Sierra. Revenues that remained in Quito, those not sent to Spain as part of the *quinto real,* or royal fifth, were not usually reinvested in productive activities by rich landowners but went for the construction of churches. This practice led to stagnation in the textile industry, Quito's primary economic activity, and diminishing production in the obrajes, which produced fabrics comparable to the finest woven goods in Europe at the time.[22]

The stagnation of the obrajes during the colonial period ultimately contributed to an economic recession in the central and northern Sierra during the eighteenth century. The production failures of the mining districts of upper Peru, the principal market for Ecuadorean textiles, added to the economic difficulties of the Sierra.[23] This recessionary period was characterized by a decrease in the indigenous population, low agricultural and cattle yields, and almost nonexistent commercial activity.[24]

The recession in the Sierra did not affect the Coast, however. That area remained immune because of its export-oriented economy and the free-trade policies of the reformist French Bourbon kings who had attained the throne of Spain in 1700. For Guayaquil, the eighteenth century proved to be a period of real growth, with the exportation of cacao, its major agricultural crop, increasing significantly. From around 1700 until 1821 cacao production increased sixfold, and from 1788 to 1820 exports doubled. By the end of the colonial period, cacao sales represented two-thirds to three-fourths of the Audiencia's exports. In turn, the increased importance of cacao caused a demographic shift as people migrated out of the Sierra in search of labor opportunities on the plantations of the Coast. For the wealthy inhabitants of the Coast, who were fast becoming an oligarchy, increased cacao production brought more capital for reinvestment. The resulting prosperity led to the diversification of agriculture and the cultivation of tobacco, which became an important cash crop that further enhanced the economy of the Coast.[25]

The differences that arose between the economy of the Coast and that of the Sierra during the eighteenth century had a profound effect on the independence movement in Ecuador. Because of recession, the Sierra took the lead toward independence, while the Coast, reaping the rewards of prosperity, delayed in taking that step. Only later, after cacao sales began to decline in the early 1820s, did the Coast demonstrate an interest in joining the independence movement against Spain. In the Sierra, the church, claiming it was motivated by economic hardship, aided the movement for separation. According to Espinosa Polit, the church assisted the movement for liberation by protecting it with its authority and directing it with its spirituality. The rallying cry at the inception of Ecuadorean independence was "a country of our own, but with the traditional religion under the protection of the eternal cross!"[26]

The Ecuadorean movement for independence had its earliest phase in Quito in 1809. At that time, creoles, mestizos, and Indians rose up in defiance of Spain. In Ecuadorean history, this movement has been characterized as the first outcry for independence in Latin America. For many, it was a holy war. From 1810 to 1812, the people of Quito lived in a republic under the leadership of Bishop José Cuero y Caicedo, who served as the ruling member of a civilian and clerical junta. In that early attempt for independence nearly one-third of the insurgents were clerics, and almost half of the churches in the city endorsed the movement. The Republic of Quito, which claimed jurisdiction over territory between Pasto in Colombia and Riobamba in Ecuador, had in its service 114 clerics, of whom 18 were troop captains and 13 were in charge of supplies, weapons, and recruits. These clerics were of humble origins, belonging primarily to the Mercedarian, Augustinian, and Franciscan orders. They were ill-equipped and poorly trained, but they fought bravely. Part of their duties included preaching in the central plazas of the towns they passed through to gain new recruits. Many Indians were recruited by the clerics to serve as soldiers. In December 1812, when the Republic of Quito finally surrendered, the clerics were the last to do so. The republican insurrection of Quito possessed strong elements of millenarianism and resembled the initial stages of Mexico's fight for independence from Spain. It gained for Quito a reputation as "La Luz de América," the first light of the Independence Era in Latin America.[27]

The Republic of Quito strongly exemplified the key element in Ecuadorean tradition and national spirit: the central role of religion in its history. Throughout the nineteenth and early twentieth centuries this trend continued as Conservatives (usually proclerical) focused on retaining the church's power and Liberals (usually anticlerical) strove to limit it. According to Hurtado, this power struggle could not be equated with the European model, in which liberalism developed as a result of territorial discoveries, growing world trade, increasing agricultural production, scientific and industrial revolutions, and growing capital accumulation in opposition to an entrenched conservative landowning aristocracy and feudal system. In Ecuador, the Liberals merely advocated diminished central authority, expanded political liberties, amplified legislative powers, and fervent anticlericalism, while Conservatives believed in a strong centralized system, limited freedoms, and a close affiliation to the Catholic church.[28]

As representatives of the above dichotomy, two men, the Conservative, Gabriel García Moreno (1821–75) and the Liberal, Eloy Alfaro (1842–1912), stand out because of their adherence to their respective ideologies and political parties. Many Ecuadoreans consider them the two greatest presidents in the history of their country. Both were traditional Latin American *caudillos,* or strongmen, who maintained firm convictions, especially in religious matters. García Moreno, president of Ecuador from 1861 to 1865 and from 1869 to 1875, was a staunch Catholic who saw church and state as partners in government. He placed education in the hands of the church and at one time during his second presidency dedicated Ecuador to the "Sacred Heart of Jesus."[29] Eloy Alfaro, president from 1897 to 1901 and from 1906 to 1911, was also a Catholic, but he viewed the church as retarding the country's political development and believed strongly in the separation of church and state. In governing strategies there was very little difference between them; they suppressed all opposition firmly. Ultimately their dictatorial tendencies and intransigence led to their brutal assassination at the hands of their enemies and rivals for power. Ecuadorean historians write not of their presidential terms but of the "Ages" dominated by each.[30]

García Moreno's age, from 1861 to 1875, was a period of Conservative control. He served as Ecuador's president all of that time except for 1865–69, when two hand-picked assistants, Jerónimo Carrión and Javier Espinosa, held the office because Ecuadorean law in 1865 prohibited election of the president to consecutive terms. García Moreno first came to power after helping overthrow the Liberal military dictatorship of 1851 to 1859. Prior to his election as president at the Constituent Assembly of 1861, he had formed part of a three-man ruling junta, which he dominated.

García Moreno used the church as his ally throughout the period that he governed Ecuador. At the beginning of his first term, the Constituent Assembly of 1861 ratified a new constitution that provided for the continued exclusive legal establishment of the Roman Catholic church; no other public worship was allowed. The constitution allowed free expression of thought with respect to religion, decency, and public morality, subject to the responsibility imposed by the laws of the land. It proclaimed the government's duty to defend the church and cause it to be respected.[31] Later in his first term, García Moreno used the church to further strengthen state authority and weaken his Liberal enemies. He allowed the Jesuits, expelled from Ecuador in 1857, to return. In 1862 he concluded a concordat with the Vatican that enlarged the role of the church in affairs of state in return for the right of patronage and the authority to name ecclesiastical dignitaries. The concordat gave the church greater privileges than it had enjoyed under the Spanish crown. Article 3 of the document, for example, gave it the right of instruction in all public and private schools at all levels. It declared that instruction must conform to the doctrine of the Catholic religion. It also stated that "the Bishops will have the exclusive right to designate texts for instruction," to prohibit books "contrary to religion and good customs, and to see that the government adopts proper measures to prevent the importation or dissemination of said books in the Republic."[32]

In his second presidential term, García Moreno increased his theocratic and political powers. In 1869 he imposed a new constitution designed to permit the use of religion and its teachings to serve the needs of the state. Liberal opponents called it the Black Charter or the Charter of Slavery to the Vatican. Roman Catholicism became a requirement for Ecuadorean citizenship. The Constitution of 1869 increased the powers of the executive branch of government. It made the presidential term of office six years and allowed for reelection. It limited certain liberties, including liberty of thought and press, and stated that abuse of those limitations would be severely punished. It also called for the complete centralization of power and the executive's right to name Supreme Court justices.[33]

Liberal opposition to the Constitution of 1869 was intense. In spite of the danger posed by García Moreno's repressive tactics, including the use of secret police, Liberals conspired to overthrow him. The soldier Eloy Alfaro and the writer Juan Montalvo led a unified opposition by "sword and pen."[34] From Panama, Alfaro called for an insurrection in the coastal provinces of Ecuador. He sought assistance from others including General José María Urbina, the Liberal caudillo of the 1850s, in exile in Peru. Alfaro obtained arms and planned an invasion, led by his brothers Idelfonso, Medardo, and José Luis, to begin on July 10, 1871, in the province of Manabi in his hometown of Montecristi. García Moreno was informed of Alfaro's plan and quickly suppressed the invasion. Alfaro's brothers escaped to Peru, and Alfaro remained in Panama, unable to mount another military threat against García Moreno.

Although Eloy Alfaro's sword failed to undo García Moreno, the pen of Juan Montalvo succeeded.[35] On October 2, 1874, in Panama, Montalvo published a pamphlet, called "La dictadura perpetua" (The perpetual dictatorship). It was a response to the publishers of the bilingual newspaper *Panama Star and Herald,* who supported García Moreno's reelection as president of Ecuador. The editors recommended García Moreno because, in their opinion, he had led a peaceful administration, had brought a great deal of material and moral well-being to Ecuador, and had made revolution impossible. Montalvo believed it was every man's duty to conspire against tyrants. For him, García Moreno was not indispensable, and the material progress of Ecuador was overrated.[36]

The publication of "La dictadura perpetua" led to García Moreno's downfall. Eloy Alfaro promoted its distribution. The church lashed out against it, excommunicating anyone caught reading it. "La dictadura perpetua" incited many young Liberals, among them, Roberto Andrade, Abelardo Moncayo, and Manuel Cornejo Astorga, who, after reading the pamphlet, arose and said: "Let us conspire."[37] They joined other conspirators in working out a plan to assassinate García Moreno. On August 6, 1875, Faustino Lemus Rayo struck down García Moreno on the steps of the presidential palace with a machete blow to the head and neck. Rayo was killed after the military jailed him. García Moreno died following a move to a nearby chapel and the administration of last rites. Upon hearing of García Moreno's death, Montalvo exclaimed, "My pen killed him!"[38]

With the assassination of García Moreno, one of the most influential political leaders in Ecuadorean history passed from the scene. He had governed for fifteen years with the assistance of the church, and Catholicism remained a potent political force after his death. In spite of his dictatorial style and repressive measures, his tenure was a period of stability. In a larger sense, García Moreno's Catholic fanaticism, considered undesirable by Liberal opponents, ensured the continuation of Ecuadorean tradition and religion. After his death, Ecuador went through a twenty-year period of indecisiveness in which Conservatives and Liberals alternately held power. The church, emboldened by its past power, remained involved in politics, advising Conservatives to continue the policies of García Moreno. This boldness fed Liberal anxiety and led to the rise of Eloy Alfaro in 1895.

Alfaro's tenure in office, from 1895 to 1912, was a revolutionary period in which "El Viejo Luchador" (the Old Warrior), as he was called, guided the political fortunes of Ecuador. Within the Liberal party, Alfaro represented the radical or *machetero* tendency, which demonstrated a propensity for militaristic solutions and a lack of concern for dialogue with the Conservative opposition. In the late 1800s radical liberalism was a more recent manifestation of Ecuadorean liberalism. It was in opposition to the original Liberal faction made up of doctrinairians who emerged out of the political conflicts of church and state during the age of García Moreno. The original or moderate Liberal response to the Conservatives was civilian in nature, carried out in the press and through the legislative process.[39]

Throughout his presidency, Eloy Alfaro seized power in moments of crisis. In 1895 he rode into Quito at the head of Liberal armies and proclaimed himself supreme commander. In 1906 he led an insurrection against his former liberal compatriot Leonidas Plaza Gutiérrez that placed him again in command of the country. In 1912 Alfaro once more tried to assume power, only to find coordinated opposition from Conservatives and

Liberal moderates. This last attempt failed and led to his imprisonment and death. It stands as Alfaro's gravest miscalculation and in marked contrast to his earlier successes, when he was confirmed as president by constituent assemblies.

Eloy Alfaro believed in the separation of church and state and the secularization of the educational system. He embodied Liberal opposition to the policies of García Moreno and the Conservative-clerical alliance. Alfaro's main purpose throughout his period as Ecuador's dominant leader was to weaken the church and lead Ecuador into the modern era. One of the first acts of his first presidential term, which began in 1897, was the formulation of a new constitution. This document was reminiscent of past Ecuadorean constitutions in that it continued to recognized Roman Catholicism as the state religion. Ecuadorean liberalism, in contrast to the movement elsewhere in Latin America, was not antireligious; it understood the Catholic beliefs of the Ecuadorean people very well. Its opposition to Catholicism was based principally on the church's privileged position, its influence in public life, its hindrance of freedom of thought and conscience, and its intervention in the political affairs of the country.[40]

The Constitution of 1897 differed from previous ones in that it provided for the first guarantee of complete religious toleration in Ecuadorean history. It stated that "the State respects the religious beliefs of the inhabitants of Ecuador and will cause to be respected the manifestations of them. Religious beliefs do not hinder one in the exercise of his political and civil rights."[41] This carefully worded clause represented the first of many steps taken by Alfaro to subdue the church's power. The constitution also prohibited the entry of additional foreign religious orders and forbade the clergy to hold public office.

Following the enactment of the Constitution of 1897, Eloy Alfaro and his successor for the presidential term of 1901–05, Plaza Gutiérrez, further reduced the church's role in Ecuador. Both men firmly believed in secularizing the state to create the *Estado Laico* (Lay State).[42] In 1901 the government established new secular schools, among them the Instituto Nacional Mejía, the Instituto Normal Manuela Canizares, and the Instituto Normal Juan Montalvo. Most of the teachers were North American Methodists (see chapter 2). Schools designed to teach specialized skills included the Colegio Militar, the Conservatorio Nacional de Música, and the Escuela de Bellas Artes. The government also created night schools, which gave adults and workers the opportunity to study for the first time in the country's history. At the same time, the church lost its right to oversee the publishing and distribution of books, and priests were forbidden to teach anything but religion. In 1904 the Congress passed the Ley de Cultos (Law of Religions) establishing freedom of religion and offering government protection to ministers of other faiths. The law also authorized Congress to sell or transfer church property and to prohibit mandatory tithing and other forms of church income. In addition, a law that permitted civil marriage and divorce was enacted during Plaza Gutiérrez's term of office.

With Alfaro's return to the presidency in 1906, a new constitution, the twelfth in the country's history, was enacted. It gave formal status to the secularization of the state, called for the complete separation of church and state, and suppressed Catholicism as the official religion of the republic. Furthermore, it established the constitution as the law of the land, balanced the functions of the three powers of state, and amplified the attributes of the Council of State as an organ of supervision and regulation in times of congressional recess.[43]

The Constitution of 1906 threatened the Conservative opposition. Adding fuel to the flame was Alfaro's attempt to overturn the selection of the popular Federico González Suárez as archbishop of Quito. In 1907 González Suárez led the opposition against Alfaro when the latter contracted with the Frenchman Daniel Conde de Charnace to build a railroad in the Oriente in return for 35,000 hectares of uncultivated Ecuadorean land. González Suárez thought the Charnace contract "not convenient for the national interest."[44]

The conflict over the Charnace contract also manifested itself in uprisings against the regime in 1907 and 1908. Alfaro moved swiftly to quell those rebellions, and this further increased the opposition. The president steadfastly pursued his anticlerical program. On October 14, 1908 Congress added the final nail in the coffin of Ecuador's long-standing church-state conflict by passing the Ley de Beneficencia (Law of Charity). This law nationalized real property held in mortmain (an inalienable right to possession) by the church. In 1908 the church lost twenty-seven large landholdings belonging to various religious orders as a result of the Ley de Beneficencia. It retained, however, important properties that were expanded in later years in conjunction with religious missions in the Oriente.[45] The Ley de Beneficencia called for the creation of three regional offices, in Quito, Guayaquil, and Cuenca, to collect and distribute funds from the nationalized properties. Some of the collected money was returned to the church, but much of it was destined for charitable projects in the regions from which it was collected.[46]

From 1908 to the end of Alfaro's presidential term in 1911, tension and violence increased between the Liberal and Conservative factions. Alfaro also faced opposition within his own party from those who foresaw only more problems if he remained in power. After 1910 political attacks against him grew in intensity. Much of the opposition came from the country's newspapers. In Guayaquil, *El Telégrafo, El Grito del Pueblo,* and *El Guante* all censured Alfaro. In Quito the criticism came from *El Comercio, La Prensa, La Constitución, El Ecuatoriano,* and *Fray Gerundio,* the last of which was the voice of the Catholic church in Ecuador. From that newspaper González Suárez lent his voice to the onslaught. Alfaro left office in 1911 and went into exile in Panama after he reneged on his choice for a successor. He had chosen the Guayaquil businessman Emilio Estrada, but after some thought he came to view Estrada as an agent of the Conservatives. He proceeded to work against Estrada's nomination but was overridden by the moderate wing of the Liberal party.

In 1912 Alfaro attempted to return to Ecuador and take power amid feverish political agitation. He was arrested in Guayaquil along with his brother Medardo, his nephew General Flavio E. Alfaro, General Ulpiano Paez, General Manuel Serrano, General Pedro J. Montero, and the newspaperman Luciano Coral.[47] From there, all of them but Montero, who was shot and killed by a noncommissioned officer in a Guayaquil courtroom, were transported to Quito and thrown into the Panóptico Prison. Soon after their arrival, prison guards brutally murdered Alfaro and his men and gave their bodies to a mob outside the prison, where, in a most barbaric fashion, they were dragged through the streets of Quito and incinerated.[48] This act, known as the *hoguera bárbara* (savage flame) was the Conservatives' revenge on the Liberals and an effort to rid the country once and for all of what they considered the evil of "Alfarismo."[49]

The death of Eloy Alfaro ended a transitional period in Ecuadorean history, after which the country ushered in its plutocratic period of government under the control of a monopolistic coastal oligarchy. Power passed to the bankers and plantation owners of Guayaquil. The church remained influential, but not a serious challenge to governmental authority. Much of what Alfaro accomplished in limiting church power remained. Because of him, Ecuador threw off the past and opened its doors to the future. North American Protestants were among those who entered.

CHAPTER 2

The Second Religious Conquest Begins: Early Protestant Groups, 1896–1931

THE NORTH AMERICAN PROTESTANT groups that established missions in Ecuador in the years of Eloy Alfaro and the Liberal Revolution were the aforementioned Gospel Missionary Union (GMU) in 1896 and Christian and Missionary Alliance (CMA) in 1897 (see introduction), the Seventh-Day Adventist Church (SDA) in 1905, and the Methodist Episcopal Church in 1907. These early missions represented official North American Protestantism; they were not the first attempts of Protestants to implant some aspect of their religion in Ecuador. That honor belonged to the British and Foreign Bible Society and the American Bible Society, who, in keeping with their work elsewhere in Latin America during the nineteenth century, sent salesmen into Ecuador to sell Protestant Bibles. These salesmen appeared in the 1820s, when Ecuador was the Southern District of the Gran Colombia; in the 1830s, during the presidency of Vicente Rocafuerte (1835–39), who admired the Protestants; and in the 1880s and 1890s with the governments of the "progressive" Catholics: José María Plácido Caamaño (1883–88), Antonio Flores Jijón (1888–92), and Luis Cordero (1892–95). While the Protestant Bible societies encountered much popular resistance and Ecuadorean constitutions that prohibited all religious activity except Catholicism, they nonetheless laid the groundwork for the arrival of the official missions.[1]

Of the early groups, all except the Methodists established long-term missions that endured throughout the 1895–1990 period. The Methodist church ended its mission in 1910 because of the lack of financial and administrative support from its board of directors in the Untied States. A first

Methodist effort failed in Guayaquil in 1880. At that time the Methodists sent one of their pastors, J. G. Price, from their western South American mission in Lima-Callao. He arrived with a plan devised by William Taylor, the director of the Lima-Callao station, to open an English-language primary school and establish a self-sustaining mission supported by the school's tuition. Price arrived, however, during the government of General Ignacio de Veintemilla (1876–83), who had just completed a new concordat with the Vatican similar to the one signed by García Moreno.[2]

Price's mission lasted only a year. Immediately after his arrival, he ran into difficulties with the Ecuadorean government, which would not allow him to remove from customs the books he had brought with him. The government claimed it was against the law to import "heretical" books. He also contracted a coastal fever and was forced to leave the country after Ecuadorean doctors denied him treatment because of his Protestantism. Price was not the only example of the Ecuadorean medical profession's hostility toward Protestants in the late 1800s. In 1892 German Von Lagerheim, a leading medical bacteriologist from Hamburg, well known for continuing the work of Robert Koch and Louis Pasteur and for introducing the microscope into Ecuador, was forced out of the country because of his Protestant beliefs.[3]

Except for the Methodists, the early missionary groups were part of the late-nineteenth-century fundamentalist Protestant movement in the United States.[4] Fundamentalism possessed a basic ideology that stressed the literal interpretation of the Bible, the doctrine of virgin birth, Christ's divinity and redemptive sacrifice, his resurrection, and his imminent return. The SDA, founded in an earlier period and different in its ritual practices, was still considered by many to be part of the fundamentalist movement. The SDA can be compared to the CMA and GMU because it uses the same Bible, literature, and ideology. Furthermore, like the other groups, it emphasizes the Puritan work ethic, individualism, apoliticism, proselytism, and millenarianism. The SDA in Ecuador has often been referred to as "fundamentalists among the Fundamentalists."[5]

The fundamentalist movement that gave birth to the early groups grew out of the economic conditions in the rural areas of the United States and the imperialistic tendencies of the period, which reached their peak with the Spanish-American War. In the late nineteenth century, small farmers and petty merchants suffered because of avaricious railroad owners, usurious bankers, and corrupt government officials. With the economic recovery after 1893, these rural people and petty merchants found themselves abruptly integrated into the expanding market system. It meant new prosperity for them, but at the same time a loss of identity, shifting family ties, and changes in social life and patterns of morality. The resulting stresses and anxieties led to a religious movement that provided simplistic solutions to problems. Fundamentalism, with its strong millenarian component, believed it was destined to save the United States and the world.[6]

When North American Protestantism began establishing permanent missions in Ecuador in 1896, that country was also adjusting to change, and it offered an open field for evangelistic work. Ironically, Ecuadorean Liberals viewed the Protestants, who in their own country were reacting against modernity, as facilitators of change. Therefore the Protestants entered Ecuador knowing that the Liberal government welcomed them. They also understood that there would be Catholic opposition, but Eloy Alfaro and the Liberals assured them that they would be protected and that help would be given to secure the success of their missions. The Constitution of 1897 first legalized this offer of protection.

Between 1896 and 1912, the year when the Alfaro period ended, the Protestants took important strides forward. They increased their numbers with the arrival of new recruits and established missions on the Coast, in the Sierra, and in the Oriente. After 1912 they continued their advance, although at a slower pace. They relied less on direct Liberal protection and moved about the country more freely. At the same time, the nature of Ecuadorean politics changed as religious tension between Liberals and Conservatives took second place to the more immediate concerns of Ecuador's economic and political future. The Liberals, who remained in charge of the government, had to pay debts owed to the Commercial and Agricultural Bank of Guayaquil and to build extensive public works projects. As a result, the Commercial and Agricultural Bank became a force in national politics, picking and choosing presidents. This situation lasted until 1925, when the Ecuadorean military took over the government after the Revolución Juliana (July Revolution). This uprising, on July 9, was the result of the failure of the coastal bankers to solve the economic, social, and political problems of the country. It ended with the naming of a civilian junta to run the government. Eventually one of the junta members, Isidro Ayora, became the provisional president.[7]

Ayora placed Ecuador in the hands of the Kemmerer Mission from Princeton University, which made recommendations for economic reform.

The idea was to put the country's economic house in order by analyzing and making suggestions in all areas of government. Among the recommendations made and followed were the creation of a central bank and the placing of Ecuador on the gold standard. These measures linked the country to the world international monetary system. Ultimately the Kemmerer Mission's suggestions helped stabilize Ecuador, and in 1928 Ayora turned the country back to constitutional government. In 1929 he was elected president and a new constitution was written. By 1931, however, because of damage to the economy from worldwide depression and the demands of Ecuador's popular sectors and the military, Ayora was deposed.[8]

The early Protestant groups proceeded amid the political and economic upheaval between 1896 and 1931. They exemplified perseverance in the face of great hardship. The Methodist Episcopal Church, the first early group discussed here, was important, in spite of its inability to establish an enduring permanent mission, because it played a critical role in the development of the Ecuadorean educational system as defined by the Liberal government at the turn of the twentieth century. Methodism's work in Ecuador paralleled what it had already accomplished in Mexico and Peru in the late 1800s. In Ecuador the Methodists helped to found schools that served as competition to the Catholic system and fostered an educational network more in tune with Liberal ideals.

The Methodist missionaries who arrived in Ecuador were few, but there were enough of them to provide teachers at the normal schools established by the Liberal governments. The driving force behind their activities was Dr. Thomas Wood, the president of the Methodist Mission in Lima-Callao. Wood tried hard to establish an independent official mission in Ecuador but was unable to convince the Methodist board of directors to provide the necessary funds. In fact, they decreased the amount of money sent to him each year. As a result, Wood sidestepped the board's stinginess and its restrictions by serving as a voluntary representative of the American Bible Society in Ecuador. From that position he initiated Methodist activities.

In November 1899 Wood came to Ecuador accompanied by Andres Milne, the American Bible Society agent in charge of most of South America (Brazil and Venezuela excepted). Wood and Milne arrived with the objective of reorganizing and strengthening the institutions they served. In Guayaquil they met with some of their missionary colleagues and the North American consul-general, Perry De Leon. There they learned that De Leon and William Fritz of the CMA had written to Andrew Carnegie soliciting

$600,000 to finance schools in the principal cities of Ecuador. Their plea to Carnegie centered around the Ecuadorean government's lack of money to implement the educational plan. Carnegie never answered the letter, but Wood thought the idea a valid one. He raised the point that education had long been a primary objective of the Methodist church.[9]

Following the meetings in Guayaquil, Milne and Wood traveled to Quito, where, with the assistance of General Archibald J. Samson, the American ambassador and a devout Protestant, they obtained a meeting with Eloy Alfaro. In that meeting Wood and Milne expressed their ideas on education. Alfaro listened attentively and instructed Equadorean minister of the interior José Peralta to draw up a contract with Wood that would allow North Americans to teach in the normal schools. The contract, signed on December 22, 1899, determined that the teachers would have to be in the country by September 1, 1900. It called for six to twelve principals and teachers to work in the various schools in Quito. It also provided teachers and principals for Guayaquil and Cuenca; the payment of the teachers' passage and Wood's travel expenses; a five-year contract for each teacher; the hiring of complementary Ecuadorean teachers; and the specification that the Methodist teachers would not be asked to work on Sunday, nor would they teach or take part in religious practices contrary to their beliefs. Wood had made the argument that the Methodists should have Sunday for evangelistic endeavors.[10]

The Methodist teachers who came to Ecuador as a result of the contract with the Alfaro government were recruited from among North Americans in Chile and the United States. In February 1900, Wood traveled to Chile, where he hired three teachers: Rosina A. Kinsman, Alice H. Fisher, and the Reverend Henry Williams. In June of the same year, Wood went to New York City to present the plan to the Methodist board of directors. Initially he faced hostility; he persisted, however, and they permitted him to recruit the teachers he required. He hired Merritt M. Harris, Charles M. Griffith, and William T. Robinson. On August 30, 1900, Wood and the three teachers from New York arrived in Quito. On the following day, Alfaro and his cabinet called them into a meeting to give them all a warm welcome.[11]

The propitious beginning of the agreement between the Alfaro government and the Methodists did not endure. The plan began to unravel almost immediately because of Conservative opposition and the fear among Ecuadorean parents of enrolling their children in schools run by Protestants. In November 1900, on the day the schools were supposed to open, students did not appear. Some parents may have wished to send their sons and daughters to the schools, but they faced serious reprisals if they did so. Ultimately two schools, Juan Montalvo and Manuela Canizares, opened in Quito on February 14, 1901. Later that same year, after Leonidas Plaza assumed control of the government, the Instituto Normal para Varones (Normal Institute for Boys) was inaugurated in Cuenca under the directorship of the Reverend Harry Compton. Compton, with his wife Rebecca, had recently arrived after previously working in Chile, Argentina, and Uruguay. They faced an overwhelming task. Along with Conservative hostility and the small enrollment, the missionaries lacked financial support from the Ecuadorean government. This was not unexpected, given the economic drain caused by the Liberal Revolution. The Methodist teachers became discouraged, and one by one they began to leave; by 1903 most had departed. In 1905 Thomas Wood retired as president of the Methodist District of Peru. Only the Comptons completed the contract, which ended in September 1907. They remained because, in that year, the Methodist board of directors decided to establish a District of Ecuador and name the Reverend Mr. Compton its director.[12]

The Methodist missionaries' work in education in Ecuador planted the seeds for the subsequent growth of the state-run secular educational system. Eventually, in spite of harassment and fear, some students graduated from the state schools. In 1905 five Ecuadorean teachers received diplomas from Juan Montalvo, and seven graduated from Manuela Canizares. In 1906 twelve more students graduated from Manuela Canizares. These graduates formed the base of a teaching staff that helped establish other schools around the country and replace the departed Methodists in the normal schools. The Methodist teachers, while not present to witness the fruits of their labor, were successful in that they assisted in the ideological renovation of the country and, in so doing, gave impulse to the advance of Protestantism in Ecuador.

The end of the Methodist mission in Ecuador came in spite of Compton's efforts. In 1908 and 1909 he tried unsuccessfully to obtain teachers to establish new schools in Guayaquil and Riobamba. It was evident that the Methodist board of directors did not share his optimism for the mission and believed the Methodist cause would be better served by concentrating on Peru. They refused to listen to Compton's appeals, and soon after, he was recalled to the United States. There he languished for a period of time, and four months before he was scheduled to return to Ecuador, he received new instructions to proceed to Panama to take charge of that district. Reluctantly he accepted the position, thereby terminating the Methodist mission in Ecuador; the Methodist board did not choose anyone to replace him.[13]

The second important Protestant group of the 1896–1931 period was the Gospel Missionary Union (GMU). It was organized in Kansas City at the end of the nineteenth century as a "faith mission" that incorporated missionaries of diverse evangelical denominations. George S. Fisher, the director of Kansas City's YMCA, founded the GMU. The YMCA itself had been established in London in 1844 by George Williams for the purpose of evangelizing young people. It began operating in the United States in 1851 and by the turn of the century had become one of the most respected Protestant institutions in the United States. It was not part of the fundamentalist movement but connected more closely to historic Protestantism.

In 1892 Fisher and other staff members of the Kansas City YMCA tried to convert the organization into a center for the recruitment and indoctrination of young people to be sent abroad as foreign missionaries. The directors of the association rebuked him for this effort and forced him to leave. Subsequently Fisher formed the World Gospel Union, which later became the GMU. Originally he did not want to start a new denomination but rather to prepare missionaries for work in other countries as part of already established missionary organizations. The first missionaries he trained went to Africa as members of the CMA. In the years that followed, however, Fisher consolidated his organization, and the GMU became a full-fledged member of evangelical Fundamentalism.

The first GMU missionaries to enter Ecuador were Fisher, J. A. Strain, and F. W. Farnol. They arrived in July 1896 at the precise moment when Alfaro was suppressing a Conservative rebellion in the South. The GMU missionaries were warned by U.S. Ambassador James D. Tillman in Guayaquil that it would be better if they turned around and left the country.[14] They refused to listen and began work in Guayaquil and in Alfaro's hometown, Montecristi. According to Washington Padilla, their decision to remain was insanity, especially since they had arrived with very little money and without anyone who could provide for their personal safety.[15]

The GMU missionaries first made contact with the few Protestant residents of Guayaquil, including Rosaura Gonzaga, an Ecuadorean teacher who had worked for the Methodists in 1880, and an Englishman, George Ashton, the manager of Guayaquil's telegraph company. Ashton helped the GMU missionaries immensely during the early weeks of their stay by ar-

ranging a meeting with Alfaro, at which they presented a letter of introduction to him from the Ecuadorean ambassador in Washington. In that
meeting Alfaro offered his personal guarantee of protection but cautioned
the missionaries that, for the moment, it would be better if they remained
on the Coast. A short time later the missionaries again met with Alfaro, and
he gave them letters of recommendation addressed to the army comman-
dant in Ambato and the governor of the province of Pichincha, which
opened the way for them to go to Quito and the Oriente. After these initial
meetings with Alfaro, the GMU missionaries viewed the Ecuadorean leader
with fondness and called him "an instrument of God for the opening of Ecuador to the Gospel."[16]

Almost immediately, in spite of their euphoria over the meetings with Alfaro, the GMU missionaries ran into difficulties. Strain and Farnol became
ill. This caused Fisher to postpone his trip to the interior while he waited for
his companions to recover. In the interim he wrote a letter to Zabulon
Yates, a Christian he had met in Panama, asking him to join them in
Guayaquil. Fisher wanted Yates because he had expressed an interest in
working in Ecuador, he spoke Spanish, and he knew how to cook. He arrived in Guayaquil in September.

Eventually Fisher became tired of waiting for Strain and Farnol to recover and left alone on an exploratory mission to Quito, where he found no
reason not to attempt the evangelization of the local population. With his
spirits buoyed, he designed an overall plan for the GMU that called for two
missionaries to work in Manabí, three in Quito, and two others to go to the
Oriente after they learned Spanish and Quechua. He returned to Guayaquil
in late September. On October 13, two more GMU missionaries, Charles
Chapman and Charles M. Polk, arrived. Fisher also had one more meeting
with Alfaro to discuss the details of the mission's progress. At the end of
October, he and Farnol left for the United States, leaving Chapman in
charge of the GMU mission in Ecuador.[17]

About the same time as the GMU organized itself in Ecuador, the National Constituent Assembly deliberated the Constitution of 1897. The missionaries were careful to wait to begin work until after this document went
into effect; article 13 called for civil and political rights for all people irre-
spective of religion. On January 12, it was ratified, and on the following
day Eloy Alfaro was elected president of Ecuador with a mandate to serve
until August 31, 1901. For the GMU missionaries this was a moment of
triumph; there was a president in office who favored their entrance and had

given them guarantees of protection. They were now free to begin chipping away at Catholic hegemony.

The early Protestant missionaries of the GMU worked in the three distinct ecological zones of the country, the Coast, the Sierra, and the Oriente. According to Scott Robinson, these three zones of Ecuador represent a "microcosm of social conflicts in different habitats . . . where the foreign missionary apparatus has invested heavily since early in the century."[18] On the Coast, where people were more receptive, the GMU initiated its work in an open manner. Two new missionaries, William E. Reed and Homer G. Crisman, arrived at the port of Manta on January 26, 1897, to assist. Charles Chapman met them and escorted them back to the mission's coastal headquarters in the city of Portoviejo in Manabí, where they joined Polk and Yates. On March 7, the GMU missionaries celebrated their first public revival meeting, which was received favorably by the local population.[19]

In the Sierra the reception was somewhat different. J. A. Strain and Charles Chapman were assigned to work in Quito. Upon their arrival in the capital, they saw that open meetings would not be tolerated by the city's inhabitants. They proceeded slowly, talking about the gospel or reading the Bible only to those who seemed most interested. Chapman left in late March for the United States because of his mother's illness, and William Reed replaced him as director of the GMU. Strain remained in Quito until April 13 before returning to the Coast. The trip back took him through highland towns and almost cost him his life. In Guaranda an angry mob found out that he was a Protestant and attacked him. A local army commander saved him from a lynching, put him on a horse, and accompanied him out of town. In Chimbo another mob attacked him, and this time the local police chief rescued him. He finally arrived in Guayaquil, where he gratefully rested before heading out for Portoviejo and his companions.[20]

After its first attempts in the Sierra, the GMU remained content to continue its work for the time being in the province of Manabí. Through the efforts of Polk and Yates, the GMU strengthened its center of operations, and its missionaries made trips into the remote regions of the province. It also began to hold regular meetings in Portoviejo. On October 24, 1897, the GMU missionaries were joined by the wives and children of Strain and Reed and by two new workers, Lettie Basore and Jerome B. Altig. On November 9 the GMU again attempted the conquest of the Sierra. This time the mission was composed of William Reed and his family, Lettie Basore, and Jerome Altig. Their objective was the city of Ambato, Juan Montalvo's birthplace and a purported Liberal stronghold. The GMU missionaries determined that it was impossible, for the moment, to try to establish a mission in Quito. They agreed with the view that Quito was "the capital of the fanatical world."[21]

In Ambato the first experiences of the GMU missionaries were reminiscent of the hostile reception given Strain. A week after their arrival, they received a letter signed by the townspeople "Los Ambateños" that ordered them to abandon the city under the threat of violence. Almost immediately a hostile crowd appeared outside their rented house, demanding that they leave. Some soldiers and a group of young men rescued them and guaranteed their safety. In Ambato, forces loyal to the Alfaro government managed to control the situation. Though the missionaries had escaped harm, the threat of violence underlined their tenuous position. Conservatives were stirring up the population not so much because they wanted to hurt the missionaries but because they hated the Alfaro government intensely.[22]

The turning point for the GMU missionaries in Ecuador came when an Ecuadorean salesman for the American Bible Society, Antonio Viteri, returned home to Ambato after working many years in Chile and Argentina. With his assistance the GMU missionaries began a small Bible-study class. From that base in Ambato, a city geographically well situated at the junction between the routes to the Coast and to the Oriente, the GMU missionaries directed their aims northward toward Quito and eastward to the Oriente. In July 1898 William Reed began making discreet contacts in Quito, seeking out ways for the GMU to begin work there. He also tried to determine if opening of the Oriente and establishing foreign colonies there were feasible. The latter possibility had been on the minds of the GMU missionaries from the moment they arrived in the country. They viewed the colonization of the Oriente as a progressive venture that would be helped along by their work and by British and North American railway builders. The Catholic church opposed the idea on the nationalistic grounds that the railway builders and foreign colonists would all be Protestants and would do little for the citizens of Ecuador. As events developed, railroad construction in the Oriente failed to take place, and colonization never advanced along the lines that the GMU had hoped for.[23]

In September 1898 Reed, his family, and Lettie Basore went to Quito and installed themselves in a centrally located house. They immediately received visits from people who had remembered Strain and Chapman. To the missionaries' surprise, Catholic reaction was minimal. They went out and freely distributed their literature in stores and parks. After a short while they came to believe they would be in the capital permanently. This experience, along with continued progress in Manabí, gave the GMU great hope for the future. On December 13, 1898, a new group of GMU missionaries, headed by Charles Chapman, arrived in Guayaquil. This group included Chapman's wife, Charles S. Detweiler, E. E. Cady, and Julia Anderson. From Guayaquil they traveled to Quito, where they participated in the first GMU conference in Ecuador (January 5 to 11, 1899). At that conference it was determined that Reed and Lettie Basore would continue their work in Quito; Mrs. Chapman and Julia Anderson would also remain in the capital and study Spanish; Altig would continue in Ambato, aided by Cady; Homer Crisman would go to Mocha, south of Ambato in Chimborazo province; Chapman and Detweiler would go to Archidona in the Oriente; and Strain would remain in Guayaquil.²⁴ The conference of 1899, the decisions taken there, and the contacts made throughout the country helped to establish the GMU mission firmly in Ecuador by the end of Alfaro's first term. By then the agency was organized and working in all regions of the country. It had made an auspicious beginning and had scouted new ground for others to follow.

The third early Protestant group to enter Ecuador was the Christian and Missionary Alliance (CMA). Founded in 1879 as an interdenominational faith mission, the CMA followed the ideals of the post–Civil War holiness movement. That movement, a precursor of Fundamentalism, believed that humanity could be sanctified by the personal experience of salvation and that all life activity from that moment on would be a demonstration of the act of salvation. Holiness affirmed the idea of the spiritual equality of opportunity and gave impetus to the belief that everyday life was a religious experience and a manifestation of God's grace. The founder of the CMA was Dr. Albert B. Simpson, a conservative evangelical leader who wanted a mission to deliver the gospel to needy people in urban areas. The earliest activities of the CMA emanated out of the first fundamentalist Bible college established in the United States, the Nyack Missionary College. Bible colleges such as Nyack were the fundamentalist movement's most important institutions. They gave it some unity, appearing in response to the demands of urban ministries and the desire to train lay leaders for evangelism. They brought together many different evangelical organizations and served as training centers for missionaries slated to go into the foreign field.²⁵

The first missionaries sent to Ecuador by the CMA were William G. Fritz and Mr. and Mrs. Edward Tarbox. They arrived in 1897 and faced many difficulties. Fritz, a student of law and a member of the Congregational church, began work in Guayaquil distributing CMA literature. The Tarboxes, experienced missionaries, initially spent six months in the port city learning Spanish before traveling to Quito to begin their work. In the capital, they distributed literature, heard testimonials, and held Bible meetings in their living room. They had to deal with language and cultural differences, illness, and the lack of financial support. Fritz in particular had problems with the Spanish language. He never learned to speak it well enough to be able to hold a church service in Guayaquil.

In Quito the CMA missionaries were the targets of religious persecution. In March 1899 Edward Tarbox and Fritz came under a direct attack at the Tarbox home by a mob led by a Catholic priest, Father Matens, who demanded that the missionaries come outside and allow themselves to be baptized as Catholics. The mob warned them that if they did not do so, they would be stoned. The CMA missionaries refused to leave the house, and the mob began throwing stones and breaking windows to the cries of "Protestant Devils." Their anger intensified, and they had almost broken down the door of the house when police arrived and dispersed them. Nine people were arrested on the spot. Later, U.S. ambassador Archibald J. Sampson protested the attack to the Ecuadorean government. As a result, the government promised to protect the missionaries and to send agents to masses celebrated at the various churches in Quito to make sure that the priests were not inciting their parishioners by their sermons.[26]

The mob attack at the Tarbox home underscored the grave problems of the early CMA missionaries. They faced hostility and uncertainty every step of the way. In 1900 Fritz ended his mission in Guayaquil because of a lack of money. He sold his typewriter and his clothing and returned to the United States. The experience did not embitter him, however. He believed he had accomplished a great deal during his stay in Ecuador. In 1899, in Guayaquil, he had distributed 5,000 pamphlets and 400 Bibles, in many cases to people he thought would never accept them. His departure left a vacancy for the CMA in Guayaquil that Charles Polk, a former member of the GMU, filled late in 1900.[27]

The Tarboxes stayed in Quito until the end of 1901, when they retired from missionary work because of bad health. In late 1903 they left Ecuador for good. In their four years there as missionaries for the CMA, they laid the foundation for the future progress of the mission. They influenced the work in the Sierra and helped recruit new personnel for the CMA staff. Prominent among these new recruits were Homer Crisman and his wife Lettie Basore, who, after leaving the GMU, joined the CMA in November 1903.[28]

In the years that followed the work of Fritz and the Tarboxes, the CMA made slow, steady progress in Ecuador. It recruited and organized personnel, built churches, and moved into new regions of the country. In 1904 the organization welcomed the Ecuadorean Alfonso Muñoz and his family, who went to work with the Crismans in Manabí. In 1905 Charles Polk and his family moved to Quito and reestablished the mission left by the Tarboxes. In 1909, in Junín, Manabi, the CMA held its first baptismal service in Ecuador, baptizing Manuel Bravo and Trinidad Pito. In 1913 Pito and Bravo became the appointed elders of the newly organized Junín congregation. They are considered the first national Protestant church leaders of Ecuador.[29]

In 1916 two new CMA missionaries, Mr. and Mrs. Howard Cragin, joined the work among indigenous people in the Sierra. They immediately combined their efforts with those of Homer Crisman and organized a two-week trip on foot to the city of Ibarra, ninety miles north of Quito, to search for a proper place to establish a new mission. They originated the work among the Otavalan Indians of Imbabura. In 1918, in Quito, the CMA held its first field conference, which was attended by seven of its missionaries.[30]

William Reed, who had separated from the GMU and taught English at the Vicente Rocafuerte High School in Guayaquil, joined the CMA in 1922 and became an important force in the mission's work in Ecuador. He also held services and Sunday school in his home. In 1924 he was appointed the CMA's superintendent of the Ecuador field. His accomplishments included publishing a weekly newsletter, the *Little Sunday Paper,* which reportedly had a circulation of 6,000, and constructing a church with a seating capacity for 600 people in a rundown Guayaquil neighborhood known as the Fisherman's Quarter.[31] Reed became its pastor and remained there until his death in 1946, a year after he helped organize the first national Protestant church in Ecuador, La Iglesia Evangélica Ecuatoriana Alianza Cristiana y Misionera (the Ecuadorean Christian and Missionary Alliance Church). With the opening of this church, Ecuadorean Protestants could fully administer their own house of worship free from North American influence.[32]

As an outgrowth of Reed's successes in Guayaquil, the CMA gained confidence and broadened its objectives throughout the entire region. In 1923 it moved into neighboring Colombia, in areas under Liberal control, where it established one of the first Protestant missions in that country's history.[33] In 1926 it founded at Sucua its most important and lasting mission in the Ecuadorean Oriente. There George and Muriel Moffatt evangelized the headhunting Shuar, or Jívaro, Indians.[34] At the same time, the CMA instituted itinerant Bible schools in the coastal backwoods regions outside of Guayaquil. The missionaries who taught in these schools traveled by launch, on horseback, and on foot to hold Bible classes at beaches and in towns and plantations all along the coastal plain.[35]

In 1928 the CMA founded the Alliance Bible Seminary in Guayaquil with an initial enrollment of six students; in 1929 it opened the Realidades Bookstore and the Alliance Academy in Quito. These institutions are still in existence and are still important to the organization. Finally, in 1931, the CMA helped found the HCJB (Heralding Christ Jesus' Blessings) radio station, which ushered in a new age in Protestant evangelism in Ecuador and Latin America. With HCJB, the CMA firmly established itself and took its place alongside the GMU as one of the most important early Protestant missions in Ecuador.

The final early Protestant group to enter Ecuador was the Seventh-Day Adventists (SDA). It dated its origins back to 1818, when William Miller began the Advent Christian Church by preaching the second coming of Christ, which he predicted first for 1843 and later for 1844. In 1863, with the second advent movement and the rise to prominence of Ellen G. White, Seventh-Day Adventism was given renewed vigor. Through her relevations and writings, White gave the SDA its name and organizational structure.

The SDA believes in the imminent second coming of Christ, the millennium, and the final judgment. It affirms the unique authority of the Bible, although its interpretations are oriented by White's writings.[36] As the name Seventh-Day Adventists indicates, the SDA observes Saturday as its day of worship and believes strongly in certain precepts of the people of ancient Israel and the Old Testament—for example, the ritual washing of feet and giving 10 percent of personal income to the church. Members abstain from alcohol, tobacco, drugs, shellfish, and pork. Some are vegetarians. SDA members are also pacifists and do not use weapons, though they will perform military service as nonbelligerents. In recent years the SDA movement has been stronger outside the United States than in it. By the 1970s it was the largest non-Catholic church in Mexico, Honduras, Costa Rica, Colombia, Ecuador, Peru, and Bolivia. By 1984 it had grown so fast in Latin America and Africa that only 15 percent of the denomination's 4.4 million followers were North Americans.[37] In Peru and Bolivia this growth was directly linked to the educational and health care services provided among the Quechua- and Aymara-speaking Indians, which brought about conversions.[38]

The first SDA missionary to enter Ecuador was Thomas H. Davis, a Bible salesman who arrived in Guayaquil in August 1904. He came with his family and went to work immediately selling SDA publications. George W. Casebeer, a minister, and his wife followed Davis in November 1905. A few months later the South American Union Mission, the governing body of SDA activities in South America, determined that Ecuador should be detached from the West Coast Mission (Chile, Bolivia, Peru, and Ecuador) and turned into a separate mission. Ecuador was seen as fertile ground for SDA work.[39]

In 1906 Davis and Casebeer moved to Ambato because of its strategic location. A key junction on the Quito-Guayaquil railroad, it was viewed as prime territory for SDA evangelistic work. During the rainy season, thousands of Southern and Coastal Ecuadoreans escaped the diseases and pests of their regions by moving to Ambato. The SDA missionaries saw Ambato as a place to make contact with many people from different regions of the country who would then take their literature and, it was hoped, new religious convictions back home to other Ecuadoreans.[40]

In 1907 J. W. Westphal baptized the first SDA convert, C. E. Yepez, in Ambato. Under the direction of Casebeer, the SDA opened an English-language school to meet the great demand among the youth of Ambato for instruction in the language. There it taught English to both adults and children. The school helped the SDA make many contacts with influential people for the purpose of evangelization.[41]

In the early years the members of the SDA were subject to illness, religious persecution, and the disdain of other Protestants. In 1907 Mrs. Davis died in Ambato and because of her religion was not given the right to a burial in the local cemetery. Her husband had to take her body outside the city and dig a grave with his own hands.[42]

The persecution and the unhealthy climate caused both the Davis and Casebeer families to leave Ecuador in 1908. They went to Chile to continue their work. Octavio Navarette and William Steele took their places, and

Steele became the mission's director. A few months later William W. Wheeler, a minister and practical nurse, arrived with his wife. Illness continued to plague the SDA mission, however, and Steele and his family left the country. John Osborne and his family arrived in Ecuador some time before October 1910 to replace the Steeles.[43]

Other Protestant groups disliked the SDA because of its attempts at evangelizing people already converted. The GMU's William Reed was more than a little distressed when he wrote about Davis, "We have felt a bit bothered by the work of an Adventist colporteur who has presented his literature to our people; however, we are confident that God will protect us from the errors that he is circulating."[44]

In 1910 the SDA moved its center of operations to Quito, where it had long wanted to establish a mission but had lacked the personnel to do so. It was given impetus by the departure of the North American Methodist teachers who had worked in the normal schools. Much to Reed's chagrin, the SDA moved in to fill the void and proselytized among the Ecuadorean Methodists left behind by the teachers. Reed gained a measure of revenge, however, when he and the GMU resumed their work in Ambato in August 1911.[45]

Early in 1911 the second Ecuadorean SDA convert, who was known as Brother Espinosa of Machala, was baptized by Wheeler. By the middle of the year, it seemed that the SDA had gained a foothold. Health problems continued to haunt the mission, though, and by the end of the year both Osborne and Wheeler had contracted tropical diseases. Osborne recovered and remained in Ecuador, but Wheeler left. In early 1912 the Osbornes were joined by César López of Peru and Santiago Mangold of Argentina, and on June 15, the first local SDA church was organized in Quito with eight members. The opening of the church gave new hope to the mission, but that was soon dashed by the death of Mrs. Mangold and the return of her husband and children to Argentina in 1913.

In 1914 C. E. Knight arrived from the United States, and Enrique Mangold came from Argentina. Knight took over the superintendency of the mission from Osborne, who was sick, and Mangold canvassed new territory. The new arrivals were also hampered by disease, and the activities of the mission came to a virtual standstill for the next few years.[46]

In the subsequent decade, the 1920s, the SDA mission went from hard times to the beginnings of a firm and permanent base in Ecuador. Important to its success was the arrival in 1921 of Mr. and Mrs. Orley Ford, who had formerly worked with Indians in Peru, and of G. A. Schwerin and his family in 1927. The Fords opened a mission station in Colta, in Chimborazo, and the Schwerins helped increase SDA membership.[47] When the Schwerins arrived, there were 31 converts to the SDA. By the following year, through their efforts, that number had risen to 65. By 1931 both the Schwerins and Fords had helped increase SDA membership to 108 followers. By the early 1930s, this growing membership solidified the SDA in Ecuador and led it to construct the first SDA church building in Quito in 1941.[48]

The early Protestant groups that came to Ecuador and flourished there from 1896 to 1931 opened the door for others to follow. The Methodist Episcopal Church, the GMU, the CMA, and the SDA were pioneers who faced the Conservative opposition head-on and made inroads in a country that had long been considered the exclusive domain of Catholicism. It could be said that the Protestants began a second religious conquest of Ecuador that emphasized missionary endeavor. They did not act alone, however; they were assisted by the government of the United States and by national governments who, by promulgating liberal constitutions, legalized Protestantism's presence and offered it protection. In effect, the Liberals in Ecuador and the North American Protestants entered into a symbiotic relationship. The Liberals used the Protestants to weaken the Conservatives' hold on power, while the Protestants utilized the Liberals to gain a foothold from which to build their movement.

In the larger picture of Latin American church history, the Ecuadorean experience with Protestantism mirrored what took place in much of Latin America in the latter half of the nineteenth century and the early part of the twentieth century. With Liberal assistance, Protestants entered Mexico, Central America, and the Andean region, where they helped change the sociopolitical and religious landscape of those areas. Everywhere the Protestants went, they established bases from which to diffuse their doctrine into the hinterlands. They established missions along trade routes, in populated areas, next to railroads, and near American investment.[49] Few in number but determined in spirit, the early North American Protestant groups in Latin America worked in the name of the United States. Like the Spanish priests of the colonial epoch, the Protestant missionaries in the late nineteenth and early twentieth centuries helped build the ideological framework around which a new and powerful empire expanded.

CHAPTER 3

The First Specialized Group:
HCJB Radio, "The Voice of The Andes,"
1931–1990

FROM 1931 TO 1990 PROTESTANTISM in Ecuador evolved into a movement that incorporated modern technology into its repertoire of evangelistic tools. During those fifty-nine years, North American fundamentalist
specialized groups entered the country emphasizing evangelization through
radio and television, health care, linguistic studies, Bible translation, and
development projects.[1] These specialized groups, multinational and multi-
denominational in nature, helped Ecuador become an important base of
operations from which North American fundamentalist Protestantism
could pursue its objectives of Latin American and world evangelization.

For much of the 1931–90 period, most Ecuadorean governments, as
their predecessors previously had done, viewed the North American Protestant influx as benevolent and an aid to national development. Throughout the period, government arguments in favor of the Protestants were
strengthened by the assistance they rendered during times of great natural
disaster. Roman Catholics, indigenous people, and nationalists, however,
had strong reservations about them. As the period progressed, opposition to
the specialized Protestant groups was laced with calls for their expulsion,
and in 1981 one specialized group was officially expelled.

As the specialized Protestant groups advanced, each decade during the
1931–90 period brought something unique in societal upheaval. In the
1930s there was a prolonged power struggle in which new factions and political parties were added to the age-old Liberal-Conservative rivalry. Important among the new political groups were the Fascist Compactación

Obrera Nacional (National Worker Compact) or "Camisas Sucias" (Dirty Shirts) and the Nueva Alianza Revolucionaria Ecuatoriana (New Ecuadorean Revolutionary Alliance). The former helped overthrow Isidro Ayora in 1931 and place in power an independent landowner, Neptalí Bonifaz Ascázubi. The latter gave an ample majority to one of the most important political leaders in Ecuadorean history, José María Velasco Ibarra, in the presidential election of December 1933. Allegedly the Camisas Sucias and the Nueva Alianza Revolucionaria Ecuatoriana were broad-based movements made up of the poor masses of workers, artisans, and campesinos of the Sierra who had united for common economic and political goals. In reality these movements were manipulated by Conservatives who wanted to win back political and economic power lost in the Liberal Revolution some thirty-six years earlier.[2]

The 1930s proved to be the most unstable decade in Ecuadorean history. The presidency was held by no fewer than fourteen individuals. The most important of these were Velasco Ibarra (September 1934–August 1935), and Federico Páez (September 1935–October 1937). Like all the presidents of the decade, however, they accomplished little. Further complicating the situation were diseases that savaged the cacao crop, Ecuador's principal export commodity.[3]

The deterioration of political and economic conditions during the 1930s caused dissension among the diverse sectors of the dominant classes and led to middle- and lower-class demands for action. The popular struggles that resulted gave birth to labor syndicates that asked for salary increases, work clothes, humane treatment, tools, overtime for evening work, an eight-hour workday, a week's annual vacation, a minimum wage, woman and child labor regulation, accident insurance, medical attention, and collective contracts for workers. During this period workers actually won certain concessions. In 1937 the government established the Instituto Nacional de Previsión (National Social Security Institute), which later became the Instituto Ecuatoriano de Seguro Social (Ecuadorean Institute of Social Security); the Congress passed the Ley de Comunas y de Cooperativas (Community and Cooperative Law), which legitimized land and property ownership for peasant community organizations; and the Syndicato Nacional de Educadores (National Educators Union) was formed. Furthermore, in 1938, the government produced a work code intended to normalize labor-management relations and promulgated the Ley de Enseñanza Superior (Higher Education Law).[4]

The majority of the gains made by labor during the latter years of the 1930s appeared only after a period of intense governmental repression. This was especially true during the Páez administration. Páez believed that Communists backed by Moscow inspired the demands. In an attempt to stem the tide, he persecuted labor leaders, arrested those who did not agree with him, and dictated the Ley de Seguridad Social (Law of Social Protection), which so deprived citizens of civil liberties that the military and the national police were authorized to fire upon anyone considered suspicious. The Ecuadorean military, who had placed the dictator Páez in power, were ultimately embarrassed by his actions, however. This led to his removal from office and the naming of General Alberto Enríquez as his replacement. During his nine months in office, Enríquez helped pass the aforementioned social legislation.[5]

The 1940s brought continuing difficulties for Ecuador. In July 1941 a so-called border war broke out with Peru. This short war had minimal casualities but disastrous consequences for Ecuador in terms of territorial loss. When it ended, Ecuador ceded half of its land to Peru. In reality, the war had little to do with Ecuadorean-Peruvian boundaries and everything to do with British and North American oil companies who were battling over petroleum concessions in the Amazon. The companies involved were two of the "seven sisters,' the world's largest oil companies, Standard Oil of New Jersey and Royal Dutch Shell. The war began after Standard Oil, upset by a 10-million-hectare concession of land given by the Páez government to Royal Dutch Shell in 1937, called upon the Peruvian military and expansionists within the government to attack Ecuador. Standard Oil had historically thought of the concession as its own and as early as 1938 drew up a plan to take it back by force if necessary.[6] In the end, Standard Oil and Peru defeated Royal Dutch Shell and Ecuador, forcing the latter out of the Amazon Basin in territory near the Marañón River. Subsequently Standard Oil turned the conquered and annexed land over to the International Petroleum Corporation (IPC), its Peruvian subsidiary, and on January 29, 1942, under the threat of continued military action, Ecuador signed the Rio de Janiero Protocol, which upheld Peru's claim to the disputed territory. Four nations—Argentina, Chile, the United States, and Brazil—guaranteed the Protocol. The United States, the principal guarantor, pushed for a quick, conclusive settlement because of its involvement in World War II. Ecuadoreans today perceive the Rio Protocol in the same light as the Treaty of Guadalupe-Hidalgo is perceived by Mexicans; it represents a national disgrace and the dismemberment of their country. The slogan "Ecuador has been and will always be an Amazonian Country" is still printed on all government stationary.

The defeat by Peru and the loss of territory tore Ecuador apart politically during the 1940s. Nationalists criticized the Liberal president, Carlos Arroyo del Río, for signing the Protocol and giving away half the country. This unhappiness led to a military uprising in Guayaquil on May 28, 1944, that forced Arroyo del Río from power and paved the way for Velasco Ibarra to assume the presidency for the second time.[7] Velasco Ibarra, however, again proved incapable of governing; the caudillo who once boasted, "Give me a balcony and I will govern" resorted to repressive tactics to silence his critics. In 1947 a new military coup forced Velasco Ibarra into exile in Argentina; he was replaced as president by Galo Plaza Lasso. In 1948 Plaza Lasso was elected for a four-year term. During his administration, with the help of the UFCO (see Introduction), Ecuador became the largest producer of bananas in the world.[8]

Compared to the two earlier decades, the 1950s were years of relative peace. Because of banana prosperity, Plaza Lasso, Velasco Ibarra for the third time (1952–56), and Camilo Ponce Enríquez (1956–60) all completed their terms as president of Ecuador. Banana dollars fostered economic, educational, and infrastructure development.[9] Unfortunately the banana boom was brought to an end by the close of the decade by Central American competition, Panama Canal tolls, severe weather, and dependence on foreign markets. The end of the banana boom led to rioting in Guayaquil, where hundreds were shot. In 1959 a desperate call went out for Velasco Ibarra to return to the presidency once again.[10]

The 1960s began with Velasco Ibarra's election as a "leftist reformer." The Ecuadorean people had brought him back to fulfill his traditional role as a mediator. He immediately came up against the U.S. government, which had determined that there would be no more Cuban-style revolutions in Latin America. Because of that, the anti-Communist, pro–North American Ecuadorean military, through the Alliance for Progress, received vast sums for military and financial aid, which enabled them to depose Valasco Ibarra and place his vice-president, Carlos Julio Arosemena Monroy, in power in November 1961. Arosemena Monroy also ran afoul of the United States by taking a pro-Cuba stance. In July 1963 the Ecuadorean military removed him from office after he purportedly insulted the U.S. government in a toast at a banquet honoring Admiral McNeil, the president of Grace Lines. Arosemena said, "To the people of the United States, but not to its government which exploits the peoples of Latin America."[11]

After the fall of Arosemena, a repressive right-wing military dictatorship took over the Ecuadorean government. It remained in power until July 1966, when civilian rule returned. In 1968 Velasco Ibarra was elected president for the final time. He declared himself dictator in 1970 and governed until 1972, when the military again deposed him. In retrospect it is apparent that José María Velasco Ibarra dominated Ecuadorean politics for four decades. His place in Ecuadorean history can be compared to that of Gabriel García Moreno and Eloy Alfaro.[12]

In the 1970s petroleum production boomed. According to the military and dominant elite, this boom augured in a period of modernization in which, because of increased revenues, Ecuador would develop its infrastructure and industry. In 1972, leadership fell to General Guillermo Rodríguez Lara, a leftist on the model of Juan Alvardo Velasco of Peru, who boasted that he would "sow the petroleum" in economic and social development. He accomplished little, managing only to make Ecuador a member of the Organization of Petroleum Exporting Countries (OPEC) and angering the United States by taking an extreme nationalistic position in the so-called tuna war, a conflict in which Ecuador detained North American fishing boats that had entered its territorial waters.[13] As a result, in 1976, a right-wing military faction strongly in favor of opening Ecuador's economy to foreign investment ousted Rodríguez Lara. This military government managed to achieve some semblance of independence from the United States by nationalizing foreign oil interests. The petroleum multinationals did not complain; they discovered that providing technical assistance to Ecuador could be as profitable a business as exploration and exploitation.[14]

In 1977 political change once again overtook Ecuador. At that time the labor movement agitated against the military government, and large numbers of campesinos and indigenous people migrated to the cities, a process that undermined economic reform. At the same time, the downturn in the world price of petroleum put a stop to the military government's development plans and forced it to accede to demands for a presidential election. In 1978 the Ecuadorean people elected the idealistic and youthful Jaime Roldos Aguilera. He took office on August 10, 1979, but ultimately failed to control warring political factions and curb the inflationary spiral that was ruining the purchasing power of most Ecuadoreans.[15]

In the decade of the 1980s, renewed border conflict with Peru, external debt, the sudden death of a president, and political rivalries dominated the course of events. In January 1981 Ecuador and Peru almost went to war again after their troops clashed in the Oriente. This conflict lasted for a month and ended with an agreement to abide by the 1941 Rio Protocol. Later in that year, on May 24 (Ecuadorean Independence Day), the Roldos Aguilera government came to an unfortunate and abrupt end when the president, his wife Marta Bucaram de Roldos, and the minister of defense were killed in a plane crash on their way to Loja in the southern Sierra. This accident shocked and saddened the Ecuadorean people, and to this day many suspect the crash was the work of a conspiracy.

Oswaldo Hurtado Larrea, who replaced Roldos Aguillera as president, promised to continue the work of his predecessor as outlined in a comprehensive development plan calling for the construction of roads, schools, hospitals, and rural electrification projects. Because of external debt, however, Hurtado Larrea could not deliver all he promised. Ultimately he and his Democracia Popular (Popular Democracy) party were harshly criticized, and, in 1984 the Ecuadorean people, in a turn to the right, elected the Guayaquil businessman León Febres Cordero to be their next president. Febres Cordero attempted to pay off the external debt and reactivate the national economy. To his discredit, he did neither. Furthermore, he was dictatorial and repressive. In 1987 he was kidnapped by a military faction and taken to an air force base on the Santa Elena Peninisula, where he was released only after promising reforms. In 1988 Febres Cordero was replaced by Rodrigo Borja Cevallos of the Izquierda Democrática (Democratic Left) party. In his election campaign, Borja Cevallos promised to unify all Ecuadoreans and to cure the economic ills of the country. In August 1989 he proposed a program for debt reduction following the guidelines of the Brady Plan, which called for cutting one-third of the debt by 70 percent and allowing the government to buy back the rest at a discount. Ecuador's creditors rejected the plan, citing that the country was too rich in oil and could afford to pay more.[16]

The specialized Protestant groups believed that the social, political, and economic tensions of Ecuadorean life between 1931 and 1990 only made their work more relevant. They viewed Ecuador as a country in dire need of evangelization, one with an important role to play in the worldwide Protestant movement. The groups that entered Ecuador during these years accommodated themselves to Ecuadorean instability and made progress in spite of it.

The first specialized Protestant group to take up the challenge of Ecuador was "The Voice of the Andes," HCJB Radio. Founded by the World Radio Missionary Fellowship (WRMF) in 1931, HCJB became the longest-lasting and most powerful specialized Protestant group in Ecuador. Its principal visionaries were Clarence Jones, who had prior experience in evangelical radio in the United States, and Reuben Larson, a CMA missionary who had worked some years among indigenous groups in the Oriente. The WRMF itself had only recently been incorporated—in March 1931 in Lima, Ohio. Clarence Jones's father-in-law ran a rescue mission there, and the incorporation of WRMF took place in the mission's library.[17]

HCJB was the first evangelical radio station to operate outside the United States. In addition to Jones and Larson, D. Stuart Clark, John Clark, and Paul Young, all missionaries with the CMA, contributed to its early development. The call letters HCJB were devised by Jones and Larson. They stand for Heralding Christ Jesus' Blessings in English and Hoy Cristo Jesús Bendice (Today Christ Jesus Blesses) in Spanish. Jones and Larson based the concept on the Chicago evangelical station WJBT, the call letters for which signified Where Jesus Blesses Thousands.[18]

The establishment of call letters for the new station was the first step in a blueprint for development that envisioned HCJB's growth from a local station in Quito to one that would ultimately reach out to all of Ecuador, its neighboring republics, and later the rest of Latin America and the world. The plan called for incremental increases in transmission power, to which the success of HCJB was in fact tied. In evangelical terms, the blueprint for the worldwide diffusion of HCJB was linked to the Bible and "the consecutive steps to be taken in reaching the holy objective of making Christ known as his 'witness.' " The Bible said that the gospel should be taken first to Jerusalem, second to all Judea, third to Samaria, and fourth to "the uttermost part of the earth." For the Protestants of HCJB, Jerusalem meant Quito; Judea, Ecuador's neighboring republics; Samaria, South and Central America; and "the uttermost part of the earth," the world.[19]

HCJB went on the air for the first time on December 25, 1931, powered by a 200-watt transmitter. A sheep shed on the outskirts of Quito served as its studio.[20] This initial broadcast went out to a city and country in which radio was virtually nonexistent, a situation that improved greatly after one of the leading commercial houses owned by William Reed's two sons, John and Alan, began importing radio receivers. In 1934 HCJB's management realized that the cost of a radio receiver was out of reach for most Ecuadoreans, and it began to lend cheap used receivers to people interested in the station's transmissions. This program of loans, known as El Círculo de Radio (the Radio Circle), called for the sharing of radio receivers among friends and relatives. It was so successful that it increased the number of listeners and brought the gospel to many people who would have otherwise remained without it.[21]

HCJB increased its transmitting power to 1,000 watts by 1937 and 10,000 watts by 1940.[22] In later increases HCJB grew to 50,000 watts in 1956, enough to send its signal around the world, and 80,000 watts in 1960. Eventually HCJB grew to an output of more than a million watts. By 1988 it operated an antenna and transmitter complex near the town of Pifo, fifteen miles east of Quito, consisting of eleven shortwave transmitters and a medium-wave transmitter. The Pifo complex had thirty-one different antenna systems, including a 417-foot steerable antenna designed and built by HCJB engineers. HCJB maintained additional transmitters at Esmeraldas, Guayaquil, and on Mt. Pichincha towering high above Quito. Most of the energy to power the station's transmitters came from its own hydroelectric plant in Papallacta, to the east of Pifo near the continental divide. There two generators produced up to 6 million watts of power. HCJB employees and engineers maintained the power station and all service lines themselves.[23]

The HCJB blueprint developed by Jones and Larson also called for a strong, globe-girdling signal to disseminate the gospel in many different languages. In the early years, with its weak signal, HCJB had to content itself with broadcasting in English and Spanish only. Jones, Larson, and Clark, with technical assistance provided by Eric Williams, the designer and builder of the earliest HCJB transmitter, handled the English-language broadcasts.[24] For Spanish broadcasting, HCJB hired Dr. Manuel Garrido Aldama, a former priest from Spain who had converted to Protestantism. His strong clear voice went out daily throughout Latin America and impressed all those who listened to him. He knew Latin American culture and language, and he appealed most directly to the Catholic majority by relating his conversion experience. His listeners even included Catholic clergy. According to accounts of the day, his audience considered him a Latin American and did not care what doctrine he preached.[25]

With time and increased wattage, HCJB began to fulfill its goal of broadcasting in many different languages. In 1941, ten years after its initiation, the station transmitted its first broadcast in Quechua, the principal indigenous language of the Andes. The Quechua broadcaster was Carmela Ochoa, an Ecuadorean from Cuenca who had learned the Indian language at an early age from a relative and had been drawn to Indian culture by that experience. Upon moving to Quito, she became interested in the work of HCJB and made contact with Clark and Larson, who, after converting her to Protestantism, persuaded her to work for the station. Her broadcasts pioneered HCJB's Quechua service, which grew to provide more than a hundred hours a week in the language and reached an audience that may have exceeded 14 million listeners in Southern Colombia, Ecuador, Peru, Bolivia, and Northern Argentina. By the late 1980s HCJB was broadcasting in eleven different languages to all parts of the world. In addition to English, Spanish, and Quechua, it provided radio services in Chinese, Czech, French, German, Japanese, "Nordic," Portuguese, and Russian. All of the languages could be broadcast simultaneously from the Program Automatic Control System (PACS), the computer-controlled nerve center in Quito. Most programs were prerecorded, but HCJB also had the capacity for live broadcasts and even international call-in shows. English, Spanish, and Quechua were the languages most broadcast; Russian (forty-three hours a week) and Portuguese, aimed at Brazil (forty-two hours a week), were next in frequency.[26]

HCJB also expanded into television. In 1956 WRMF's board of trustees went on record as favoring a television ministry in Ecuador, and in 1958 the Ecuadorean government granted HCJB the permission to import, duty-free, the equipment necessary to set up a television studio. On August 10, 1960, HCJB aired the first television program ever produced in Ecuador. This beginning led to the station's receiving a provisional license to telecast test programs three times a week. On May 18, 1961, the minister of public works signed an official contract with WRMF that allowed it to own and operate a television station in Quito and later one in Guayaquil.[27]

HCJB-TV, Channel 4, "The Window of the Andes," was the first missionary television station in the world. Though it engendered much hope within Protestant circles, however, it never reached its full potential. It was plagued by its staff's technical inexperience in the medium, the lack of proper facilities, shortages in suitable programming, and ultimately, new Ecuadorean laws and regulations governing the management and operation of television stations. These problems affected daily operations so much that even though there were plans for expansion, the broadcasting rights were transferred to local business interests on April 27, 1972. With that act, Channel 4 became a commercial station devoid of any religious content. Later, however, HCJB developed the capacity to produce evangelical programs and home videos targeted at specific groups. The production unit, Producciones Vozandes, made programs such as "Prisma," a show for young people, and "Family in Crisis," a home video series designed to promote biblically based marriages and families. These programs, made for worldwide consumption, were distributed by HCJB's own distribution department.[28]

HCJB-TV can be viewed as a prelude to the avalanche of North American religious television programming in Latin America. Beginning early in the 1980s, programs such as Pat Robertson's "700 Club" and "One Hour with Jimmy Swaggert" appeared on regular television. As the decade progressed, cable television from the United States introduced its broad array of stations, including the Christian Broadcasting Network (CBN). This costly service was used most by elites who viewed it as a sign of development. For many other Latin Americans, however, including fervent nationalists, U.S. television and Protestant religious programming was an intrusion. They questioned the motivations behind the "electronic church" and its modern marketing techniques.[29]

In addition to its activities in radio and television, HCJB also provided a health-care delivery system that evolved around hospitals and community-based services. It committed itself to training health-care specialists and researching health problems in rural communities. HCJB built two hospitals in Ecuador, the Rimmer Memorial Hospital (Hospital Vozandes-Quito) and the J. B. Epp Memorial Hospital (Hospital Vozandes-Shell Mera), and furnished medical caravans that traveled around the country taking care of the health needs of the rural population, particularly addressing the treatment and prevention of waterborne intestinal diseases.[30]

HCJB first became involved in health care in January 1946, when the president of WRMF, Clarence Jones, wrote to its trustees about the needs of HCJB in Quito. Jones believed a doctor was needed to care for HCJB personnel and local indigenous people, for developing a supervised recreation program, for broadcasting a regularly scheduled hygiene class on the air, and for traveling with HCJB's sound bus. The traveling sound bus (or "radio rodante") was an integral part of HCJB's early history in Ecuador. A studio on wheels, it was designed to go quickly from town to town. It proved to be a novelty in out-of-the-way places and attracted crowds wherever it went. It carried all the necessary equipment for remote radio broadcasts: an electric generator, a portable transmitter, an antenna, phonograph turntables, loudspeakers, and 16-millimeter movie equipment complete with a tripod for a projector.[31]

The petition of HCJB's president resulted in a plan for raising funds to purchase land suitable for an Indian clinic on the Pan-American Highway in Quito Norte (North Quito). Responsibility for completing the plan went to Dr. Harry Rimmer, who enlisted help from missionaries in the United States and appeared on a gospel broadcast in Philadelphia, "The Morning Cheer Hour," directed by Dr. George Palmer, to obtain backing for the project. Palmer became an enthusiastic supporter and helped raise the necessary funds.[32]

On April 28, 1950, HCJB inaugurated the Alberque y Dispensario Indígena (Indian Hostel Clinic), housed in a modest building that doubled as a church. The clinic had an examination room, a dispensary, and two small rooms with eight bunk beds to accommodate patients. It became the center of HCJB's medical department. Almost immediately after its opening, however, HCJB deemed it inadequate to meet its needs and made plans, with the help of George Palmer, to erect a hospital in Quito in memory of Dr. Harry Rimmer, who had died before the opening of the Indian clinic. On October 4, 1953, HCJB broke ground for the new hospital, and nine months later, on June 16, 1954, it opened. During its first year, the Hospital Vozandes-Quito treated more than 16,000 patients and boasted that "many men, women and children found the lord as their own personal Saviour." It became an important fixture in Ecuador. By the late 1980s it had become a general hospital that offered services in most specialties and was the only hospital in North Quito that provided twenty-four-hour emergency service. It also became a teaching hospital affiliated with Ecuadorean medical schools.[33]

The Hospital Vozandes-Shell Mera was conceived in the mid-1950s with the help of the Missionary Aviation Fellowship (MAF), a nondenominational evangelical agency that supplied aviation, radio, health care, and technical assistance to national churches and other agencies in foreign countries. Nate Saint of the MAF had established a base at Shell Mera, a site on the western edge of the Oriente that formerly belonged to Royal Dutch Shell. From there he flew missionaries and supplies into the deepest reaches of the jungle. He saw a great need for a hospital in the Oriente, because the area's population was isolated from civilization.[34]

Two members of HCJB's medical staff, Dr. Paul Roberts and Dr. E. Fuller, favored Saint's idea.[35] To get the project rolling, Saint offered to deed some land in Shell Mera to HCJB for the hospital. HCJB accepted the offer and began construction, using people from various missions in the region. The GMU's Roger Yoderian, who had experience in construction, and Ed McCully and Jim Elliot of the Plymouth Brethren helped build the hospital. Later the Huaorani (Auca) Indians killed Saint, Yoderian, McCully, Elliot, and Peter Fleming (see chapter 4).[36]

Financial aid and promotional assistance for the project came from the Back to the Bible Broadcast in Lincoln, Nebraska. One of its executives, the Reverend G. Christian Weiss, was a former president of the GMU who visited the Oriente and knew Ecuador well. He spoke to Dr. Fuller, became a supporter of the project, and promised to work hard in the United States to fund it. He helped initially by getting the board of directors of the Back to the Bible Broadcast to donate $10,000.[37]

Ultimately HCJB, the GMU, the CMA, the MAF, the Plymouth Brethren, and the SIL all contributed to the completion of the Hospital Vozandes-Shell Mera. It was inaugurated on May 10, 1958, and provided beds for eighteen inpatients in one building and facilities for outpatients in an adjacent building. It served as a base for medical work throughout the Oriente and as an example of radio and medicine working together toward realizing North American Protestant goals in the region.

For HCJB, the two Vozandes hospitals served as a means to draw people to Christ. The Protestants viewed people who entered the hospitals as in need not only of medical help but also of spiritual help. They believed there was no better captive audience than a person in bad health. Frank S. Cook wrote:

The whole thrust of the Gospel message is that by any and all means men and women should come to the knowledge of Christ as Saviour. Radio is a wonderful and modern means of disseminating the seed of the Word, but the whole worldwide radio ministry of HCJB is dependent on a strong base in Quito. What better way to help strengthen those ties that bind us to the country of Ecuador and its people than by helping them in their distress? Medicine, as one of the HCJB doctors has said, is a magnet to draw men to Christ.[38]

In its history in Ecuador, HCJB's zeal gained it the goodwill of many Ecuadoreans. Conversely, however, it alarmed others who viewed its activities as contrary to the prevailing cultural and religious traditions of the country. These critics viewed HCJB as setting itself apart from the surrounding cultural environment and espousing solutions that failed to take into consideration the structural nature of Ecuador's problems. They considered HCJB's fundamentalism and profound conservatism an imposition of North American cultural values that did more harm than good. As evidence of HCJB's detachment, Ecuadorean nationalists pointed to the station's fenced-off compound in Quito, which they jokingly referred to as the Protestant Vatican. Located within that compound and in the adjacent vicinity were housing, the Vozandes hospital, a school, a book store, transmitting studios, and administrative offices. The compound functioned as the principal North American Protestant center in Ecuador and was the entry point for North American groups like World Vision and Billy Graham's Evangelical Association.[39]

Controversy beset much of HCJB's work in Ecuador. Abundant criticism came from nationalists within Ecuadorean Protestantism itself, who believed that HCJB worked to divide the Ecuadorean and Latin American ecumenical movements. Their criticism first surfaced in a time of marked conflict, between 1965 and 1967, during which HCJB and the Confraternidad Evangélica Ecuatoriana or CEE (Ecuadorean Protestant Brotherhood), the governing body of the Ecuadorean Protestant church, clashed over the question of ecumenism.[40] The national Protestants held a negative view of HCJB that contradicted the one generally held by Ecuadorean governments, which lauded HCJB's assistance in times of great need and its pioneering work in the fields of communication and health care. One example often pointed to was the assistance that HCJB provided in the aftermath of the Ambato earthquake of 1949, which killed thousands of Ecuadoreans. During that tragedy, HCJB helped establish communications with the disaster area by sending a portable transmitter. It also arranged with NBC in New York to take movies of Ambato for television broadcast in the United States and opened its studios for President Galo Plaza Lasso to speak to the world. The three major networks rebroadcast his speech in the United States. HCJB also sent members of its medical team to the stricken area.[41]

During the period of conflict between the national Protestants and the North Americans, there were two instances when criticism of HCJB came to the fore. The first was at the Third Assembly of the CEE, held in Alangasí, outside Quito, on March 21, 1966. At that meeting Washington Padilla, the president of the CEE, reported that HCJB and other fundamentalist groups including the GMU had attempted to set up a rival organization. He stated that HCJB and the others feared that the CEE board of directors was moving too far to the left and becoming an instrument of the World Council of Churches (WCC). Padilla told the meeting that after deliberations, the board had expelled the GMU from the organization and was on the verge of doing the same to HCJB. He condemned the GMU and HCJB as blind and irrational and stated that they were defensive even though they were unsure of what they were defending. He told the assembly that the GMU and HCJB were attempting to divide and subdivide the organization by raising the specter of ecumenism within the CEE. He accused the North American Protestants of paternalism and said that they resented the board of directors because it believed in freedom of choice and was against making the organization a prisoner to a foreign ideology. He emphasized that the board refused to be managed by groups with a sectarian spirit. He believed, he said, that HCJB was reacting to members and groups that accepted the doctrine of ecumenism, not because it was a threat, but because an all-Ecuadorean directorship now controlled the CEE. He also accused HCJB and the fundamentalists of hypocrisy because many of them received support from churches in the United States that belonged to the WCC.[42]

The second instance of national Protestant criticism of HCJB took place after Frank S. Cook, HCJB's director of the Bible Institute of the Air, wrote a letter to Padilla on March 15, 1967. In that letter Cook expressed his sorrow that the upcoming annual assembly of the CEE was scheduled for April 17–21, the dates for the World Vision meeting in Medellín, Colombia. Cook regretted that the CEE meeting might not have a quorum because World Vision had already invited some seventy national Protestants to the meeting and could not change its date. Cook also protested an invitation the CEE had extended to Dr. José Miguez Bonino, a leading advocate of liberation theology and an important Latin American Protestant scholar. He was especially irked because Miguez Bonino was a professor at the progressive ecumenical College of Theology in Buenos Aires.[43]

Padilla's answer to Cook, dated March 20, 1967, analyzed the relationship between the North American Protestants and the national Protestants.[44] Padilla wondered why World Vision did not have the courtesy to check with the CEE before the World Vision meeting was scheduled. He stated that he found out about the conflict of dates by accident and was surprised that no one at any of the foreign Protestant missions, including HCJB, had warned him in time to change the date of the CEE assembly. He also wondered why Cook thought it impossible for World Vision to change its date and easy for the CEE to do so.[45]

As to the invitation of Miguez Bonino, Padilla responded to Cook in terms that defended his choice. He stated first that Miguez Bonino was an expert on the changes that were occurring in the Catholic church, that the Methodist church had sent him to the Second Vatican Council meeting in Rome a few years before as an observer, and that it would be positive for Ecuadorean Protestants to gain a greater understanding of what was happening in the world, in Latin America, and in Ecuador. Second, he said that he considered it necessary to give support to "brothers" who looked at problems from a positive and Christian approach rather than from a negative and anti-Christian one. Third, he stated that "the day had passed in which we had to limit ourselves and receive the approval of the Protestant 'popes' before being able to invite and listen to brothers of the faith who can contribute to a better understanding of the problems we face."[46]

In sum, Padilla took a strong nationalistic stance. He was interested in the problems of Ecuadorean Protestants and not those of church politics in the United States, he said. His reaction was not simply a case, as he put it, "of juvenile rebellion nor a disparaging of authority nor the desire for irresponsible independence." He clearly saw it as a "revindication" and a demonstration of the right to religious freedom.[47]

Padilla's criticism of HCJB went to the heart of Ecuadorean nationalism and showed how strong those patriotic feelings really were. Ultimately, however, nationalism did little to weaken HCJB's position in Ecuador, in Latin America, and around the globe. After 1967 HCJB expanded its services both nationally and internationally. It began local FM broadcasts in Quito; the new radio station HCJB-2 in Guayaquil; and a Center for Evangelism and Discipleship (CED) that organized monthly music and film crusades, private correspondence courses, and Bible study seminars for pastors. In 1984 HCJB founded the Christian Center of Communications (CCC), an institution of higher education dedicated to training Latin American Christians in communications, Bible study, and music. At the CCC, Christian professionals studied to be future leaders in the fundamentalist Protestant movement in Ecuador and Latin America.[48] National Protestants viewed the CCC as HCJB's answer to the Ecuadorean ecumenical movement. For

HCJB, the CCC underscored its determination to proceed along fundamentalist sectarian lines.

Elsewhere in the world, HCJB cooperated with other radio ministries, such as Far East Broadcasting, Trans World Radio, and SIM Radio. Together they devised a plan called World by 2000, which had as its prime objective the transmission of the gospel by radio to all the inhabitants of the Earth by the year 2000. In addition, HCJB affiliated with Radio HOXO in Panama and the World Radio Network along the Mexican-U.S. border. HCJB considered its joint ministry with the World Radio Network necessary because the Mexican government did not allow Christian radio to transmit from within its boundaries.[49]

By 1990 HCJB had become an important institution in Ecuador and a base of operations for North American fundamentalist Protestantism in Latin America. It attributed its survival and prosperity in the face of social, political, and economic barriers to two important rules: first, it did not attack other religions or beliefs; and second, it maintained absolute political neutrality.[50] Some Ecuadoreans believed that nothing was further from the truth; HCJB, they thought, was deeply involved in politics, as demonstrated by its presence in Ecuador and by its promoting an antiecumenical, anti-Latin American religious doctrine. Those who believed in its missionizing message, on the other hand, lauded HCJB because it demonstrated an ability to stay the course and lead the way for others to follow.

The Second Specialized Group (I): The Summer Institute of Linguistics, 1952–1981

In the end, man destroyed the place called earth.

The earth had been lovely
until man's spirit moved over the face of the earth
and destroyed all things.

Iglesias, Mexico City, October 1987
Quoted from "Anti-Genesis," *Latinamerica Press*
November 12, 1987

THE SECOND IMPORTANT North American fundamentalist Protestant specialized group to establish itself in Ecuador between 1931 and 1990 was the Summer Institute of Linguistics (SIL). A division of an evangelical organization that has branches in many countries, the SIL includes the Wycliffe Bible Translators (WBT) and Jungle Aviation and Radio Services (JAARS) in its structure. The basic objective of the SIL is to complete linguistic studies and Bible translations in the missionary field. The WBT, the operational wing of the organization, works in funding, recruitment, and public relations in the United States. JAARS, staffed by pilots, mechanics, radio technologists, computer specialists, and construction workers, is the SIL's technical and transportation support arm. As of 1985, the WBT/SIL/JAARS conglomerate comprised the second largest Protestant overseas missionary agency in personnel and the seventh largest agency in reported income for overseas ministries, with earnings of $36.8 million.[1]

Officially, the SIL began its work in Ecuador in 1952, at the end of the presidential term of Galo Plaza Lasso. Unofficially it may have been in the country prior to that time helping HCJB in the Oriente.[2] There is evidence that the SIL entered through Peru in 1946 when its translators worked on or near the undelineated border with Ecuador. At that time HCJB's Clarence Jones lauded the work of the SIL:

> Already widely known for its linguistic school for missionary candidates, the Wycliffe translators, under the direction of Mr. W. Cameron Townsend, represents a tremendous step forward in scientifically attacking the problem of Bible translation. For years past, the Bible societies and missionary societies have laboriously reduced to writing the languages of hundreds of tribes and peoples. Not until Mr. Townsend, with Drs. [Kenneth] Pike and [Eugene] Nyda [Nida], developed and perfected a new approach to the problem of linguistics have missionaries had such a large opportunity for a wholly new type of preparation at home to approach this vital problem on the field. Since translation is basic to giving the people the Word of God in their own language, few advances in the mission field of the last century augur such important reaction upon missionary endeavor of the future as the work being done by Wycliffe translators. Their work is thoroughly spiritual and scientific and has won the approbation and admiration of Christians and governments alike wherever it has been introduced. The Church dare not shun the use of scientific methods in carrying out its work where the objectives of such methods are spiritual.[3]

Further evidence of what may have been early SIL involvement in Ecuador is that when it made its first contract with the Ecuadorean government in 1953, it already had a network of cooperation in place with HCJB. HCJB provided the SIL with fixed-band radio receivers, and the SIL, through JAARS, provided the radio station with aircraft to transport medical emergencies out of the Oriente.[4]

Since its founding in 1934, the SIL has been governed by what it considers to be important operating principles. First, it believes no group too insignificant for linguistic study nor any language too difficult to translate. It views itself as a missionary organization that goes forth to work "among the unnoticed, unreached, remote areas of the world." Second, the SIL postulates that the gospel must be presented to people in their own language, meaning that at least some of the scriptures should be translated into native languages. Third, it does not attempt to establish any ecclesiastical organization or denomination in the field; it only cooperates with other evangelical groups. Fourth, the SIL believes that it upholds the highest linguistic and translation standards through extensive training at its International Linguistics Centers in Dallas; at the universities of Oklahoma, Washington, and North Dakota; and at sites in Australia, Canada, England, France, Germany, Japan, and New Zealand. Fifth, the SIL asserts that it serves everyone, not only Christians, and cooperates with governments in community development, education, agricultural programs, and medical aid; it professes that one of its most important functions is to teach people to read. Finally, the SIL assumes that God will provide whatever is necessary for the organization to reach all the language groups of the earth and claims that its revenue is derived solely from home churches and individual donations.[5]

The SIL believes its work is fundamental to the task of translating the Bible into all the languages of the world by the year 2000. It reported in 1987 that Bible translations were still lacking in 3,303 of the world's 5,665 languages. Those 3,303 included 765 definite languages still in need, 234 probably in need and 2,304 possibly in need of translation. In terms of world population, these figures meant that there were more than 300 million people still without the Bible. Furthermore, the SIL contended that of the 1,708 languages already worked on, 256 had all of the Bible translated into them, 552 the New Testament only, and 900 at least one book. It reported that Bible translations or linguistic studies were under way in 1,101 languages, including 813 languages that the SIL worked with and 288 that other groups worked with. The SIL boasted of having completed translations of the New Testament or having had substantial involvement in their completion in 257 languages and of finishing its work in Bolivia. The number of language projects that the SIL had been involved in through 1987 totaled 1,105; that number represented work in 53 countries among language groups that varied in population from as few as 100 to more than 23 million.[6]

With respect to personnel the SIL needed to reach the goal it had set by its deadline, the year 2000. The organization claimed in 1987 to have 5,630 career members and short-term assistants working in the Americas, Africa, Asia, and Australia. These workers were recruited from twenty-eight different countries. The SIL admitted, however, that it needed additional personnel. As a result, it asked for several thousand people to come forward to "help bring the knowledge of Christ to Bibleless peoples through Scripture translation in their own language . . . in this century." It called for "dedicated Christians" to work as translators and linguists, academic publicists, accountants and bookkeepers, administrators and managers, anthropologists, ethnomusicologists, aviators, center operations and service workers, community development employees, computer-related workers, construction and maintainance mechanics, educators, librarians, literacy workers, media and video specialists, medical services workers, artists, public relations experts and journalists, radio and electronic technicians, secretaries, and technical studies advisors.[7]

W. Cameron Townsend, known to his followers as "Uncle Cam" founded the SIL. He originally came to Latin America in 1917, beginning his career as a Bible salesman for the Central American Mission (CAM) in Guatemala. He became well known for translating the New Testament into the Cakchiquel Indian language, a task he undertook in 1919. This work took him ten years to complete and demonstrated to the Protestant missionary world that language translation could be of value in the evangelization of native peoples.[8]

In 1934, after a bout with tuberculosis interrupted his work in Guatemala, Townsend returned to the United States. He joined with L. L. Letgers, whom he had met in 1920, to begin the SIL as a summer translation program in a farmhouse rented for $5 dollars a month in Sulphur Springs, Arkansas.[9] The site became known as Camp Wycliffe in honor of John Wycliffe, the fourteenth-century religious reformer and the first person to translate the Bible into English. Townsend and Letgers invited all who wanted to study aboriginal languages for the purpose of Bible translation to come to the camp. During the first summer, two students attended. Townsend taught grammar, literacy, and Indian village life. Letgers taught anthropology, and Dr. Elbert L. McCreey taught a two-week course in phonetics. In the summer of 1935, five students attended, including Kenneth L. Pike, who later became president of the SIL.[10]

In that same year, as a result of Camp Wycliffe activities, Townsend, now recovered from tuberculosis, returned to Latin America and took along many of his students. He chose Mexico as the first place to work because of his interest in the Nahuatl language and an invitation extended by the Mexican Presbyterian educator Moises Sáenz. His students followed his lead and began studying Maya, Tarascan, Mazatec, Otomí, Mixe, Tarahumara, Mixtec, and Totonac.[11]

Lázaro Cárdenas, the president of Mexico (1934–40), aided Townsend and the SIL. Cárdenas saw a link between the work of the SIL and help for poor Mexicans. He and Townsend became good friends. Cárdenas served as the best man at Townsend's second wedding in 1946, and in 1952 Townsend wrote a book about Cárdenas's life.[12] Their friendship even carried over to the next generation of the Cárdenas family, including Cuauhtemoc Cárdenas, who ran for president in 1988 under the banner of Mexican socialism. In 1971 the younger Cárdenas wrote the foreword to Townsend's book about the SIL leader's first two of eleven trips to the Soviet Union to investigate the possibility of translation in that country. The younger Cárdenas lauded the work of the SIL among the indigenous peoples in Ecuador and Colombia and spoke highly of its translators; he wished their humanitarian attitude could be expressed everywhere, he said, "so that humanity as a whole might benefit from the progress of science and creative capacity of men in peace."[13]

On a more pragmatic level, above and beyond friendship, Lázaro Cárdenas and Townsend each stood to gain by their relationship. By keeping Mexico's doors open to North American Protestantism, Cárdenas vented his anti-Catholic feelings and hoped to weaken the church even more than it had already been weakened. He believed he could accomplish this easily by collaborating with a group that hid its proselytizing behind a veil of linguistic investigation and at the same time could shield himself from his Mexican critics. Townsend saw Cárdenas as a link to the future and the leader through whom he could gain a permanent base in Latin America from which the SIL could expand its activities to its ultimate target, the indigenous people of the Amazon Basin.

In 1942 both the SIL and the WBT were formally incorporated in the United States. The latter was founded to represent the SIL's aims to church groups that did not understand the organization's policies. Also in 1942 the original Summer Institute of Linguistics, Camp Wycliffe, moved to the University of Oklahoma at Norman under the directorship of Eugene Nida and Kenneth L. Pike. During that summer, more than a hundred students enrolled in classes, and fifty-one of those went to Mexico.[14]

In 1943 Townsend took an exploratory trip to Peru as a consultant for the American Bible Society. While there, he contacted government officials and told them of the SIL's work among the indigenous people of Mexico. This resulted in an invitation to the SIL to do the same in Peru. Townsend understood that the tropical jungle environment of Peru, inhabited by tribes believed to be savage, would be much more difficult to manage than the more temperate people and climate of Mexico. He felt he needed a place where he could train his translators. In 1944 he found the perfect spot—in Chiapas, in southern Mexico, on the edge of the Central American rain forest. There he established the SIL's jungle training camp, where he planned to teach his followers skills they would need to survive the rigors of the Amazon. He accomplished this with the assistance of Kenneth L. Pike, who taught students how to make soap, how to preserve meat, what kinds of food to eat, how to build and navigate a dugout canoe, how to swim, and generally how to work productively under pioneer conditions.[15]

In 1946, a year after Townsend had signed a contract with the Peruvian ministry of education, SIL translators entered Peru to practice the skills they had learned at the Mexican training camp. They labored in jungle areas previously scouted by Townsend, many of them close to the Ecuadorean border. The SIL translators soon found out that they were ill-equipped for the work. They lacked radios and air transportation. One SIL team, Titus and Florence Nickel, had a particularly tough time of it. They worked among the Aguaruna tribe in northern Peru on the Marañón River and expected to be periodically resupplied by a Peruvian air force plane; as it happened, the plane was in need of repairs and could not fly much of the time. Exhausted after eight months, and with Florence pregnant and in need of medical attention, the Nickels chose to leave on foot and by canoe. Their trip back to the coast took twenty-one days; during its course they had to deal with swollen rivers, rapids, a drunken boatman, broken propellers, and intense jungle hiking. Their experience was sobering testimony to the reality that in river or overland travel anywhere in the jungle, it took days to cover distances that could be spanned in hours by air. It became apparent that transportation in the jungle would have to be improved if the mission were to proceed. Because of this, Townsend vowed, "no more of our translators should go into the jungles of Peru until they can be assured of adequate transportation."[16]

Thus JAARS was born in 1947 under the leadership of Captain Lawrence Montgomery, a North American who had been a combat pilot during World War II. After the war he served in Peru as a trainer of Peruvian pilots while he maintained his rank as a U.S. Air Force reserve officer. He knew the country, the terrain, and the hazards of flying in the jungle. Townsend was able to get the Peruvian Air Force to make JAARS a subsidiary through which Montgomery had responsibilities. At the organization's inception, the JAARS fleet consisted of a variety of aircraft such as Piper Cubs and PBY Amphibians. Eventually, the mainstay of what became known as the Friendship Fleet was the Helio-Courier, a plane designed for short takeoffs and landings and thus perfect for use in isolated locations with only limited airstrips. To obtain the planes, Townsend worked out a deal with the Helio-Courier Aircraft Company by which he could purchase the aircraft at cost if he would help sell them to the Peruvians. Another leading Helio-Courier buyer was the CIA, which began using the airplane to supply Montagnard guerrillas in Southeast Asia in 1961. The SIL also had contact with the Montagnards through a contract with South Vietnam's Diem government in 1957.[17]

With the operation of JAARS, the SIL acquired a capacity for moving swiftly into uncharted areas to encounter indigenous people and languages. In Peru the SIL stood only a stone's throw from Ecuador; its translators worked in a region of the Amazon that was never clearly delimited because of the Ecuadorean-Peruvian border dispute of 1941. With its increased transportation capability the SIL made use of this ill-defined border to work itself into Ecuador. Assisting in this effort was Rachel Saint, an SIL translator who longed to work in Ecuador with her brother Nate of the MAF. She was particularly interested in the Huaorani or Auca Indians, of whom she had learned from Nate when she passed through Ecuador in 1949 on the way to her first assignment, in Peru, after finishing the SIL's linguistic school at the University of Oklahoma and its jungle training camp in Mexico.[18] Nate told her of an almost mythical "savage" people who wore big plugs of balsa in their ears, carried elongated, chonta-wood spears, and controlled a vast area of the Oriente between the Napo and Villano rivers, beyond the Curaray River. She learned too that since the colonial period, the Huaorani had successfully defended their territory from all invaders. In the sixteenth century they speared conquistadors and Jesuits; in the nineteenth century, rubber workers; and in the twentieth century, petroleum explorers and foreign missionaries.[19]

As stipulated in its 1953 contract with the government, the SIL worked in Ecuador to develop a program of linguistic investigation of indigenous languages, to gather data on traditional medicine, to study regional folklore, and to be of general service to the Ecuadorean government.[20] The initial Ecuadorean contract, like those signed later in other countries, did not mention any of the evangelical attributes of the SIL and its work. Neither did the subsequent contracts signed in 1956 and in 1971. They did, however, give the SIL the tax-exempt status reserved for religious organizations that worked in the Oriente. David Stoll describes the SIL's failure to state its evangelical purpose clearly as a strategy that is part of a dual identity, the organization elaborated early in its history in response to political requirements both at home and in foreign countries. The SIL proclaims itself a nonsectarian linguistics organization offering governments technical assistance in return for operational rights to promote the "moral improvement" of native people and to translate books of "high moral value."[21] By representing itself in this manner, it gains access to native peoples in foreign countries.

This dual identity enabled the SIL to work in Ecuador for almost three decades. With the blessings of Ecuadorean governments, it concentrated its efforts among the indigenous people of the Oriente. It established a strategic base at Limoncocha, an hour by air from Shell Mera, the MAF station, close to the unreached tribes and convenient enough for Indians to be brought to school there and trained as language informants.[22] Limoncocha also became the base of operations for JAARS and its Helio-Courier airplanes. Out of Limoncocha, the SIL pursued its Bible translation work among various indigenous tribes of the region: the Cofanes, the Siona-Secoya, and most important of all, the Huaorani.[23]

Understanding the campaign to evangelize the Huaorani is fundamental to a perception of the role of the SIL in Ecuador from 1952 to 1981. It was a source of much controversy and ultimately led to the official expulsion of the mission.[24] Known as Operation Auca in its earliest stage, the campaign began when five Protestant missionaries with strong ties to the SIL—Nate Saint, Jim Elliot, Peter Fleming, Edward McCully, Jr., and Roger Younderian—attempted to establish contact with the Huaorani in the fall of 1955. This attempt was launched in secrecy to keep knowledge of it from Rachel Saint, who was convinced that God had chosen her to be the only one to work with the Huaorani.[25]

In the initial stage of Operation Auca, the missionaries needed someone to teach them the basics of the Huaorani language and called on Dayuma, a young Huaorani who had earlier escaped her tribe for fear of a revenge killing. Dayuma had originally gone to work on a hacienda, where she met Rachel Saint, who became her mentor in Christian ways. Dayuma served the five missionaries without the knowledge of Saint, who was away at the time. With Dayuma's language training, the men began making flights in Nate Saint's plane over some Huaorani huts, where they shouted out messages of friendship through a loudspeaker. They also delivered gifts by using a technique developed by Saint known as the spiraling line, in which the plane circled a target at lower and lower altitudes to plant a basket in a strategic location.²⁶ Using this method, they set down small gifts at first: an aluminum kettle, some buttons, and rock salt. Later they delivered machetes; this transaction eventually proved fatal. The gift-giving was so successful that the Huaorani reciprocated by sending up gifts of their own: feathered headbands, parrots, and cooked fish. Between October and December 1955, the Operation Auca missionaries made four-teen drops.²⁷

The opening phase of Operation Auca, in which the missionaries learned some of the Auca language and exchanged gifts with the Huaorani, gave the men hope for the next step, an actual landing at a campsite close to the Huaorani village. They accomplished this on the morning of January 3, 1956, after Nate Saint successfully set his plane down at a sandy site on the bank of the Curaray River. This site, which the missionaries later code-named Palm Beach, was only a short flight from Arajuno, the SIL's forward base in the Oriente, approximately thirty miles to the west. At Palm Beach the missionaries immediately went to work building a tree house, which they thought would provide them with safety at night. They also devised a plan that called for three of them to stay at Palm Beach each night while Nate Saint and one other missionary flew back to Arajuno to protect the plane. For defense at Palm Beach, the men brought along revolvers and .22-caliber carbines.²⁸ They hoped that they would not have to use the weapons, however, and thought that if the need arose, they would fire into the air to ward off any attack. On the first night at Palm Beach, Nate Saint and Peter Fleming flew over the Huaorani huts—or Terminal City, as they named it—and called out to the Huaorani over the plane's loudspeaker to "come tomorrow to the Curaray." No Huaorani appeared on the following day, but unexpectedly, three days later, a small band emerged in an open area across the Curaray River from Palm Beach. Peter Fleming amply documented in his diary what took place.

This is a great day for the advance of the gospel of Christ in Ecuador. Ed was at one end of the beach, Jim on the other and Roger, Nate and I in the center near the shack—all of us shouting phrases periodically. Suddenly from directly across the river a strong masculine voice began jabbering at Ed and immediately three Aucas stepped out into the open on the opposite bank, two women and a man. My heart jumped, thumped wildly as we walked slowly to join Ed and to shout phrases with him. We shouted "puinani" (come) and he replied lengthily, pointing frequently to the girl (of about 15–16) as perhaps willing to trade her for some knives. Jim started wading across the shallow, 20 yard wide river.

The Aucas were a little afraid but as Jim gradually approached them, the girl began to edge toward the water and stepped off a log into the water with the fellow following her slowly and last of all the other woman. Jim caught them by the hand and began leading them across to our side. They were uneasy but did not seem terrified as they stepped out on our side and we all laughed, smiled and told them they had come well and not to be afraid.

The man was a young fellow of 20 or so, the girl younger and the woman perhaps 30 or so. They were completely naked except for a G-string worn around the waist. We walked toward the plane and showed it to them, explaining by sign language how the propeller worked. By then the Aucas were relaxed and showed no signs of fear, jabbered happily to themselves and to us, seemingly with little idea that we didn't understand them. The young girl was still childish though physically mature, seemed dreamy, rubbing her body against the plane and waving her hands in the air imitating the plane's movements.

Soon the fellow began to show interest in the plane and we guessed from his talk that he was willing to go to his house to call his comrades. We put a shirt on him and he climbed in the plane with no sign of any emotion except eagerness to do his part. Nate taxied down the strip and took off while the fellow shouted all the way. After circling and shouting briefly Nate landed again, thinking to give the fellow a rest before making the flight to Terminal City. Nothing doing! He was ready to go right then—I guess he shouted all the way over and back and thoroughly enjoyed his trip.

My theory is that he had been sent with the girl and her mother (?) to give us the girl in exchange for paring knives and beads. We are praying that the others will come over and invite us to go over to their place—this fellow has seemed reluctant whenever we mentioned the subject and it may be he lacks the authority to invite us on his own.[29]

After the encounter ended, the three Huaorani left as quickly as they came, slipping back across the Curaray and into the jungle. On the following day all was quiet and there were no signs of the Huaorani. On Sunday morning, January 8, Nate Saint flew in from Arajuno; he stopped briefly to eat and then took off once again to fly over Terminal City. On this pass, he saw only a few women and children. On his way back, however, he spotted a group of Huaorani men heading for Palm Beach. When he landed, he shouted excitedly to his companions, "They're on the way."[30] Saint then made one last entry in his diary.

Heart heavy that they fear us. Saturday night I was wide awake at 1 A.M., thinking of the many ways we might have tried to keep our visitors around on Friday. I guess the thrill of being with them and of their casualness quite disarmed us of keen constructive thinking. Perhaps it is the Lord's goodness that we had a quiet day yesterday (Saturday). Song and prayer service. Spirits high on *playa* [beach]. Put beans on to cook. Arrange shack for company. Arrange "sand table." Eat lunch. Song and prayer service. Short flight—no men at *chacra* [compound] now. Going for bath now.[31]

A half-hour later, Saint talked to the operations camp over the radio. "We are hoping for visitors at about 2:30," he said. "I'll call you again at 4:35." He never called back, however, and as 4:35 came and went, the wives of the missionaries began to show their concern. One source reported that Saint's last words to the base camp were "Here come a group of Aucas whom we have not known before."[32] On the following day, Johnny Keenan, Nate Saint's fellow MAF pilot, flew over Palm Beach and radioed back that he had sighted Nate's plane ripped apart on the sandbar. Three days later, rescue parties were organized, one made up of Ecuadorean civilians and soldiers to go in on foot, and another to go in by helicopter, under the auspices of the Panama-based U.S. Air Force Air Rescue Service. On the next day, the Air Rescue Service arrived at Palm Beach and discovered the tragic scene. Nate Saint's body was found in the Curaray with a spear through it. His watch had stopped at 3:12. Jim Elliot's body was downstream in a tangle of debris. Roger Youderian's had a spear protruding from the right hip. It was evident that the Huaorani had used their machetes on some of the victims.[33]

In the wake of the discovery, back in the SIL base of operations, the wives of the five dead missionaries carried on as best they could and expressed the hope that the Huaorani would still be converted. They all claimed they felt no bitterness toward the Huaorani and were pleased when the Ecuadorean government promised not to take reprisals against the Indians. They all agreed on one thing: someone had to continue the work among the Huaorani for which their husbands had given their lives.[34] Sharing in that desire was Rachel Saint, who determined for herself and the SIL that she should be the one.

There have been subsequent attacks by the Huaorani. In 1977 three members of a French oil exploration company General Geophysical were speared; and in 1987 two Catholic missionaries, the Capuchin Archbishop of Aguarico, Alejandro Labaca, and his aide, Sister Inés Arango, met a similar fate.[35] In both cases, all those who died had been under contract to Petroecuador, the state-owned Ecuadorean petroleum corporation.[36] In the first attack, the Frenchmen were on Huaorani lands exploring for oil. In the second, the Catholic missionaries were attempting to help the oil company remove a Huaorani clan known as the Pucachaquis, or Red Feet, from lands where petroleum had been found. The name Red Feet is derived from the fact that during warfare, these Huaorani adorn their bodies and their feet with red achiote paint. The Red Feet do not refer to themselves as such but as Los Tagaeri, meaning the Warriors of the Cacique Taga.[37]

The latter incident, like Operation Auca, made headlines worldwide. It represented another case in which foreign missionaries, in this instance elderly Spanish Basques, intruded upon an isolated indigenous people. In both Operation Auca and the Labaca-Arango affair, missionary fanaticism clouded the judgment of the victims, and they foolishly miscalculated the intentions of the Huaorani, ignored their reputation, and acted carelessly in the manner in which they approached. As one writer pointed out in discussing the Labaca-Arango incident, the missionaries made many mistakes. They intimidated the Huaorani by approaching from the air, failed to recognize the red stripes on the roofs of the Huaorani huts as a declaration of war, and mistook the Huaoranis' smiles as a sign of friendship. Further, their appearance in civilian clothes led the Huaorani to believe that they were colonists or oil company emissaries.[38]

In both cases, it is not exactly clear what precipitated the attacks. It is evident, though, that the Huaorani were angered by the intrusions. This was exemplified by the fact that the victims were found to have multiple spear wounds. Labaca and Arango each had twenty-one, a number that points to the Huaorani custom of having each male member of the tribe pierce a victim with his spear as a show of defiance. After Labaca and Arango were found, their missionary colleagues continued to misread the Huaorani by removing the twelve-foot-long, rope-ornamented spears from the bodies, taking them to the Capuchin mission in Coca, and displaying them in Quito. The Huaorani believe that spears are important symbols, much as flags are for Europeans and North Americans. Their removal signified to the Huaorani that the white man had taken up the challenge of war.[39]

The deaths of both the Operation Auca missionaries and Labaca and Arango, spanning a period of thirty years, shocked and saddened the missionary community in Ecuador. These incidents underscored the long-standing bitterness felt by the Huaorani and other indigenous peoples toward all missionary activity. For the Red Feet, the second incident was an admonition declaring that all white men and mestizos who entered their territory would perish. In a greater sense, both Operation Auca and the case of Labaca and Arango called into question missionary understanding of indigenous peoples everywhere and the mental stability of those who pursue indigenous peoples even though they know it might eventually cost them their lives.

The tragedy of Operation Auca set off a chain of events that turned five Protestants missionaries into martyrs and led the SIL under Rachel Saint to move into the forefront of the evangelical movement in Ecuador and Latin America. Petroleum multinationals and the Ecuadorean government also profited from the incident. They worked in conjunction with Rachel Saint to remove the Huaorani from lands under which vast reserves of petroleum existed. The Huaorani were the losers; they were forced from their territory into an SIL protectorate where their way of life was severely disrupted, and they fell victim to disease and greed. A few of them, including the Red Feet, managed to escape after running into the deep reaches of the Oriente, where they continued to live apart from the encroaching modern world. In times of invasion by outsiders, however, the isolated Huaorani have been forced into the open to retaliate. As a result, their numbers have declined even further, and as of 1990 only a few of them still survived in their natural habitat.

CHAPTER 5

The Second Specialized Group (II):
The Summer Institute of Linguistics—
Salvation or Genocide?

"RACHEL SAINT IS THE most famous missionary of our time, a missionary super-star," acclaimed Jerry Bledsoe in his *Esquire* article in 1971.[1] The Huaorani intrigued her. In 1949 she promised that when she finished her assignment in Peru, she would return to Ecuador. In 1954 she made good on her promise and began working with the Huaorani refugee Dayuma along with SIL coworker Catherine Peeke. Saint quickly became fluent in the Huaorani language and gained a knowledge of their culture. Dayuma told her that Huaorani life was a great circle of hatred, fear, and revenge in which no one lived to die of old age. That knowledge made Saint even more determined to bring Christianity to the Huaorani. She never expected that her brother and his companions would try to do that first. She refrained, however, from criticizing the five missionaries for Operation Auca, even though she felt they may have overstepped their bounds. She professed to believe they had done everything possible to assure the safety of their operation. When Bledsoe asked Saint if she would have tried to stop them had she known what they were going to do she replied that she would not have. For her, it was all part of God's plan.[2]

After a respite of three months following the deaths of the five missionaries, Saint returned to her work with Dayuma. According to Bledsoe, some years later she learned from Dayuma what had happened at Palm Beach. Dayuma told Rachel that her relatives were responsible.[3] She related that the two women at the first meeting were Dayuma's aunt, Mintaka, and her younger sister, Gimari. They were also present on the day of the attack along with Dayuma's mother, younger brother, and uncle. During the actual attack, Mintaka and Gimari had gone ahead of the Huaorani men to distract and separate the missionaries. Dayuma said that one of the missionaries became frightened by the rattling of spears and reached for his gun, causing Dayuma's mother to scuffle with him. Then the gun went off, hitting her son Nampa in the head. Nampa died six months later, but it was unclear whether his death was the result of the bullet wound or something else. Bledsoe wrote that Nampa was crushed by a boa constrictor.[4] David Stoll believed that the boa story was part of the SIL cover-up and that Nampa died from the bullet wound.[5]

As the attack persisted, the missionaries fired into the air, scaring off the Huaorani. Gikita, Dayuma's uncle and the leader of the attack, rallied the band, and they returned to kill the missionaries after the latter had expended all their ammunition. Initially Nate Saint made it safely to his plane, but he returned to help the others. According to Dayuma, Gikita speared him as he pleaded for his life. After that, the Huaorani destroyed the plane and threw all the missionaries' belongings into the Curaray. In Dayuma's account, the primary motivation for the attack was that the Huaorani thought the missionaries were cannibals who were trying to lure them into their cooking pots.[6]

In the aftermath of the revelations about the killings, Rachel Saint and Dayuma became close companions and coworkers. With the aid of W. Cameron Townsend and the SIL propaganda apparatus, the story of the martyred missionaries and Rachel's friendship with Dayuma gained notice around the world. In 1957 Saint and Dayuma traveled to the United States, where they appeared on Ralph Edwards's television program "This is Your Life," which spotlighted Rachel Saint. Another famous SIL Indian convert, Chief Tariri of the headshrinking Shapra tribe of Peru, also appeared on the show.[7] Thirty million North Americans watched them. The entourage then traveled to New York City, where they appeared with Billy Graham. Later they toured the United States, and even Dayuma's young son Sam was brought over to be with her. As an adult, Sam "Caento" Padilla became an important contact for the Huaorani in Quito. He was only half Huaorani; his mestizo father had worked on the hacienda with Dayuma. Later in his life Padilla studied at the fundamentalist Florida Bible College in Miami. He disliked Bible study, however, and returned to Quito, where he worked for Metropolitan Tours on its Flotel Orellana, a floating hotel that sailed the Oriente offering tourists a view of the rain forest.

Sam Padilla was well known for profiting from the deaths of the five missionaries. He devised a plan that called for tourists to be flown into Palm
Beach, where they would be welcomed by an "authentic" Auca Princess,
Dayuma, and then taken to a shrine built to the Protestant martyrs. Padilla
would show off the massacre site, and the story would be told there by some
of the "participants." He also arranged to have twenty or thirty "Aucas"
demonstrate "their daily lives." The tourists could pursue whatever interests they had, and he would assign them individual Indian guides to take
them wherever they wanted to go.[8]

In 1988 Padilla ran Caento's, a bar in the Amazonas red-light district of
Quito. Caento's was a North American hangout where tourists could enjoy
beer, food, and a game of pool or darts and could buy so-called authentic
Auca spears and blowguns.

During the time that Rachel Saint, Dayuma, and Sam Padilla were in the
United States, Jim Elliot's widow, Elisabeth, made contact with Dayuma's
aunts, Mintaka and Maegamo, in the Oriente. She gained their confidence
by playing tape recordings made by Dayuma in the United States that told
the two women not to run away and to do what the SIL translators asked of
them. In the spring of 1958, Rachel and Dayuma flew back to the Oriente,
where Dayuma met her aunts and heard from them about the deaths of
Nampa and a second brother, Wawae, who died in a spear attack from a
rival Huaorani clan. As a result, Dayuma became despondent and returned
to her people to teach Christianity. A month later she went back to Elliot's
house, appearing at the edge of the jungle with a band of Huaorani. She
brought with her an invitation for Saint and Elliot to come and live with
them. That was the opening the missionaries had prayed for; they could not
refuse it. They went first to Palm Beach and later to a site on the Tiwaeno
River.[9]

At Tiwaeno the SIL set up a mission under Rachel Saint's control.
Dayuma served as Saint's liaison to the Huaorani. Elliot departed two years
later, and Catherine Peeke was brought in to replace her. Accounts vary as
to the success of Rachel Saint's mission at Tiwaeno. Bledsoe stated that the
Huaorani took to the teachings of Saint and Dayuma. According to him,
they shed many of their old ways, built an airstrip, and started wearing
clothes flown in by the missionaries. They quit wearing balsa earplugs, taking multiple wives, using spears against each other, strangling their babies,
and burying their sick and feeble alive. They also opened a church.[10]

David Stoll offered a different picture, one that demonstrated that the

SIL's ascendancy at Tiwaeno was based upon the Huaorani's desire not for Christianity but for trade goods, particularly steel cutting tools. He believed that Dayuma controlled the trade goods business as a means of coercing the Huaorani into wearing new clothes and getting haircuts. In reality, the Huaorani did not accept Christian beliefs. Stoll wrote that, according to Elisabeth Elliot, Dayuma was still the only Christian convert at Tiwaeno as late as 1960.[11]

The SIL's intrusion into Huaorani life coincided with the "discovery" of petroleum in the jungles of Ecuador's northern Oriente in the 1960s. This period marked a new export boom similar in some ways to the earlier export booms in cacao and bananas on the Coast. Petroleum augured an unprecedented surge in wealth for the Ecuadorean government. The location of the oil fields in the Amazon suggested that infrastructural improvements from which the Coast had benefited in the earlier booms would now take place in a region of the country that never profited from cacao or bananas. Roads and airports were built to help link the Oriente to the Sierra and provide access to unsettled lands within the region. This construction occurred because the oil companies needed to transport men and supplies to the oil production sites. In 1971 a Texaco-Gulf consortium completed a 280-kilometer (175-mile) third-class road between Quito and Lago Agrio, the center of Ecuadorean petroleum production. It was the first road connecting the Sierra with the northern Oriente.[12]

The new infrastructure brought colonists to the eastern jungle. Early in the petroleum boom, the Ecuadorean military sponsored free flights from Quito for colonists who wished to settle in the region around the oil fields. The military claimed that increased colonization would prevent Colombian settlement and the loss of Ecuadorean sovereignty over the territory. They urged conscripts and unskilled laborers to settle in the Oriente as agricultural workers. Between 1971 and 1978, six thousand families settled in the region.[13]

The initiation of petroleum production, the development of infrastructure, and the influx of colonists portended little that was good for the Huaorani. They faced a modern army of developers invading their lands, and their relationship to the outside world changed drastically as they were caught up in a struggle for their cultural and physical survival. The SIL was also concerned about the new turn of events. It wanted the Huaorani for its religious and linguistic work but understood that the colonization of Huaorani lands could not be stopped.

The organization responded to this dilemma by working with the Ecuadorean government and the petroleum companies to help remove the Huaorani from the petroleum rich lands. It honored the clause in its contract
which called for general service to the Ecuadorean government, and the oil
companies supplied financial aid to the SIL to help in the Huaorani displacement. The arrangement benefited all parties except the Huaorani who
lost much of their territory. The petroleum companies and the government
received oil profits and, with the SIL controlling the Tiwaeno mission, they
finally had the Huaorani together in one place where their activities could
be effectively monitored. For its part, the SIL could now pursue its objective
of evangelizing the Huaorani.[14]

The SIL devised a plan that called for setting aside a reservation for the
Huaorani. This was accomplished in 1969. The original request came from
Rachel Saint. Dayuma drew up the plans for the reserve, consisting of
160,000 hectares bounded by the Nushina and Chullua rivers, only a por-
tion of the original Huaorani lands. It was too small to support the tribe,
which subsisted primarily by hunting. But the SIL had little choice and began the process of bringing the rest of the Huaorani who remained outside
the mission to Tiwaeno to ready them for removal to the reservation. According to Bledsoe, the roundup of the Huaorani was a difficult task that
involved the Operation Auca techniques of flying over, dropping gifts, and
talking over loudspeakers. The SIL chose Christian Huaorani at Tiwaeno to
go in and talk to the "downriver" bands. Slowly they began to come in, and
the population at Tiwaeno grew. As a result of this process, heathen Huaorani outnumbered Christianized ones at the mission. By 1971 about half of
the Huaorani were at Tiwaeno. The other half still lived on a ridge some
ninety miles downstream from Tiwaeno and were pressed in from all sides
by the oil companies and colonists. To facilitate bringing these people in,
Saint dispatched to the region a young Christian Huaorani named Tonya,
who had a brother and sister in the group. He flew in on an oil company
helicopter carrying a radio and a Huaorani translation of the Book of
Mark. He stayed with the ridge group a few months before they speared
him at the instigation of his own brother. Tonya thus became the first Christian Huaorani martyr.[15]

The death of Tonya led the SIL to redouble its efforts to bring the outcast
Huaorani into the reservation. They sent in other Christian Huaorani, who
eventually convinced the ridge group to build an airstrip; this enabled the
SIL to bring in trade goods and persuade the ridge group to join the rest of

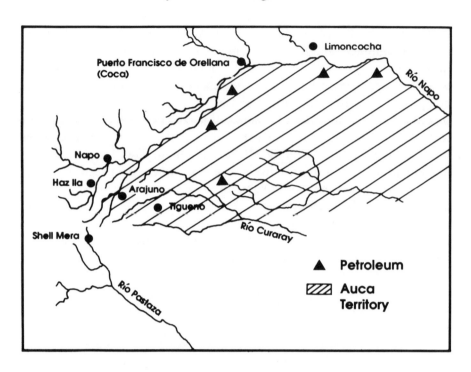

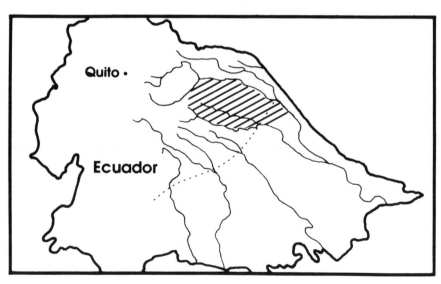

Auca Territory

the tribe at Tiwaeno. From that point Huaorani life and culture deteriorated. Bledsoe described what he saw upon his arrival at Tiwaeno in 1971.

> I arrived at Tigueno (Tiwaeno) to find once wild Aucas wearing oil company T-shirts and caps and Auca kids cutting little swaths through the jungle undergrowth playing oil company. Oil company workers were complaining that the Aucas who have made oil-worker watching a favorite pastime were stealing things from them, particularly transistor radios.[16]

Bledsoe witnessed what he recognized as the cultural destruction of the Huaorani, a view shared even by SIL workers. Catherine Peeke had written with remorse two years before:

> There is something pathetic in the plight of those who having failed to find isolation through remoteness, are driven to hide their thatch huts under the trees, thus exposing themselves to natural dangers (snakes and falling branches in a windstorm) which they would normally avoid. How can they assume goodwill when we ferret them out so relentlessly, approaching from the very sky, the sphere which they do not control? They are desperate to hide from forces which they do not understand—but how much more desperate they would be if they really did understand! The swallowing up of their resources, their liberty, even their identity is inevitable. And they will meet the even greater frustrations of modern man.[17]

Although the removal disturbed Peeke, Rachel Saint felt the SIL had done the right thing. She told Bledsoe, "We've worked hard on this [coexistence]. . . . It hasn't just happened. What we tried to do was work ahead of the oil companies to prepare the people, and we also tried to prepare the oil companies, and that wasn't easy either. We had to work both ways. I mean, they have a tendency to say, 'a handful of Aucas out there, what difference,' you know?" She added when asked about the meaning of oil for Ecuador, "I think it's a wonderful thing." And for the Aucas? She replied:

> The most I can say good is that it has forced us all into contact long before we would have had the courage to tackle it especially after the first. The head-on collision was so horrible that we never, any of us, would have had the courage to attempt such a thing again, except for the fact that these people knew their relatives would kill the oil company people and they wanted to protect the oil

people. They also knew that the sickness would hit their people, and that they would die from outside sicknesses brought in, plus wanting all along to teach them about the Lord. So if you look at the allover picture . . . maybe oil has done us a big favor. I will say too that the companies have been very cooperative especially when it was to their advantage.[18]

By 1971, with the Huaorani for the most part ensconced under the SIL's wing at Tiwaeno, the future appeared certain for the SIL, the Ecuadorean government, and the petroleum companies. According to Stoll, however, almost immediately problems emerged in the SIL reservation. One centered around the fact that Tiwaeno was a domain shared by the Huaorani and an oil exploration company. In 1971 the oil company drilled a well three miles from Tiwaeno. Ultimately it proved uneconomical, but it left its mark. The Huaorani took the company's leftovers, and every one of the Indians' huts except Rachel Saint's ended up with a corrugated metal roof. In addition, the cross-cultural exchange between lowland Quichua oil workers and the Huaorani proved disastrous because the Quichuas who had been displaced by colonization resented the Huaoranis' special land privileges embodied in the reservation.[19]

The most serious threat came from Huaorani demands on the SIL for trade goods, which the SIL did not want to meet. This led to rebellion and defection from Tiwaeno. One band of Huaorani ran off and moved west toward the Napo River looking for better trading partners. That group eventually settled on the northern boundary of the reservation at Dayuno. There the escaped band passed on to the control of the CMA. They became handicraft workers and attracted large groups of North American and European tourists. They sold necklaces and toy blowguns and asked for ladies' underwear and aspirin in return. Stoll, who passed through the area, described Dayuno as being in "a middle stage of disintegration."[20]

Another serious problem faced by the SIL was Rachel Saint herself. She had become increasingly autocratic in her control of Tiwaeno, and the SIL's main governing body found this difficult to accept. They did not want her acting as spokesman for the SIL. She presented an unflattering view of its mission by repeating on more than one occasion, without really explaining why, that it was dangerous for any male colleague to reside there and that spearings could occur. Doubting her word, the SIL hierarchy sent one of their anthropologists, James Yost, to evaluate the Tiwaeno branch.[21]

Saint did not welcome Yost; she feared that he was setting up her departure. Yost, however, did not let her hostility stop him, and he made discoveries that called her leadership into question. He found the Huaorani in possession of shotguns that came through Dayuno, dynamite obtained from oil crews, and DDT from malaria spray teams. These commodities were used in new methods of hunting and fishing that depleted the stock of fish and game and thus led to Yost's most telling observation: that the Huaorani had lost weight. He tried to persuade some of the ridge group to return home. None would, and he believed that their pursuit of trade goods was the reason. In 1975 the SIL team, without the blessings of Rachel Saint, urged Huaorani dispersal from Tiwaeno and curtailment of the flow of trade goods to the airstrip. The following year all the SIL members were pulled out for a while as the first step in reducing Huaorani dependency on the organization.[22]

As the SIL expected, the Huaorani dispersed; they continued, however, to maximize their contacts in the vicinity of Tiwaeno with the Quichuas, who in many cases had become godparents to Huaorani children to gain access to the reservation. Godparenthood provided trading partners, intermediaries in other transactions, and a place to stay where outsiders could be observed. In addition, a few of the Huaorani men went to work for an oil company that hoped their continued presence would prevent trouble with the Huaorani who remained to the east of Tiwaeno.[23]

Rachel Saint rejected the antidependency campaign of her fellow workers. This led to further problems with the SIL leadership, who in August 1976 ordered her into retirement. She also was not well, suffering from the aftereffects of polio, which she had contracted in an epidemic that hit Tiwaeno in 1969, and from eye trouble. She considered the Huaorani her pet project, and she had made serious mistakes by refusing to accept the opinions of others and preventing people from visiting Tiwaeno without her approval. Among other offenses, she had refused to help the Ecuadorean military carry out a census of the ridge group in 1974. In November 1976 she appealed her expulsion to the SIL branch executive committee and lost. In March 1977 she left Tiwaeno on furlough. According to Stoll, by early 1980 Rachel Saint still believed she could retire among the Huaorani; the SIL did not agree.[24]

In the end, the internal struggle between Saint and the SIL leadership proved harmful and counterproductive, fueling the growing Ecuadorean opposition to the SIL. The removal of the Huaorani to the SIL reservation had touched a raw nerve in Ecuadorean national consciousness. It became a cause of intense concern among students, intellectuals, politicians, church leaders, and above all indigenous organizations who called for rescinding the SIL contract. This demand was in keeping with the trend established in other countries around the world: after 1975 the SIL lost government contracts first in Nigeria and Nepal and later in Brazil, Mexico, and Panama.[25]

In 1981 the outcry against the SIL led to its expulsion from Ecuador. This was mandated by Presidential Decree 1159, signed by President Roldos Aguilera on May 22, 1981, two days before he died. The decree ended Ecuador's official relationship with the SIL. It called for all the programs and services initiated by the SIL to be transferred to national organizations and stated that the activities of the SIL "were incompatible with the priorities of development in the Ecuadorean Amazon and with national scientific investigation."[26]

Despite its legal expulsion, however, the SIL never completely left the country. It went underground to wait for a more auspicious time to reappear. That time came in 1986, during the Febres Cordero regime, when the SIL's supporters called for a new agreement with the Ecuadorean government that would last until 1990. The driving force behind the establishment of a new contract was Vice-President Blasco Peñaherrera, who argued that the work of the SIL had been abruptly and unfairly interrupted by pressure from the Roldos-Hurtado administration.[27]

Supporters of a new government-SIL contract pointed to the failure of the Instituto Anthropológico y Lingüístico de Limoncocha (Limoncocha Anthropological and Linguistic Institute), the Ecuadorean agency that took over the work of the SIL, to carry out the bilingual education and acculturation of indigenous groups. They argued that the SIL could help impede any guerrilla activity that might spring up in Oriente, possibly emanating from Colombia. Furthermore, they believed that the government of Ecuador could not finance linguistic and educational programs among the indigenous people in times of burdensome external debt and falling crude oil prices.[28]

A draft of a proposed contract drawn up by the Febres Cordero government in 1986 lauded the SIL for its past thirty years of work in Ecuador. In particular, it mentioned accomplishments in the beneficial and rational integration of the Huaorani to Ecuadorean national life. It praised the thousands of Indians in bilingual education programs and the hundreds of indigenous men and women who had been trained as bilingual and bicultural teachers, mechanics, carpenters, nursing aides, and cooks. It also praised the SIL's promotion of home maintenance and infant care among the Indians and the organizational contribution to a more literate and educated community. The new contract denigrated evidence that cattle ranching destroyed the rain forest by noting how the SIL had played a role in helping to improve the quality of cattle produced in the Amazon region and the concomitant betterment in economic conditions for its inhabitants. Finally, it recognized "the cultural and moral labors of the SIL that put aside all sectarianism and advanced the work of the translation of indigenous languages to studies of high spiritual, moral, and cultural value."[29]

The terms of the proposed contract surpassed earlier agreements and were exceedingly generous. As a consequence, it raised a firestorm of protest, particularly from indigenous groups who resented the paternalism in the agreement. They denounced the contract as a threat of new intrusion into indigenous life and an attempt by the Febres Cordero government to introduce an antinational policy of turning over the Oriente to foreign transnationals. The indigenous people believed the contract was part of the government's policy of removing them from their lands in order to promote large-scale agricultural endeavors and petroleum exploration. They called the government racist and declared that the organized indigenous people of Ecuador would oppose with all their energy any new formal intervention of the SIL in Ecuador.[30]

In the 1988 presidential election, the victory of Rodrigo Borja ended the possibility of any new government contract with the SIL. Fears remained high among indigenous groups, however, that the evangelical translators could return to the position they had once held. In 1990 these groups knew that JAARS still maintained an office and a linguistic center in Quito, and they understood that the SIL still worked in other Latin American countries that had also formally rescinded contracts. Their sentiments were engendered by some thirty years of what they saw as genocide and dubious accomplishment. Ultimately, they were determined not to let Ecuador follow the path taken by its neighbors and leave the door open for future SIL evangelization.

Figure 1. *The Cross in the garden at the Jesuit-owned Aurelio Espinosa Polit Library, Cotocollao. The Library is named for the former rector of the Catholic University of Ecuador, who referred to Protestantism's role in establishing Ecuador's secular educational system as anti-Catholic.*

Figure 2. *An anti-Protestant graffiti calling for the expulsion of the Summer Institute of Linguistics and World Vision from Ecuador. Otavalo marketplace, Imbabura.*

Figure 3. *The facade of Vozandes Hospital at the HCJB Radio complex, Quito.*

Figure 4. *The interdenominational chapel at HCJB Radio, Quito.*

Figure 5. *A message announcing Seventh-day Adventism in Ecuador. On the road from Quito to the oil-producing region of Lago Agrio in the Oriente. This spot is near the highest point on the road, near the continental divide of the cordillera orientale (eastern range) in the Ecuadorean Andes.*

Figure 6. *The entrance to HCJB Radio's hydroelectric facility. The sign reads "to the glory of God, serving Ecuador and the world," Papallacta. The Transandean Pipeline is in the background.*

Figure 7. *The way the two black golds of Ecuador are transported: by oil pipeline and Coca-Cola truck. Lago Agrio road, Napo Province.*

Figure 8. *Otavalan textile weaver and entrepreneur reading HCJB literature, Otavalo marketplace.*

Figure 9. *Pentecostal tent-revival and faith-healing campaign comes to the north. The sign declares, "Jesus Christ, healer of body and soul." Ibarra.*

Figure 10. *Newly completed Episcopal church in the center Ciudadela Ruminahui, Quito. The church towers above other structures in the neighborhood and is a sign of change.*

Figure 11. *The front entrance of Episcopal church in Ciudadela Ruminahui.*

Figure 12. *An example of the spread of Protestantism on a local level. The storefront Iglesia Tabernaculo Evangelistico, Quito.*

Figure 13. *Homegrown Pentecostalism among the poor. The Templo Evangelico Filadelfia, Calderon, Pichincha Province.*

Figure 14. *The front entrance of the independent Pentecostal church Iglesia Bautista Vida Eterna, Calderon, Pichincha Province.*

Figure 15. *The Assemblies of God in the countryside. Advertisement for a faith-healing crusade, Calderon, Pichincha Province.*

CHAPTER 6

The Third Specialized Group: World Vision,

1975–1990

THE CAPTION "World Vision Equals Division" headed a November 18, 1983, letter written by the *cabildo* (town council) of La Compañía, a freeholding community in the northern Ecuadorean province of Imbabura. In Ecuador, freeholding communities like La Compañía are typically situated on poor land among indigenous people. They are characterized by both communal and family-owned landholdings. In a freeholding community, most communal land is pasture; no one member can hoard any part of it for his exclusive use. In Imbabura, individual family-owned parcels of land are seldom able to provide enough for each family to survive; alternative economic activities are usually required. Most families, therefore, work in the production of textiles, which, for the most part, are sold to tourists on Saturday morning in the Otavalo marketplace. Communal labor is used in freeholding communities for building houses, digging irrigation canals, and harvesting crops. In Imbabura and the Ecuadorean Sierra in general, this shared work, called the *minga,* not only increases productivity but also fosters long-standing reciprocal work relationships among community members that help bring about a unified social structure in which all members act as guardians of the community's land and labor. Members of freeholding communities generally view any outside intervention as an intrusion and a call to arms.[1]

Imbabura is often referred to as La Provincia de los Lagos (the Lake Province) because it is home to three crystal-clear lakes: San Pablo, Cuicocha, and Yaguarcocha. It is also home to two myth-shrouded mountains, Imbabura and Cotacachi, which to the indigenous people of the province represent the father and mother of the universe. Lake San Pablo is situated beside Mount Imbabura, and Lake Cuicocha is in the crater of Mount Cotacachi. These two mountains stand at opposite ends of the Otavalo Valley. Yaguarcocha, in the north of the province, is the site of a historic pre-Colombian battle between the region's native Caranqui Indians and the Incas. "Yaguarcocha" means Blood Lake; the name was given in memory of the many indigenous people, including women and children, who were massacred there.[2]

In La Compañía, the accusing town council missive appeared in *La Bocina*, a bimonthly publication of FEPP, the Fondo Ecuatoriano Populorum Progressio (Ecuadorean "Populorum Progressio" Foundation), a Catholic liberation theology organization that derived its name from an encyclical written by Pope Paul VI. It denounced World Vision as attempting to destroy traditional systems of community, reciprocity, and self-protection. Furthermore, it declared that the town council members of La Compañía had been the targets of physical attacks by Protestant Indians whom World Vision supported. The council members related that these assaults resulted in injuries requiring medical attention, and, in spite of their meager financial resources, calling upon expensive legal assistance for protection. The assaults were also reported to have wrecked property but, notwithstanding this damage, to have met with a noticeable lack of interest by local government authorities, who the council members believed were bought off with World Vision money. The letter stated that after most of the attacks, the Protestants had gone to the authorities first and presented a contrary version of events.[3]

The denunciation named the indigenous Protestants involved—Andrés Otavalo, Rafael Ascanta, and Segundo Otavalo—and declared that as salaried members of World Vision they had terrorized the community. Council members accused the Protestants of leading a group of sixty fellow believers, armed with stones, sticks, hoes, and axes, in an attack on Juanita Males in her home some eight days earlier, which left the property totally destroyed. They stated this allegation could be proved by photographs taken and judicial inspections made after the incident. Town council president Antonio Padilla, Vice-President Francisco Morales, and treasurer Carlos Males signed the letter. By this act they underscored the controversy in Ecuador over the work of World Vision among indigenous people.

In the 1980s, many Ecuadoreans thought that World Vision, in its professed determination to assist indigenous people, did more harm than good. It was likened to Santa Claus's bringing gifts in return for passivity and a belief in the New Testament.[4] World Vision was also compared to the SIL and accused of the cultural and physical destruction of indigenous people. Because of this, many secular and religious organizations worked to expel World Vision from Ecuador. They argued that it exacerbated divisions between Catholics and Protestants and ruined traditional communal arrangements, claiming that World Vision introduced into indigenous communities new values that placed undue emphasis on individual and material wealth. It was also argued that World Vision threw money into development projects such as irrigation systems, sanitary and health works, pig and chicken farms, textile and embroidery factories, community stores, childcare centers, and community parks without making proper preliminary feasibility studies or training local personnel. Often, World Vision failed to control its money, they charged, and much of it was pocketed by local community officials or employees. Furthermore, World Vision was criticized for competing in the developmental field with Ecuadorean state agencies responsible for carrying out projects among indigenous people. With abundant money, World Vision promised to complete projects faster and in many cases did so, though critics demonstrated that its projects did not always correspond to the needs and aspirations of the indigenous communities involved. According to the late Catholic archbishop of Riobamba, Leonidas Proaño, who was well known for his work among the indigenous people of Chimborazo, with World Vision "there is no growth, no attention to the man, and no road toward economic liberation."[5]

In the wake of the violent incidents in La Compañía and because of the overall lack of support for its programs among Imbabura's independent textile-weaving Indians, World Vision asked its indigenous administrators to resign, accusing them of misuse of funds and blaming them for the failure of the agency's programs. In their places, World Vision hired two mestizos who it claimed would not be involved in the internal problems of indigenous groups and who would work only in communities that invited them. World Vision also stated that these agents would have no political or religious connections and would merely pass along requests from the town councils of each community to the World Vision offices in Quito. Generally, however, the projects financed after this strategy change in Imbabura demonstrated concern only for infrastructural development.[6]

World Vision regards itself as a humanitarian fundamentalist Christian organization that attempts to help the poor and marginalized people of the world. It is an interdenominational agency of evangelical tradition that operates out of offices in Monrovia, California, and engages for the most part in projects involving child care, community development, emergency relief, evangelism, leadership development, and public health.[7] It includes representation from autonomous support operations in Canada, the United States, Australia, New Zealand, and South Africa. Since its founding, it has worked in 110 countries giving aid and counsel to most of the world's major Protestant denominational and interdenominational churches, among them the SDA, the CMA, the Assemblies of God, the Baptists, the Angelican/Episcopal Church, the Lutherans, the Mennonites, the Methodists, the Pentecostals, and the Presbyterians. In 1986, in Latin America, World Vision had a presence in Argentina, Bolivia, Brazil, Colombia, Ecuador, El Salvador, Guatemala, Nicaragua, Panama, Peru, Uruguay, Mexico, and Venezuela. It also had twelve missions in Africa, fifteen in Asia, eight in Europe, and four in the Middle East.[8]

According to its own *Mission Handbook,* in 1985 World Vision worked in sixty-three countries and employed a total of 707 people worldwide. Its total income was more than \$127 million, with \$83 million coming from its overseas operations. These figures placed it second among the twenty-five largest missionary agencies worldwide.[9] Other sources reported that it operated in more than eighty countries with 2,200 child and family assistance projects reaching some 400,000 children. It also worked on more than a hundred emergency and rehabilitative projects, four hundred community development plans, and a hundred leadership programs.[10]

Bob Pierce, a North American newspaper correspondent and fundamentalist Protestant evangelist, founded World Vision. He developed the idea while working for Youth For Christ (YFC), a movement that employed Billy Graham and sponsored what it called World Vision Rallies in the mid to late 1940s in Philadelphia, Chicago, and Los Angeles. These rallies helped raise money for global evangelistic enterprises. Initially Bob Pierce helped publish the YFC's magazine, but he spent much of his time as a rally organizer. By 1947 the movement had grown and gained recognition both nationally and internationally. At that time, YFC named Bob Pierce its vice-president-at-large, and his first assignment took him to China, where he organized a series of youth rallies following an invitation from Nationalist Chinese leader Chiang Kai-shek. Pierce spent a month in China preaching in Shanghai, Soochow, Hangchow, Sian, Nanking, Chungking, and Chengdu. His trip became legendary; one source reported that during that month almost 18,000 Chinese men and women converted to Protestantism.[11]

In 1950 Pierce again set his sights on Asia. Just before the outbreak of the Korean War, he went to South Korea where he organized rallies and orphan-sponsorship programs. He returned to the United States with strong anti-Communist views and stories about what he described as Communist atrocities and the courage of the South Korean people facing the threat from the North. He worked extensively at raising money to help Korean Christians, whom he perceived as suffering victims of Communist aggression. In August Pierce spoke at the Billy Graham Crusade in Portland, Oregon. His eyewitness accounts stunned the audience and elicited an outpouring of prayer and money. Pierce mentioned the need for an international evangelical organization to aid in the Christian struggle against communism. His words impressed those present, including Frank C. Phillips, the director of the Billy Graham Crusade and Portland's YFC branch, who lent Pierce the use of his office and a secretary to begin his world organization. A month later, in Los Angeles, Pierce's dream became a reality when he and fellow officers Paul and Thelma Myers signed the minutes of World Vision's first meeting. With this incorporation, in 1950, Pierce officially became World Vision's first president.[12]

In the 1950s and 1960s, with Pierce at the helm, World Vision prospered. Under his tutelage it became an evangelical development agency. Its activities included the production of church films, which were distributed freely to denominations and their missionaries in return for affiliation. These World Vision films promoted the organization's vehement anticommunism. Twelve films were produced in the two decades of Pierce's administration. They included *38th Parallel* (1950), *The Flame* and *New China Challenge* (1952), *Dead Men on a Furlough* (1954), *Other Sheep* (1955), *The Red Plague* and *Of Such Is the Kingdom* (1957), *A Cry in the Night* (1959), *The Tokyo Crusade* (1962), *So Little Time* (1964), and *The Least Ones* and *Vietnam Profile* (1965). The promotional copy for one of the films read in part, "To help your church and your missionary, World Vision makes this magnificent film available to all churches with this stipulation—that you take an offering for your own foreign missionary program."[13]

Also during Pierce's presidency, World Vision initiated its child-sponsorship program; built clinics, hospitals, and Bible training schools;

opened new national and international offices; held pastoral assemblies around the globe; published the World Vision magazine; incorporated the Missions Advanced Research Communications Center (MARC); the publisher of the *Mission Handbook;* and sponsored the Korean Children's Choir. Pierce worked hard, and it cost him his health and family, from which he separated. The suicide of his eldest daughter, Sharon, at the age of twenty-seven after the failure of her marriage added to his distress. In 1967, with his mind and body exhausted, Pierce resigned as president of World Vision and entered a medical clinic in Basel, Switzerland. His place was filled by Richard C. Halverson, who served as acting president until 1969, when World Vision named a former member of the Billy Graham Crusade, W. Stanley Mooneyham, its chief executive.[14]

During Mooneyham's administration, which lasted until 1982, World Vision changed its focus. While it still produced church films and carried on with child sponsorship and other activities, it became sensitive to criticism that it had received too much AID money and that it had worked with the CIA in Vietnam and Cambodia.[15] It toned down its anticommunist rhetoric and distanced itself from its relationship with the U.S. government. Because of Mooneyham, who displayed an understanding of world social problems, particularly hunger in the Third World, World Vision assumed more progressive positions on the key issues of poverty, the environment, and the population explosion. In 1975 Mooneyham wrote,

> The food crisis does not stand in isolation from the rest of the world's problems. If we were dealing with just an agricultural shortfall, the solution would be relatively simple. But add changing climatic conditions and you complicate the problem. Link it with an uncontrolled world population—as you certainly must—and you further intensify the dilemma. . . . Now compound it by introducing ecological factors plus deficiency of medical services, inadequate educational programs, discriminatory distribution systems, global economic inequity and repressive political regimes—add these and you've got an apocalyptic situation.[16]

Mooneyham also moved World Vision away from a strict fundamentalist view. He rejected the idea that because of the threatening nature of the times, people must concentrate on the eternal and not worry about human suffering.

I have accepted my dual citizenship—earthly and heavenly. The earthly was not negated when I took on the heavenly. Rather, for me, the second enhanced the first.[17]

Under Mooneyham, World Vision showed signs of a liberalization of its ideals. Evidence, however, persisted that the agency still played rightist politics. One indication of this was in Honduras, in 1981, during the Salvadorean refugee crisis, when World Vision was given the job of administering refugee camps. At that time it remained silent in the face of the Honduran army's accusations that the camps harbored guerrillas; their silence became all the more appalling after the harassment and murder of some refugees. It was pointed out that four out of the six camp administrators hired by World Vision had links to the Honduran military. In addition, refugee testimony demonstrated that the four administrators had given the military reports on new arrivals, had denied entrance to some refugees, and had withheld food to coerce people to attend church. It was also reported that Cuban exile Mario Fumero, a Pentecostal preacher and the top man hired by World Vision, not only was retained despite allegations of wrongdoing but remained to harass those refugees and executives of other relief agencies working in the camps who criticized him and World Vision. It was only after the near collapse of the Catholic relief agency Caritas and the Protestant Comité Evangélico de Desarrollo y Emergencia Nacional (CEDEN) that World Vision dismissed him.[18]

According to David Stoll, the near collapse of CEDEN was not the work of Fumero alone but also the doing of Honduran fundamentalists with CEDEN who were pushed by World Vision into thinking that CEDEN was working too closely with Catholic and ecumenical organizations in New York. These fundamentalists accused CEDEN of helping Salvadoran guerrillas, and in June 1982 they took over administrative control of the organization by electing a new board of directors. They immediately severed their relationship with the WCC and stated that, in the future, CEDEN would accept money only from World Vision and AID. In the end, CEDEN's ecumenical backers were unsure as to what really happened in the Honduran camps. They thought it strange, however, that Fumero was replaced only after he had done much harm to CEDEN.[19]

World Vision made its entrance into Ecuador in 1975, working in conjunction with HCJB to furnish disaster relief. In 1978 it opened a field office in Quito, and in 1980 it obtained legal recognition from the Ecuadorean government and authorization to operate in the country for fifty years.[20] From 1979 to 1985 World Vision provided Ecuador with more than $4.7 million in assistance. It rendered many services, including the provision of food, medicine, and transportation during the coastal floods of 1982, caused by the Pacific Ocean El Niño current, which destroyed half of the cotton and soybean crops and a third of the rice and bananas.[21] In recent times El Niño has caused further devastation along the Ecuadorean and Peruvian coasts. Scientists believe it is the result of atmospheric disturbances set off by volcanic activity. Such was the case when Mexico's El Chichón volcano erupted in 1982. The effects of El Niño have sometimes been global, felt in such a range of places as the Pacific coast of North America, the South Pacific, Asia, and Europe.

During the 1980s World Vision worked on many projects in Ecuador. Its entrée into Ecuadorean communities was its "Plan Padrino," a program that by 1985 had claimed sponsorship of 8,200 children, most of whom resided in the Quechua-speaking highland Indian communities in Imbabura, Cotopaxi, Tungurahua, and Chimborazo. The indigenous people of these provinces, with the exception of Imbabura, were for the most part subsistence farmers who worked on small plots of poor land. In many areas potable water was nonexistent, and parasitic diseases and malnutrition were common.[22]

In Ecuador, mistrust of the white man and mestizo is endemic among the indigenous people of the Sierra. During the period from 1975 to 1990, many indigenous groups particularly feared World Vision's individualistic, one-sided approach. Nowhere was this truer than in Chimborazo, which contained the largest indigenous population of all the provinces of Ecuador—250,000 out of a total population just exceeding 320,000.[23] In 1980 the Ecuadorean census bureau related that not only did indigenous people predominate in Chimborazo, but they controlled some areas of the province.[24]

During the 1975–90 period Chimborazo was a major battleground for World Vision in Ecuador. The organization first entered the province in 1979 and remained relatively low-key until its 1983–84 strategy change in Imbabura. In Chimborazo it made use of indigenous land tenure systems, the *ayllu* and the *huasipungo,* to propel itself into development activities. The ayllu, the traditional, local sociopolitical unit of the Andean region, was characterized by long-standing mutual cooperation, close kinship, and reciprocity, all relationships that were not easily broken in a region that suffered from poor soil and scarce production. The huasipungo was a feudal arrangement by which small plots of land, water, and pasture were given to indigenous people in return for free labor on haciendas. This latter system enslaved indigenous people as they amassed huge debts to hacienda owners who provided them with credit to purchase needed supplies.[25] Both the ayllu and the huasipungo tied Chimborazo's indigenous people to a sedentary way of life that kept them from upward or outward mobility. For World Vision's evangelical aims, they were in a propitious position.

The Ecuadorean agrarian reform laws of 1964 and 1974 were intended to prohibit the huasipungo; in Chimborazo, however, it persisted in an altered form and caused indigenous people to become more dependent on producing cash crops that they sold to regional markets. In a practical sense, the laws led to less diversity in production and the increasing importance of money (of which World Vision had plenty) to indigenous people.[26]

World Vision was not the first Protestant group to work in Chimborazo. It had been a center of evangelical activity from the first years of Protestantism's arrival in Ecuador. The GMU showed the earliest interest, arriving in 1902 to open a missionary station at Caliata, south of the provincial capital of Riobamba. In 1921 the SDA had opened a station in the Colta Lake area; in 1933 it sold that facility to the CMA, who sold it in turn to the GMU in 1953. The GMU has remained there ever since.[27]

Until the entrance of World Vision, the GMU was the primary Protestant group in the region. It represented a stabilizing force for many indigenous people. In 1954 it began its work in earnest by proselytizing with a Quechua version of the Bible, a strategy that helped it to attract many Indians. In 1956 it initiated basic literacy classes; in 1957 it opened a boarding school to teach classes in both Spanish and Quechua; in 1958 it completed a hospital; and in 1961 it organized HCUE-5 radio station, "The Voice of Colta Lake," broadcasting in Quechua.[28]

The GMU also helped establish two important organizations in Chimborazo: the Leadership Training Institute (LTI) and the Associación Indígena Evangélica de Chimborazo (AIECH). The LTI trained lay leaders with the intention of using them in native churches the organization planned to form. AIECH was a political organization that accepted newly formed churches into its structure; it acted as a liaison to state authorities and other national institutions. Established in 1967, AIECH was instrumental in defending the religious rights of the indigenous Protestants. By 1977 it included 137 churches and three similar organizations in nearby provinces. According to anthropologist Blanca Muratorio, the objective of AIECH was to constitute a national association of evangelical peasants.[29]

World Vision began its work in Chimborazo in Cintaguso, in the Colta Lake region. It was invited in after that community's Protestant leaders, with the help of HCJB, asked it to contribute financial assistance for the construction of a communal meeting house. World Vision accepted the offer and constructed a two-story building at a cost of a million sucres, or approximately $40,000. With that beginning, World Vision expanded throughout Chimborazo and acted on requests for development projects in the communities of San Bartolo Grande, Palmira Davalos, Llactapamba, Rayo, Guantal, Bishud, Chauzan, and Naubug. It opened an office in the town of Guamote to facilitate the requests for projects from the indigenous communities without the hardship of traveling to Quito. By 1984, 80 percent of all World Vision projects in Ecuador were carried out in thirty-nine communities in Chimborazo. More than a hundred project requests were received in January 1984 alone.[30]

In the early stages of its operations in Chimborazo, World Vision faced resistance from many indigenous people who believed it would not help without wanting something in return. Many thought its offers were not genuine, that World Vision would not do what it promised to do, and that the only reason for its assistance was to create for itself an opportunity to steal children, land, and animals. Indigenous Catholics warned that World Vision provided assistance to people only after converting them to Protestantism.

To get through this veil of mistrust, World Vision enlisted the help of other Protestant groups. One of them was AIECH, which was promised in return the credit for any new completed projects. Without AIECH, World Vision would have found its task in Chimborazo extremely difficult. AIECH's cooperation ultimately enabled World Vision to build communal houses, laundries, kindergartens, fruit and vegetable stores, community roads, medical facilities, water pumps, latrines, baths (some using solar energy), playgrounds, communal fertilizer-storage facilities, child-care centers, granaries and mills, and small-scale textile factories.[31]

World Vision used a simple system that enabled it to complete projects much faster than the Ecuadorean government could. It almost always employed native Ecuadoreans as its representatives. In 1984 it had seven salaried employees, six of whom were indigenous: a coordinator, a secretary, a photographer, three administrators, and a director of the kindergarten program. It also set up an easily implemented system for getting projects started. Each community had to fill out an application, establish a budget, and send it to the Quito office of World Vision, which then set up savings accounts for the community in Banco La Previsora in Riobamba and had the bankbooks carefully guarded in a safe in the Guamote office. Once the requests were approved, World Vision deposited funds in the name of the community that could be withdrawn in Riobamba by the town council members. They in turn gave the money to a Protestant church leader appointed by World Vision who acted as a project administrator.[32]

Though the system was simple, it was plagued by difficulties. World Vision instituted projects without proper preliminary study. It fomented opportunism and the misuse of funds through poor follow-up and control of projects, with the result in many cases that money ended up in the hands of one family. Its system led to conflicts between indigenous groups, thereby weakening the indigenous community as a whole. Ultimately World Vision debilitated state authority.[33]

In Chimborazo there were many examples of problems brought about by World Vision. In the community of Chauzan, the state agency Fondo de Desarrollo Rural Marginal, or FODERUMA (Rural Development Fund), and World Vision clashed over construction projects. In this incident, FODERUMA and World Vision were working on two separate projects at the same time. FODERUMA, which lacked money, was attempting to construct a small facility for making cement blocks. World Vision, with its abundance of funds, was involved in building a two-story communal house, a potable water system, and a laundry. The difficulty emerged when the community, impressed by World Vision's larger project, rose up in anger against FODERUMA and destroyed the block-making facility. The indigenous people of Chauzan stated that the FODERUMA project was taking too long and that it had found an organization that would provide money for more and bigger projects.[34]

A second incident involving FODERUMA and World Vision took place in San Bartolo Grande when two community groups, one working with the state and the other with the North American fundamentalist Protestants, fought over which agency would complete the construction of a child-care center. World Vision promised to finish the project immediately and also build a school. FODERUMA could not compete, and World Vision finished the construction. A third incident concerned World Vision's effective attempts to stop the work of the Oficina de la Secretaría de Desarrollo Rural Integral, or the DRI (Office of the Secretary of Integrated Rural Development), in Palmira Davalos. World Vision offered the indigenous workers a job on the condition that they force the DRI out of the community and accept World Vision as the provider of the community's development needs.[35]

Examples of World Vision's misuse of funds and lack of control and follow-up were also plentiful. In Rayo, one administrator received money from World Vision to buy 150 one-hundred-pound bags of cement; he purchased only 80 bags and pocketed the rest of the money. In Naubug and Guantal, administrators secured funds from World Vision to construct communal meeting houses, then bought inferior building materials that caused inadequacies in the construction. In the latter instance, World Vision charged the indigenous administrators with malfeasance and accepted no responsibility for doling out money indiscriminately.[36]

World Vision's operations in Chimborazo during the 1980s raised serious doubts about its effectiveness as an international development agency, justifying Ecuadorean criticism and the belief that World Vision should be expelled from the country. Many Ecuadoreans joined in a national outcry.[37] Among them was Washington Padilla, speaking for Ecuadorean Protestants:

> The great majority of Protestant groups have an excellent concept of World Vision; but a small minority criticize the fact that like other foreign missions, they confuse North American culture with Christianity. It is my impression that World Vision does this; it does not take into account the peculiarities of the communities and instead of fomenting self-sufficiency it acts like Santa Claus.

Francisco Teran, a former high official of FODERUMA, expressed a government view:

> In the concrete case of World Vision, beyond the religious question there is detected a work methodology that exerts pressure on state programs. To justify the distribution of funds for a project we must first make sure of its destiny and the technical assistance we are going to offer; imagine the problems that would occur if suddenly a minister appeared and asked, "What do you need in this community?" and immediately solved all the problems by giving

money and machinery, one, two, three. This Santa Claus vocation casts shadows and provokes questions about state programs. Because of all of this, I believe it is urgently necessary to complete studies on the influence of religion on the cohesion of rural sector organizations.

Monsignor Proaño of Chimborazo voiced a liberation theologian's view of the situation:

> As to World Vision, it is working in the province with mountains of money and as indicated by World Vision's director in Ecuador, in the first place, its labor is proselytistic and divisionistic, planting division even amongst those they have made Protestants. The way that they distribute money, without plan or control, produces envy in other Protestant groups and many conflicts with indigenous Catholics.

While some Ecuadorean leaders had grave misgivings about World Vision, there were celebrities and leaders in the United States who lauded its work. Bob Hope, Dr. Theodore Hesburgh, Gerald Ford, Edward Kennedy, and Nancy Reagan appeared on World Vision telethons asking for support for child sponsorship in the Third World. Senator Mark O. Hatfield of Oregon, who served as an honorary member of the World Vision board, offered a view of the evangelical organization that was quite different from that of leading Ecuadoreans. He remarked in a speech to government, business, and religious leaders during a visit to Africa:

> I felt . . . that there is no organization in the world which combines so effectively the meeting of human need with clear and compelling proclamation of the gospel. I have seen World Vision's work in many different places on the globe and have always been impressed with their staff people's deep commitment to a holistic gospel. My attachment to World Vision is one of my proudest associations.[38]

The view that such Americans held in the years between 1975 and 1990 contrasted with that of nationalistic Ecuadoreans, who saw World Vision and its projects in a more ominous light. The events in La Compañía, the incidents in the Honduras refugee camp, and the examples of violence and misuse of funds in Chimborazo demonstrated that, while World Vision professed humanitarian principles, it adhered to divisionistic and repressive practices. In the view of Ecuadorean nationalists, this contradiction indicated that World Vision, like the SIL, endeavored to have the best of all possible worlds; it wanted freedom to interfere in local affairs, no government opposition to its projects, and indigenous people who accepted its evangelistic message without question.

CHAPTER 7

Mothers and Daughters:
The Pentecostals and the Independents,
1950–1990

The Pentecostal movement occupies first place on the
country's evangelical scale. In less than twenty-five
years, it has managed to erect eighty churches in
Guayaquil. It is diffused among marginal groups that
look for meaning to their human, social, and religious
situations; such is the case in the slums of the port
city. In one parish alone (Febres Cordero), there are
thirty-three churches.
    María Albán Estrada and Juan Pablo Muñoz, Con dios
    todo se puede (1987)

WITHOUT A DOUBT, the most important development in Protestantism in
Ecuador and in Latin America generally from 1950 to 1990 was the growth
of Pentecostalism. This loosely structured movement, characterized by the
specific tenets of complete sanctification, baptism of the Holy Spirit, speaking in tongues (glossolalia), and faith healing, had its origins in the primitive Christian church in the communities of Rome, Thessalonica, and
Corinth.[1] Within Pentecostalism, complete sanctification means becoming
holy, being "born again" following an initial conversion called justification.
This second blessing purifies the believer and enables him to secure God's
love and that of his fellowman. The baptism of the Holy Spirit is a second

baptism in which the spirit of God enters the convert and is accompanied by the outward, emotional sign of speaking in tongues, the proof of having received a second rebirth.[2]

In the United States, Pentecostalism owes its existence to the religious awakenings or "holiness" revivals that took place from 1725 to 1750, 1795 to 1835, 1875 to the end of the century, and during and after the first and second world wars. These revivals emphasized direct inspiration and religious emotionalism, personal sanctification as a possible or necessary state for conversion, universalism (which rejected predestination and stressed that salvation was possible, even probable, for all), and the millenarian ideal of the second coming of Christ as the solution for all the world's problems.[3]

Modern-day Pentecostalism had its origins in Iowa in 1895 with the initiation of the Fire Baptized Holiness Church, founded by Benjamin Hardin Irwin of Lincoln, Nebraska. Irwin, a lawyer who left his practice to enter the Baptist ministry, came into contact with holiness teachings through ministers of the Iowa Holiness Association, a subsidiary of the national holiness movement. He received the experiences of sanctification and studied the writings of John Wesley, the founder of Methodism, and Wesley's colleague John Fletcher. Fletcher's idea of an experience following sanctification, which he called the "baptism of burning love" or "baptism with the Holy Ghost and fire," greatly influenced Irwin, who began preaching it among holiness groups in the Midwest. Irwin concluded that the experience came with great joy and ecstacy. His publications in various holiness periodicals gained him legitimacy within the holiness movement.[4]

Irwin's circulation of Fletcher's ideas caused a revolution in the Methodist holiness wing of revivalism. Other men took up the cause. In 1901 Charles F. Parham of Bethel College, a small Bible College in Topeka, Kansas, led a Pentecostal revival that took as its major tenet the doctrine of a separate baptism of the Holy Spirit following sanctification as described in Acts 2, when the apostles spoke in tongues. Parham stressed that speaking in tongues was a sign of a Pentecostal experience.[5]

In 1906 one of Parham's students, W. J. Seymour, a black preacher and leader of the Asuza Street Mission in Los Angeles, further popularized Pentecostalism. Seymour and his followers, a group made up of blacks, whites, and Hispanics, held daily meetings in which they prayed, spoke in tongues, prophesied, and healed the sick. Seymour taught that speaking in tongues was an indication that a person had been baptized by the Holy Spirit.[6]

From the Asuza Street Mission, word of the new movement spread throughout the United States and around the globe. Within a short period of time, Pentecostal revivals were taking place in Canada, England, Scandinavia, Germany, India, China, Africa, and Latin America.[7] Pentecostalism arrived in Latin America in 1909 and was disseminated there in four distinct ways: by missionaries who belonged to organized Protestant denominations, by independent Pentecostal missionaries who believed they were sent by the Holy Spirit to the new lands, by returning migrant workers who had lived in the Southern United States, and by native Latin Americans who had been healed and baptized by foreign missionaries in urban centers.[8]

During this incipient phase in Latin America, which lasted until 1915, Pentecostalism entered Chile, Argentina, Brazil, Venezuela, and Mexico.[9] Some of its early pioneers were the North American Willis C. Hoover in Chile and, in Brazil, the Italian immigrant Louis Fransescon and two Swedes, Gunner Vingren and Daniel Berg.[10] With the exception of Hoover, all of these missionaries had been indoctrinated into Pentecostalism in the United States. Hoover originally came to Chile in 1902 as the head of the Methodist Episcopal Church in Valparaiso, and it was there that he converted to Pentecostalism in 1907 after receiving a leaflet on the religion sent from India by a family friend. He subsequently corresponded with Pentecostal pastors in Norway, the United States, India, and Venezuela; and between 1907 and 1909 he passed on his newfound knowledge to the members of his congregation. In 1909 they helped him establish the Iglesia Metodista Pentecostal (Methodist Pentecostal Church), Chile's first national Protestant church.[11]

In Brazil, Fransescon, Vingren, and Berg all arrived from the midwest United States. Initially they went to work for historic denominations: Fransescon for the Presbyterians in 1909 and Vingren and Berg for the Baptists in 1910. Fransescon worked in São Paulo's Little Italy, where the resident population helped him establish the Congregacão Crista no Brasil (Congregation of Christ in Brazil), a church that eventually grew to a million members. Vingren and Berg also gained a strong following, thanks in part to their learning Portuguese. They established a church in Belém, out of which emerged the Brazilian Assemblies of God.[12]

The growth of Pentecostalism in Latin America was thus the result of the interrelationships fostered between foreign missionaries and local populations. The early Pentecostal movement would not have been successful had it not been for the receptivity of many Latin Americans. While Pentecostalism originated outside of Latin America, it ultimately expanded into a powerful homegrown religious movement.

The greatest growth in Pentecostalism in Latin America came after 1950. It was assisted by faith-healing crusades that emanated from North America. In 1952 Theodore "Tommy" Hicks had a vision while preaching in Tallahassee, Florida. He claimed he saw a map of South America covered with yellow stalks of wheat that turned into men and women who called out to him to come and that he received a prophetic message from God that instructed him to go. Three months later, in Red Bluffs, California, the wife of a local minister allegedly repeated the words of that message while praying; she stated that she had no previous knowledge of it. Because of this, Hicks gathered together all the money he could and flew to Argentina, where he met President Juan Perón, who purportedly prayed with him and gave him permission to conduct a faith-healing crusade in Buenos Aires. Perón also gave Hicks free access to government radio and press. In 1954 Hicks initiated a crusade that helped bring Pentecostalism to Argentina. This crusade lasted for fifty-two days and reached a total of 2 million people.[13]

Hicks's success in Argentina gained him the support of Pentecostals everywhere, most notably, the Full Gospel Businessmen's Fellowship International (FGBMFI), an organization made up of wealthy Pentecostal believers from the southern United States who were desirous of improving the movement's image in Latin America.[14] The FGBMFI, which had originated in Los Angeles in 1951, was led by Demos Shakarian, an Armenian-American dairy processor. By 1981, after thirty years of existence, the organization had grown to encompass 2,700 chapters around the world with a membership that consisted of so-called self-made men who were drawn to its evangelistic message. Shakerian was very active in Latin American political circles and even contacted Cuba's Fidel Castro and Nicaragua's Thomas Borge and Daniel Ortega in an attempt to open their countries to Pentecostalism. He also worked to revive the religious fervor of Latin American Catholics, and in 1974 Pope John Paul II showed his gratitude by inviting him to the Vatican to receive a papal commendation.[15]

In the years that followed Hicks's campaign in Argentina, other Pentecostal revivalists took up the call in various Latin American countries. A. A. Allen awakened Venezuela to the movement. Morris Cerrullo, an avowed anticommunist, promoted Pentecostalism in Uruguay during the 1960s and in Central America in the 1980s. He became the first North American revivalist to be barred from Nicaragua, and his Costa Rican crusade caused that country's government to break off diplomatic relations with Cuba.[16] Elsewhere, including Ecuador, the tent campaigns and faith-healing crusades of the Church of the Foursquare Gospel furthered the movement. Pentecostalism became so successful in Latin America that by 1969 it comprised 63.3 percent of the total Protestant population there.[17] By the mid-1980s it had grown to 70 to 75 percent.[18]

The rapid growth of Pentecostalism in Latin America was aided by a system of church reproduction built on the concept of centralized mother churches that would give birth to many daughter churches. This system fostered almost simultaneous growth and was successful in many Latin American countries. One example of this mother-daughter growth pattern was seen between 1970 and 1973 in Bolivia. During that time the Assemblies of God followed a program of church planting called Cada Iglesia una Iglesia en un Año (Each Church Another Church in One Year) and grew fivefold, from a denomination of only 20 churches to one of 104.[19]

Problems arose despite the success and rapidity of Pentecostal mother-daughter growth in Latin America, especially where daughter churches became too independent from their mothers. Liberated from any denominational scrutiny, such wayward daughters often developed beliefs that certain segments in each country viewed as harmful. During the 1980s, for example, many independent Pentecostal churches negated the Pentecostal apolitical doctrine and increasingly became involved in politics in Chile, Brazil, Colombia, the Caribbean, and particularly Central America. The politically involved independent daughter churches—or Reagan cults, as they were called by some—usually allied themselves closely with the religious branch of the New Right in the United States and supported the military dictatorship in Chile, the geopolitical strategy of the United States in Brazil, and the move to brand liberation theology as Marxist. Furthermore, the independents succeeded in making Latin American converts. The authors of a 1989 *Newsweek* article described these evangelists' amazing success: "Every hour, demographers calculate, aggressive 'evangelicals'—most of them independent Pentecostals or fundamentalists—convert 400 Latin Catholics."[20]

In Central America, independent Pentecostalism was viewed as something more than a religion. It was an ideology and a dynamic, aggressive social movement with serious political implications. As one source described it,

The U.S. evangelicals are coming to Central America with more than Bibles. Many of them bring a pacifying ideology that forgives the guilty and soothes the poor with promises of personal salvation. It is a U.S. manufactured anti-dote to liberation and social justice theology. In the United States, the religious right helped put a reactionary into the White House. In Central America, the emerging religious right is helping keep reactionary elites in power and may prove a serious obstacle to revolutionary transformations that are long overdue.[21]

In Latin America, the prime example of independent Pentecostalism's role in politics surfaced after the military coup in Guatemala in March 1982, which placed General Efraín Ríos Montt in the presidency. Ríos Montt was a born-again Christian and a member of a Pentecostal sect, the Church of the Word, a mission of the California-based organization Gospel Outreach. After taking office, Ríos Montt implemented a counterinsur-gency campaign, Plan Victoria 82, against leftist guerrillas in the Guatema-lan highlands. He used independent Pentecostal assistance to establish strategic hamlets designed to pacify the indigenous population and disrupt guerrilla activities. The independent Pentecostals became liaisons between the army and local communities. They served as leaders of civil defense pa-trols and informants against guerrilla sympathizers.[22]

The independent Pentecostals themselves, however, were not completely safe from the counterinsurgency campaign. Because of its fanaticism. Ríos Montt's army did not always identify the enemy correctly. In one fit of ex-cess, it executed thirty Pentecostals in the village of Tuchubuc (Tu Chobuc) in the misguided belief that they had guerrilla connections—the army claimed that it had found an empty guerrilla storage pit in the vicinity. These killings were the exception, though, and the independent Pentecos-tals even excused Ríos Montt for the mistake, despite the fact that the vic-tims throats had been cut.[23]

The true targets of the Ríos Montt counterinsurgency campaign were Catholic catechists active in the education of indigenous people in the high-land base communities. Independent Pentecostals and their churches, in fact, became obstacles to and competitors with the liberation theologians. Ríos Montt gave preferences to so-called apolitical Protestant groups who carried out programs in literacy, health care, and relief aid.[24] For his efforts, he received support from U.S. Moral Majority groups that funneled money through World Vision and other organizations. On one occasion Ríos

Montt appeared on the "700 Club" with Pat Robertson, who asked viewers to pray "round the clock" for the general and his campaign. Other North American Pentecostals and conservative Protestants became involved; Jimmy Swaggert, Jerry Falwell, and Billy Graham all raised funds to send to Guatemala's small indigenous independent Pentecostal sects.[25]

Ultimately, in spite of North American evangelical assistance, Ríos Montt's regime came to a sudden end. The military, led by many younger army officers, overthrew him on August 8, 1983, and replaced him with General Oscar Humberto Mejía Victores. These young officers had felt that Ríos Montt had gone too far in waging a holy war against peasants in the Guatemalan highlands. They accused him of leading a fanatical and aggressive religious faction that took advantage of its high position in government for personal gain. Furthermore, they believed the foreign religious intrusion under Ríos Montt threatened Guatemala by ignoring the constitutional principle of the separation of church and state.[26]

In the late 1980s Ríos Montt was still active in Protestant circles in Central America. Through a program called Operation Whole Armor, he toured Guatemalan military bases distributing Bibles supplied by Bible Literature International of Ohio, a subsidiary of the Verbo Church, another California-based evangelical organization. He also smuggled Bibles into Nicaragua. In the United States, Ríos Montt remained the darling of the religious right. One source reported:

> In many ways, the Ríos Montt tenure marked a turning point for Christian rights activists, who midway through President Reagan's first term realized that some of Reagan's promises—ending abortion, instituting school prayer, etc.—would not be fulfilled. Organizationally, the private aid campaign to Rios Montt was a dry run for later involvement in funneling aid to the Nicaraguan contras. However vicarious, the experience of a born-again Christian shepherding an entire nation reinforced the notion that they could seize the reins of power and install—by force if necessary—their version of the Kingdom of God on earth. The massive human rights violations which characterized the General's rule failed to diminish his stature among conservative evangelicals, who to this day consider him a hero.[27]

Also in the late 1980s, Ríos Montt attempted a political comeback by running again for Guatemala's presidency. He banked on the support of Guatemalans who wanted a strong-armed leader who would stamp out po-

litical corruption. Guatemalan law, however, prohibited past coup participants from running for office, and he was banned from the campaign. He
subsequently called upon his supporters to ruin their ballots and riot in the
streets, but they threw their support behind another Protestant political
leader, the born-again businessman Jorge Serrano Elías, who eventually
won the runoff election of January 6, 1990, by a landslide. As president,
Serrano Elías proved himself incapable of controlling the Guatemalan military and their death squads, as he had promised in his campaign to do. He
promoted the neoliberal fiscal policies of austerity and increased production
as a way out of the country's economic difficulties; these measures portended increased suffering for the majority of Guatemalans. According to
David Stoll, Serrano Elías, like the Catholic Fujimori in Peru, was a dark-
horse candidate who could not have won without evangelical support. His
election victory and Ríos Montt's attempted comeback were significant because they demonstrated the power of Pentecostalism in Central America
and made Guatemala the first country in Latin America to have an election
dominated by two Protestant candidates.[28]

In Ecuador, Pentecostalism did not have political leaders to rival Guatemala's General Ríos Montt or Jorge Serrano Elías. The movement did play
an important political role there, however. This was especially true in the
1960s, following the Cuban Revolution, and in the 1980s during the Reagan administration. In both decades Pentecostal activism coincided with
faith-healing crusades that served to dampen the revolutionary impulses of
Ecuador's urban and rural poor.

The first Pentecostal group to enter Ecuador, the International Church of
the Foursquare Gospel, arrived in 1953. It was followed by Christ the King
Evangelical Church in 1958 and the United Pentecostal Church (Only Jesus)
in 1959.[29] In 1962 the Assemblies of God entered and immediately joined
forces with the Foursquare Gospel Church to organize a citywide evangelical faith-healing crusade in Guayaquil under the guidance of Roberto Aguirre, a young Foresquare Gospel missionary, and Roberto Espinosa, a
Mexican Assemblies of God preacher and faith healer.[30] This crusade took
place in the Ramon Unamuno Stadium, lasted for the unusually long period
of six weeks, and drew crowds of as many as 35,000 people each night.[31]
Following the mother-daughter growth pattern of the Pentecostal movement, the one struggling Foursquare Gospel Church of thirty members became seven churches with 1,500 members. New members, most of whom
Aguirre named "instant pastors," took the Pentecostal message back to

their families and friends; as a result, within four years the Guayaquil Four-square Gospel Church bred forty-two daughter churches in various parts of the country.[32]

The 1962 Pentecostal faith-healing crusade came at a critical juncture in the political life of Ecuador, a time when Guayaquil, with a population of approximately 500,000 people—half of them poor urban dwellers—was threatened by political upheaval. Those urban dwellers, who resided in Los Guasmos, the squalid swampland *suburbios* or *barrios* (slums) on the banks of the Guayas River, were outraged at the government of the controversial populist Carlos Julio Arosemena Monroy (November 1961-July 1963) because of its failure to remedy the lack of sewers, potable water, and electricity and because they were largely hungry, malnourished, unemployed, and ill-housed.[33]

Also at the time of the crusade, the U.S. government began to interfere once again in Ecuadorean politics, attacking Arosemena for what it viewed as his flirtation with communism. Arosemena was under pressure from two sides: the Left and the poor of Guayaquil, who clamored for change, and the Right, including the United States and the Ecuadorean military, who wanted to maintain the economic and sociopolitical status quo. His difficulties mirrored those of his predecessor Velasco Ibarra who had been overthrown by the Ecuadorean military for failing to carry out reforms in industry, public housing, and agriculture promised to the urban poor.

U.S. criticism of Arosemena surfaced when he refused to have Ecuador cast its vote for sanctions against Cuba at the Punta del Este Conference in Uruguay in January 1962. This stance led to a CIA operation in July 1963 that resulted in the Ecuadorean military's seizing power from Arosemena and the suppression of his student and worker supporters. The anti-Arosemena campaign was the result of long-standing North American political and economic hegemony over Ecuador, which was exemplified by U.S. control of international lending institutions and the pro–North American and anticommunist indoctrination of the Ecuadorean military. According to Oswaldo Hurtado:

The subordination of the 1963 government to the dictates of the United States was extraordinary: the foreign policy was shaped according to strategies developed in the Department of State; the offices of public agencies were filled with Agency for International Development technicians; the embassy of the United States intervened openly in the designation of public officials; and a secret "protocol" was signed authorizing United States–based fishing boats to operate freely within Ecuador's 200-mile territorial limit. Even before assuming power, the military, at the behest of the United States, forced President Arosemena Monroy to break diplomatic relations with Cuba and to suspend commercial relations with Eastern Europe. Once in power, they unleashed a general persecution against leftist ideas and politicians, suppressed the student and labor movements, outlawed the Communist party, and dismissed public employees suspected of Communist sympathies.[34]

The Pentecostal crusade in Guayaquil and the religious expansion afterward took place in the midst of urban uprising and the anti-Arosemena, anticommunist campaign conducted by the U.S. government and the Ecuadorean military. It demonstrated that Pentecostalism, through faith-healing crusades, could serve political ends. The Guayaquil crusade effectively calmed the city's impoverished masses and removed the threat of a generalized outbreak of unrest that could have overtaken all of Ecuador.

In the years that followed the Guayaquil crusade, Pentecostalism proliferated among Ecuador's poor, with its greatest growth taking place in the 1960s. During that decade Pentecostals carried out the highest percentage of baptisms among the principal Protestant groups in Ecuador, some 53 percent of the total number. By 1970, 13,140 of a total of 24,620 Protestants received Pentecostal baptisms. This year compared favorably to 1960, which showed only 170 Pentecostal baptisms, or 4 percent of the total of 4,260.[35] Furthermore, by 1985, while the percentage of Pentecostal baptisms declined to approximately 24 percent, or 21,000 out of a total of 87,650, the number still represented substantial growth.[36] One Ecuadorean scholar pointed out that if the tendencies of Pentecostal growth in Latin America as a whole had any validity for Ecuador, then Pentecostal baptisms in Ecuador would probably show even higher percentages in the future.[37]

In the 1980s Pentecostalism expanded into all regions of Ecuador. North American televangelism and new faith-healing crusades helped accomplish this. Most significant were the campaigns of the Puerto Rican Pentecostal Yiye Avila, who visited Ecuador twice during the decade. In his crusade, Impacto de Dios 86 (Impact of God 86), Avila called himself the messenger of the Holy Spirit and preached for nine days in Quito's Plaza de Toros (Bullring), where he attracted more than 130,000 spectators. He electrified the audiences and took his followers to the point of ecstasy by speaking of the three conditions for accepting the Holy Spirit: "the fear," "the guilt," and "the reward." The following excerpts illustrate Avila's Pentecostal gospel to Ecuadoreans.

> The judgment of God is about to befall you. Earthquakes are about to befall you. Floods are coming. Most of humanity will perish. All who have sinned will die and go to hell. Smile, God loves you! Repent and escape the tragedy that will befall the earth. Only the people of God will be saved. If you are hesitating listen well, repent. There will be no more campaigns of salvation. This is the evening of your victory over sin. Smile, God loves you! The end is near. Christ will come on the clouds mounting a white horse, dressed in the finest linen. Christ is coming and the white horse of Jesus Christ will descend as here on earth the Third World War will break out. The strategists will ask themselves if this airborne cavalry is a secret weapon of Russia. Look up! No horses or horsemen are falling. No! Blessed be God! Jesus Christ's horse has eyes like fire. The horseman on top will implant the New Kingdom of God. His place will be Jerusalem. Hallelujah, Hallelujah, Hallelujah!
>
> Buy an insurance policy for your children. Convert and insure your children's salvation. You are guilty if your children go to hell. Buy insurance today. It won't cost a cent. Buy. Don't leave without Christ. Buy. Bring your children and they will be well. Break Satan's yoke. Convert. Blessed be God!
>
> There are sinners among those here. I can see you, do not hide. Your heart is full of sin. If you die in this moment you will go to hell. The *Plaza de Toros* has four doors to heaven. We only want for you to be saved. First, is the salvation of the soul. Later will come the healing of the body. I am not in a hurry. Come down, all who want to receive Christ. Do not turn your backs. This evening is decisive for you. Feel the presence of the "Holy Spirit."
>
> And when the Kingdom of God arrives, I can assure you there will be no hunger, no poverty, no anguish, no misery because Christ, in person, will imprison the devil who is the cause of all the world's injustices.[38]

Avila used psychology and marketing techniques to further the cause of Pentecostalism in a city that at one time in its history had not allowed Protestants to enter its gates. He took advantage of every moment. In one instance, he depicted a plane landing at the nearby Mariscal Sucre airport as Christ's fiery-eyed horse descending to earth. His impassioned words and his acceptance in Quito demonstrated the distance Pentecostalism and Protestantism in general had traveled in Ecuador; their acceptance in Avila's time was a far cry from the reaction against the early Protestants during the period of the Liberal Revolution.

Avila played an important role is the Latin American Pentecostal movement. For many years he traveled the region proselytizing its message. He was actually a representative of the Puerto Rican Pentecostal movement, which itself had an estimated 150,000 members. In Puerto Rico, Pentecostalism dated its origins to 1917 and Juan L. Lugo, an Assemblies of God missionary who, with financial aid from the Bethel Church of Los Angeles, established the colony's first Pentecostal church, the Iglesia de Dios Pentecostal (Pentecostal Church of God). Lugo was also credited with bringing the Pentecostal movement to Puerto Ricans in New York City when he founded a church in an old, abandoned synagogue in the Greenpoint section of Brooklyn in 1929.[39]

In addition to serving as a representative of Puerto Rican Pentecostalism, Avila demonstrated the movement's increasingly right-wing political proclivity during the 1980s. His 1986 tour took him to Sandinista Nicaragua as well as to Ecuador. He followed the example of another Puerto Rican revivalist, Jorge Raschke, who through his Clamor a Dios campaign vehemently attacked the Puerto Rican independence movement and its supporters in Latin America. Raschke believed that people advocating independence for Puerto Rico were working in league with the devil.[40]

By the late 1980s, many Ecuadoreans viewed Pentecostalism with alarm. They compared it to the SIL and World Vision and accused independent Pentecostal churches of fostering divisions in indigenous communities, precipitating clashes with Catholics and other Protestants, and causing serious problems by opening schools and orphanages that failed to register with the government agencies responsible for licensing nonprofit organizations. Ecuadorean critics of Pentecostalism claimed that human rights violations often occurred through the activities of these churches and that foreign doctrines were espoused by their adherents.

Throughout the 1980s there were examples to illustrate the validity of these concerns. In 1987 one independent Pentecostal group, the Iglesia Evangélica Nombre de Jesús (Name of Jesus Evangelical Church), attempted to undermine other Protestant groups in the communities of El Marco and Tolontag on the outskirts of Quito by implying that the other Protestants exploited the inhabitants of the communities with the imposition of a heavy tribute. Among other groups singled out for criticism were the non-Pentecostal independent Ebenezer church, with strong ties to HCJB, and the small progressive Betel church, related to the Consejo Latinoamericano de Iglesias (Latin American Council of Churches) or CLAI, an offshoot of the WCC.[41]

According to demographic data for El Marco and Tolontag in 1987, the Ebenezer church was the largest religious group in the two communities, boasting 1,800 members, or 65 percent of the total number of Christians. The second largest group, the Catholics, had approximately 530 members, or 20 percent of the total number of believers, down from 100 percent prior to 1968. The Catholics were nonhomogeneous, divided between traditional Catholics at 3 percent and charismatic Catholics (those who followed beliefs and rituals similar to those of the Pentecostals) at 17 percent. The Iglesia Evangélica Nombre de Jesús was third, with 240 members, or 9 percent of the total religious population, and the Betel church had only 150 followers, or 6 percent of the total religious population.[42]

The Iglesia Evangélica Nombre de Jesús entered the community as a consequence of the difficulties between the other Protestants. Both communities had a history of religious struggle dating back to 1968. At the heart of the problem was the conflict raging between Ebenezer and Betel over a piece of land for the construction of new churches. They had demanded that a local landowner donate the land to them, but he felt unduly pressured and did not want to cooperate. In an attempt to drive the other denominations away, he helped bring the Iglesia Evangélica Nombre de Jesús into the communities. The Iglesia Evangélica Nombre de Jesús did the landowner's bidding and criticized the other Protestants for their alleged harshness in collecting the *diezmos* (tithes) and *primicias* (first fruits), the traditional church taxes. The Iglesia Evangélica Nombre de Jesús claimed that these taxes were punitive and that people were punished severely for not paying. It promoted itself as above reproach and claimed that, as far as it was concerned, the payment of church taxes was completely voluntary.[43]

The Iglesia Evangélica Nombre de Jesús in El Marco and Tolontag professed to a degree of social concern for the people of the two communities. In reality, however, it did little more than criticize the other Protestants. Its true objective was self-serving, to help the distraught landowner, to broaden its own base in the communities, and to drive out all other religious groups. Ultimately this church only divided the communities further and kept the holy war alive. It made no real attempt to resolve the cause of the conflict, the dire socioeconomic condition of the communities caused by the scarcity of land.

Another problem centered around El Tabernáculo (the Tabernacle Church), a wayward daughter of the Church of the Foursquare Gospel in Guayaquil. El Tabernáculo was founded in 1972 by Pastor Francisco Campos, who claimed to have support from Ecuadorean residents in the United States and from Luis Noboa Naranjo, a Guayaquil banana magnate and major supporter of León Febres Cordero. Campos organized El Tabernáculo after the North American head of the Foursquare Gospel Church turned down his idea to establish a school for Guayaquil slum children. The North American told Campos that the Church of the Foursquare Gospel could not afford the additional project and that any Ecuadorean initiative would be doomed to failure. Campos reacted sharply to this response, withdrew from the mother church, and established his own congregation. By 1986 he claimed to have organized thirty churches throughout the country with 10,000 members, fifteen pastors, and a boarding school for three hundred children.[44]

El Tabernáculo never registered with any government agency. Pastor Campos stated that his church preferred to remain anonymous so that it could work freely among those in need of its services; he did not want the government interfering in church affairs. Campos claimed to have the best interests of Ecuador at heart and said that he hoped to make the country great and turn it into a community of love.

In 1986 the controversy over *El Tabernáculo* centered around the conditions at its boarding school, near the city of Latacunga in Cotopaxi in the central Sierra. Situated on a 115-hectare hacienda on an arid, windy, and extremely cold *páramo,* or mountain pass, the school contained substandard sleeping quarters where as many as six children slept in one bed. It had no sports facilities or playgrounds of any kind, no weekend or holiday leaves for the children, no entertainment, inadequate provisions of clothing and scarce food and water. In addition, it promoted Fascist ideology. Nazi swastikas were observed all over the school, on desks, walls, and blackboards. They were even seen on the children's shoes and jackets. In many cases the swastikas were included in religious drawings that also depicted doves in the form of the Holy Spirit and Christian crosses. Most tellingly, it appeared that the students were brainwashed. Asked whether or not they were hungry, most of the children at the school replied, "We are not hungry, we are filled with the 'Spirit'; the material is worth nothing."[45]

El Tabernáculo and similar institutions, in the view of Ecuadorean critics of Pentecostalism, were problems because of their uncontrolled growth.

These critics asked what was permissible in the name of religion, a questions raised as they saw poor people in need of spiritual solace being easily molded by the various doctrines of one religious group or another. The government did very little. During the 1980s government agencies were constricted by budget and personnel cuts necessitated by Ecuador's external debt. It was debatable, too, whether or not the government should take on a regulatory role, given the legal separation of church and state. For the critics of Pentecostalism in Ecuador, *El Tabernáculo* was representative of a grave problem with implications for the future, as Estrada and Muñoz noted:

> The pathetic school of Pastor Francisco is nothing more than a minute demonstration of what is happening in the country as a result of the explosive and uncontrolled division among Protestant sects. It is fundamental to find out if other fanatical religious groups, even more dangerous, are taking advantage of the ignorance and poverty of the people for the purposes of orienting our youth toward a resurgence and renovation of Fascist Nazi doctrine.[46]

The Iglesia Evangélica Nombre de Jesús in El Marco and Tolontag and El Tabernáculo exemplified negative aspects of mother-daughter independent Pentecostal expansion in Ecuador from 1950 to 1990. This growth came quite unexpectedly and was not a cause of concern until the 1980s, when sociologists, theologians, and journalists began to question it. They equated Pentecostalism to other forms of Protestantism in their country and felt, by and large, that Ecuador would be better off without the movement. Not everyone saw Pentecostalism as completely devoid of merit, however. One analyst, Tomás Bamat, pointed out that some young independent Pentecostals were themselves disturbed by the actions of their colleagues, and in Guayaquil a few of them had formed organizations that promoted literacy, adult education, women's rights, and community development. These socially concerned Pentecostals, Bamat wrote, believed that social action was implicit in the gospel of Christ. He interviewed one young woman, Tatiana Ortiz, who asserted,

> Jesus said that he came to give us life and life in abundance. The purpose of God is Man's life. Jesus showed by his example: multiplying bread—material bread—curing the sick. The church as a body is called to fight and work for life for those inside the church and those outside of it.[47]

According to Bamat, Ortiz was disturbed that the majority of Pentecostals did not think as she did. In her words:

> They don't see this dimension, because they read what has been written literally, without seeing the content and the significance. Pastoral training is individualistic and besides it is more comfortable not to commit oneself.[48]

Ortiz and her views represented a departure from the Pentecostal norm of frowning upon social action for the poor. She supported the notion that the movement could be a positive social force in the future, and she mixed the Ecuadorean nationalistic desire for social change with Pentecostal belief. By 1990, Pentecostals like Ortiz offered some hope that as the Ecuadorean Pentecostal daughters severed their ties with their North American mothers, social activism would take precedence over religious apoliticism and indoctrination.

Tatiana Ortiz's ideas resembled those of other socially active Pentecostals in Latin America. Beginning in the 1950s, important voices were heard throughout the region, including those of Gabriel Vaccaro, a Pentecostal pastor in Argentina who sounded much like a liberation theologian and talked of an option for the poor; Manuel Melo in Brazil, the leader of Brasil para Cristo (Brazil for Christ; BPC), who, in the early 1960s, called for increased democracy and social justice; and Noel Vargas Castro, a writer and poet in Nicaragua, who espoused his own "dawn theology," the idea that Pentecostal churches must work, as Jesus did in Israel, for the liberation of the poor and the downtrodden. Castro was unique to the Pentecostal movement because he made the ultimate sacrifice; he was murdered along with seven teachers and thirty-five campesinos in a Contra attack in 1982.[49]

In Chile, the activities of the CCI, the Confraternidad Cristiana de Iglesias (Christian Brotherhood of Churches), also exemplified burgeoning Pentecostal social awareness. The CCI, founded in 1985, included eight Pentecostal churches and four historic denominations that acted against the traditional apoliticism of Chilean Protestantism and publicly opposed the Pinochet government. The CCI generally supported efforts to bring about human rights and democratic reform. In 1986 it organized the Prayer Campaign for Life, Peace, and Reconciliation in Chile as a response to government repression against demonstrators in a July protest, which saw police set fire to two young people. This campaign lasted a month and ended with CCI representatives presenting to the military government a letter urging it to permit a transition to democracy and human rights.[50]

The growth of Pentecostalism in Ecuador from 1950 to 1990 mirrored what took place in many Latin American countries, including Guatemala, Brazil, and Chile. It was clear that Pentecostalism played to the spiritual needs of the many poverty-stricken Ecuadoreans and, with the exception of social activists like Tatiana Ortiz, did not seek to change the economic and sociopolitical status quo. Ultimately, Ecuadorean Pentecostalism served right-wing political aims. Furthermore, the movement was basically self-serving, amorphous, lacking in clear-cut objectives, and steeped in division-istic tactics and bizarre ideologies that called into question any long-term benefit that might accrue from its endeavors. By 1990 many nationalistic Ecuadoreans believed its presence in their country, like that of many other Protestant groups, represented nothing more than a continuation of the historical processes of domination by the local elite and outsiders.

CHAPTER 8

The Protestant "Threat" and
the Catholic Response

Jesus was born in Bethlehem,
"the smallest among
the villages of Judah,"
surrounded by shepherds
and animals.
His parents had come
to the stable
after they fruitlessly knocked
on many doors in town.
There, in oblivion,
the Word was made history
in the flesh of the poor.

Gustavo Gutiérrez, Latinamerica Press, *December 24,* 1987

IN THE YEARS BETWEEN 1895 and 1990 Ecuador's Catholic church viewed North American fundamentalist Protestantism in its country as a threat to its role of ministering to the spiritual and educational needs of the Ecuadorean people. It responded in ways that reflected the different social, political, economic, and religious trends of four consecutive periods of time: 1895 to 1917, 1917 to 1937, 1937 to the late 1960s, and the late 1960s to 1990.

In the first period, the church followed a traditional pattern of response, allying itself with Conservatives to attack Protestantism in newspapers, catechisms, pastoral letters, and sermons as a "heretic" religion. In Quito, tab-

loids such as *La Defensa* and *El Monitor Popular* said that North American
Protestantism lacked sincerity; that the Catholic church was too strong
for the Protestants to attract many converts; and that Ecuadoreans had to
protect their children against Protestant missionaries who tempted, conquered, and used them in an assortment of immoralities. In Cuenca, local
newspapers called Protestantism "a decrepit sect" and a "cadaver full of
putrification."[1]

In its catechisms, pastoral letters, and sermons, the Catholic church
instructed followers to remain loyal to the true faith and to question the
principles of Protestantism. Catholic literature denigrated the origins of
Protestantism and reiterated certain Catholic ideas: for example, that the
only true church of Christ was the Catholic church; that even though many
Protestants called themselves Christians, they had no right to do so; and
that Martin Luther and John Calvin had usurped Catholic doctrine to begin
their movements after the Catholic church had already been in existence for
fifteen centuries. In addition, the literature told Ecuadoreans that Protestantism was an evil because it failed to accept the traditional doctrine that
the pope was God's authority on earth and that Christ had named Peter the
first pope in Rome.[2]

The traditional Ecuadorean Catholic church response to North American fundamentalist Protestantism during the period of 1895–1917 took its
lead from the Conservative archbishop of Quito Federico González Suárez
(see chapter 1). Writing in Catholic periodicals and speaking from the pul-
pit, González Suárez led the attack on the North American Protestants, Eloy
Alfaro, and the Liberal governments for what he believed was an unholy
alliance that had as its prime objective the destruction of Catholicism in Ecuador. In 1917, however, after González Suárez's death, the church's outcry
became less intense, and it entered the second period of response which saw
its influence and political power reined in by a national government controlled by a coastal liberal oligarchy that enforced the anti-church legislation enacted during the Alfaro period. While the church still managed to
have a voice by virtue of its traditional position within Ecuadorean society,
this second period nonetheless represented a muted reaction that lasted until 1937.

In the third period of response, from 1937 to the late 1960s, the Ecuadorean church returned to the traditionalism of González Suárez. Church
officials called on the precepts of extreme conservatism and authoritarian
ecclesiastical control based strongly on church sacraments, theology, and

pastoral positions. The church promoted moderate social reforms through its values and educational system. As an integral part of its response, it listed secular education as the reason for the growth of Protestantism and other assorted evils, including communism. It warned that secularism in education, the result of religious indifference, was against Catholic practice and would ultimately bring about the "softening of faith." Among church leaders who participated in this response were Aurelio Espinosa Polit (see chapter 1), who in 1960 gave a sermon in Quito that celebrated the fifty-sixth anniversary of the Miracle of La Dolorosa, in which the statue of the Virgen de los Dolores (Virgin of the Sorrowful) was observed at the Colegio San Gabriel opening and closing its eyes and crying. He called this a sign that the Virgin Mary was united with all Ecuadorean children and adolescents in their struggle against educational laws that prejudiced the position of Catholic schools.[3] The Virgin was named the patron saint of antisecularism in education.

Two important developments aided the resurgence of the church's strength in the third period of response. First, in 1937 the church successfully petitioned the government to sign a *modus vivendi* establishing official relations between the Ecuadorean state and the Vatican. Second, in 1938 the church joined the political Right in founding CEDOC, the Confederación Ecuatoriana de Obreros Católicos (Ecuadorean Confederation of Catholic Workers). The modus vivendi guaranteed the church the right to organize new schools and to build new missions in the Oriente in return for which the Vatican would renew its orders to the Ecuadorean clergy to refrain from any party affiliation or to have anything to do with politics. As part of the agreement, the Ecuadorean government promised to give the church 1.5 million sucres in payment for lands nationalized during the Alfaro period if it renounced its demand for the total return of confiscated church lands. CEDOC, with antecedents in the Compactación Obrera Nacional (see chapter 3), organized artisans and workers and became the most important labor organization in the country and a stronghold of Catholic support.

The modus vivendi and CEDOC brought the church back from the fringes of Ecuadorean society in spite of some concern on the part of both the Left and the Right. The Left believed the church had regained too much power, and the Right thought it had been given too little. Specifically, the Right questioned the modus vivendi's failure to return to the church the authority to perform marriages.[4]

In the fourth period of response, from the late 1960s to 1990, the Ecuadorean church came to the conclusion that traditional methods would not stop the progress of North American fundamentalist Protestantism in Ecuador, and it responded by adhering to the doctrines of liberation theology and the opinions of the Vatican II Ecumenical Council (1962–65) and the Episcopal congresses at Medellín, Colombia, in 1968 and Puebla, Mexico, in 1979. In 1979 the Ecuadorean Bishops Conference issued Opciones Pastorales, a statement that endorsed eight key pastoral goals designed to strengthen the progressive tendencies within the Ecuadorean church. These goals included evangelization to build God's reign; the defense and promotion of human dignity, especially that of the poor; the establishment of CEBs; the encouragement of lay participation; the reexamination and purification of popular religious practices so they would become liberating experiences; the strengthening of local churches; the promotion of a missionary spirit; and the encouragement of vocations.[5]

In addition, the Ecuadorean church followed certain ideas of such church leaders as Pope John XXIII and Pope Paul VI, and it took to the teachings of two important founders of liberation theology, Camilo Torres of Colombia and Gustavo Gutiérrez of Peru. Pope John XXIII championed the liberalization of the church's liturgy at the Vatican II Ecumenical Council. He also wrote two encyclicals, *Mater et Magistra* (On Justice, 1961) and *Pacem in Terris* (Peace on Earth, 1963), that called for decent standards of living, education, and political participation as universal human rights. He elaborated the ideas that the right to private property and the church's adherence to capitalism were not unquestionable, that the church is of this world, and that it is a community of equals whose members all have something to contribute and to share.[6]

Pope Paul VI influenced the Ecuadorean church by adding to the work of John XXIII. In 1967 he wrote *Populorum Progressio* (On the Progress of Peoples), which stressed the economic, social, and political rights of all men. Directed at Latin America, it urged its bishops to hold a conference to examine the conclusions of Vatican II. This call resulted in the Medellín Congress, which became a turning point in the church's theology in Latin America. With its documents, including the "Message to the People of Latin America," the Medellín Congress called for a series of reforms intended to eradicate injustice. It was followed by the Puebla Congress, which, in amplifying the themes of Medellín, issued a more extensive call for a commitment to the poor and for human rights.[7]

Camilo Torres touched the liberalizing tendencies of the Ecuadorean church by the example he set. He was a Catholic martyr who believed that, to bring about change, he had to take a more active role in the struggle of peasants and workers. In his first combat action with the Colombian guerrilla Army of the National Liberation (ELN) on February 15, 1966, he organized his followers into a revolutionary cell called the United Front. When he enlisted in the ELN, he wrote,

> I am joining the armed struggle. From the Colombian mountains I mean to continue the fight with a gun in my hands until power is won for the people. I have joined the Army of the National Liberation because I have found the desire for and realization of unity at the base, the peasant base without religious or traditional party differences, without antagonism toward the revolutionary principles of other sectors, movements or parties, without caudillism.[8]

The effect of Camilo Torres was to bring about direct clerical involvement in the peasant movement and revolution. For many in the Ecuadorean and Latin American church, his martyrdom was a call to arms. Among those who followed his example were James (Guadalupe) Carney, a North American priest who took up the armed struggle in Honduras, his adopted country, in the early 1980s. Carney believed there was no greater joy for a Christian than to die a martyr doing "Christ's work" on earth. In 1983 he disappeared in an ill-fated guerrilla campaign.[9]

Gustavo Gutiérrez touched the progressive movement in Ecuador and elsewhere by formulating the basic doctrines of liberation theology, a task he began in the early 1960s while he was a student at the Catholic University of Louvain, Belgium. There, with the assistance of Camilo Torres, he initiated a type of Catholic theology that was rooted in the perspectives of social science and Marxism, although it was not in itself Marxist. Unlike Torres, Gutiérrez believed that it was unnecessary to give up one's life to bring about change. He favored a nonviolent approach that followed the pacifism of Gandhi and Martin Luther King. Gutiérrez's method for change was the written word, and he used it extensively to promote liberation theology throughout Latin America and the world.[10]

In 1968 Gutiérrez publicly introduced liberation theology doctrine in a sermon he delivered at a pastoral conference in Chimbote, Peru. Gutiérrez acknowledged that a class struggle existed in Latin America but contended that in the context of liberation theology, it represented an expression of love for one's neighbor and solidarity with the poor. For him, the conflict was not the Marxist class struggle that denied the existence of God but one that viewed God as an integral part of the liberating process, especially as it concerned the poor. Gutiérrez rejected the idea that capitalist development would resolve Latin America's serious economic, political, and social problems. He viewed developmentalism as the problem, not the solution, because it emanated from within the prevailing exploitative system. In sum, he saw liberation theology as the road to change and believed that an enlightened Latin American church could offer the poor an option to their poverty.[11] In 1988 he was asked if he had ever imagined the repercussions his work would have in Latin America, the church, and the world over a period of twenty years. He replied,

> No, I never imagined the influence it would have. In a meeting with pastoral agents in Chimbote in 1968, I was asked to develop the theology of development, a topic that was in vogue at the time. Preparing the talk, I became convinced that rather than a theology of development, it was necessary to talk about a theology of liberation; that is, theology of salvation in Christ, with all its present-day historical consequences.... I only wanted to help those present to develop a faith perspective on the social and historical situation in Peru and in Latin America in those years.[12]

In Ecuador, many clerics employed the tenets of liberation theology in reaction to Protestantism. They entered a conflict that raged all over Latin America, one that saw liberation theology pitted against a growing number of politically motivated and determined North American fundamentalist Protestant groups eager to pursue a religious war for the hearts and minds of the region's people. According to David Stoll, this conflict was a new type of religious rivalry, one that differed in intent and intensity from the past competition and was connected to the political struggle:

> If battles over turf used to be waged mainly between Catholics and Protestants, in terms of honor due the Pope or the Virgin Mary, now they were being overlaid by a new kind of confrontation between liberation theology and anti-Communist crusades. Where right-wing fundamentalists came up against left-wing Catholics, religious and political differences overlapped and built up what started to look like holy war.[13]

Archbishop Leonidas Proaño of Riobamba led the liberation theology movement. He had gained his position of leadership by laboring for indigenous people in Chimborazo for many years, and he understood the people of the Sierra very well. He believed they were entitled to health care, proper working conditions, and education and that getting those things for them required a clear understanding of their identity and circumstances, something that he felt the North American Protestants did not have. He wrote of them in terms sympathetic to their plight:

They are people who do not have sufficient land to extract what they need to eat, to dress, and to educate themselves. They are the people who do not enjoy the basic services such as water, electricity, and more often than not schools. They are the people exploited by other men, possessors of capital and great expanses of land. They are the illiterate on the margins of culture and of civilization. The only thing they have is a master. They are people who do not have voice to express their needs and aspirations. They are the people who easily acquire diseases that ruin their lives, that dedicate themselves to drunkenness as the only escape. They are a people who are profoundly religious with a religiosity mixed with superstition and apparent Christian forms. They are the people that as a consequence of centuries of oppressive exploitation are psychologically prostrate and wasted: timid, suspicious, troubled.[14]

Proaño believed that the indigenous people of the Sierra, in spite of the negative aspects of their lives, possessed physical and moral strength, dedication to work, community spirit, hospitality, and solidarity. He added,

Their aspirations are to become owners of the land, to satisfy their need for recognition as someone by others, to break away from their complexes, to acquire confidence in themselves, to feel themselves capable to participate in the progress of the community, to affirm themselves as people subject to rights and obligations, to transform their lives into a source of happiness and understanding of the world, to discover the true God and his son Jesus Christ.[15]

Archbishop Proaño was born in the community of Pucahuayco near the town of San Antonio de Ibarra in the province of Imbabura. Though he modeled his life on Gandhi and King, traditionalists within the church attacked him as a disciple of Karl Marx. He represented what Oswaldo Hurtado called the "committed Church." In Chimborazo, Proaño organized literacy campaigns by radio for the indigenous population, established peasant leader hostels and schools, vetoed the construction of an elaborate cathedral, stripped territorial holdings from the church in his jurisdiction, and adopted a life-style of "total evangelical poverty."[16]

The indigenous people of Chimborazo revered Proaño. He worked among them wearing a gray poncho that became his trademark; when he died, he was buried in his hometown with it on. During his life in Chimborazo, he came under the scrutiny of the Ecuadorean military and the large landowners of the province. He is best remembered for a meeting he organized that took place in Riobamba on August 12, 1976, and included seventeen Latin American archbishops, four North American church officials (Archbishop Roberto Sánchez of Santa Fé; Juan Arzube, auxiliary bishop of Los Angeles; Gilberto Chavez, auxiliary bishop of San Diego and Patricio Flores, auxiliary bishop of San Antonio), and several of the hemisphere's top theologians. The meeting, approved by the Vatican and Ecuadorean church hierarchy, was called to discuss Proaño's pastoral program in Chimborazo. It was abruptly interrupted by forty national policemen dressed in civilian clothes and armed with machine guns and tear-gas canisters. Their assault resulted in the arrest of Proaño and the others, who were taken by bus to Quito and briefly detained there after the Ecuadorean government accused them of plotting its overthrow. All were released after plans to escort them out of the country failed. One participant, the Venezuelan archbishop Mariano Parra León, suffered a heart attack during the ordeal. Parra León later told what happened:

> These barbarians pushed us into a police bus without allowing us to touch any of our personal belongings or even put on a pair of socks. For the first time in my life I knew what it was like to have a rifle shoved in my back.
>
> We were stuffed into the bus, . . . eighty people in a space meant for fifty, with armed guards pointing their guns at us. We had to take turns standing up during a three-hour trip through the mountains—we didn't know where they were taking us—and even when the bus stopped to allow us to relieve ourselves, there was an armed guard right behind us. Later, when the guards realized who we were—the government hadn't told them—some of them were so ashamed that they wanted to confess their sins there and then.[17]

Archbishop Proaño was dragged from the bus in the town of Machachi, just outside of Quito. Parra León related, "We didn't know what they were going to do with him or if they were going to kill him. . . . Those gangsters in charge of the military government will murder people without the slightest compunction."[18]

Some Ecuadoreans believed the military government did not act alone in the roundup of the clergymen but in concert with the Brazilian and Chilean military. Strengthening that argument was the fact that many of the bishops and priests at Riobamba had just come from a meeting in Vitoria, Brazil, which had been monitored by the Brazilian military. Also, at the time of the Riobamba meeting, ten Chilean intelligence officers were in Quito coordinating security operations for the Ecuadorean military. Further evidence of Chilean military involvement was the rock-throwing incident it arranged at the Santiago airport for the three Chileans who went to Riobamba.[19]

After his release, Archbishop Proaño continued to lead the Ecuadorean liberation theology movement and to serve as a major proponent of human rights and peace in Latin America. In 1986 he was nominated for the Nobel Peace Prize. Proaño's message was antimaterialistic. He believed in the nobility of mankind and taught that peace could not coexist with oppression, injustice, and torture, all of which he knew were taking place in Ecuador and elsewhere in the Americas. He believed that people must learn to be just, to pay others according to the true value of what they produce; that it was important to love the truth and to lend a helping hand to the poor; and, above all, that change could come through education and the diffusion of CEBs. He wrote, "We begin with small groups, those called ecclesial base communities, Christian communities of brotherhood that multiply Christian homes in a true community of love, ideals and aspirations. Where all are one while at the same time different."[20]

Proaño also spoke of inculcating youth at the university level with a strong respect for human rights, liberty, and justice. He called for Ecuadorean unity with the rest of Latin America and the construction of a new world by conquering hunger, unemployment, infant mortality, and servitude. He believed that all Ecuadoreans should be teachers and that change must begin in the consciousness of the poorest, the Indians and the campesinos, from whom would flow the new Christian world mentioned in the Universal Declaration of Human Rights in Algeria on July 4, 1976.[21]

Proaño died on August 31, 1988. His importance to the indigenous people of Ecuador was best summed up by Alfonso Cachimiel, coordinator for the Pastoral Juvenil Indígena de Imbabura (Pastoral Indian Youth

School of Imbabura), at his funeral. Cachimiel expressed the feelings of the indigenous people the archbishop had worked for in terms that reflected the syncretism of their native Catholicism. He compared Proaño to Bartolomé de Las Casas, who defended the Indians in the sixteenth century, and placed him in the indigenous pantheon next to other heroes and gods.

Our *Pachacamac*-God and his son *el Inti* (the Sun); light of the world, living symbol of our theology defended by the Archbishop of the Indians, are sad. . . . On the other hand, those who persecuted our Archbishop, the landowners, the masters, and other authorities that exploit the Indians are content.

Monsignor Proaño defended human rights; the rights of the Indian to his land, our mother, where we live. He rejected the celebration of five hundred years of the white man's domination and exploitation of our lands. The Catholic church must involve itself more in the option for the poor, as Monsignor Proaño did. Today, Monsignor Proaño will be together with our indigenous heroes, [and] with Bartolomé de Las Casas. They are in the realm of Pachacamac-God lighting the way for the oppressed, the exploited, the poor until a true liberation is realized, the Kingdom of God, the new society.

Monsignor Proaño will live in our conscience, and everywhere the Indian is mistreated, oppressed, abandoned. He will be there with his humble spirit, but fighting for justice, the right to the land, and a life of dignity.

For all of this, Monsignor Proaño has not died, he is alive, he is present today and forever. . . . *Huandai Monseñor Proaño* [Monsignor Proaño lives].[22]

With the death of Proaño, the leadership of the Ecuadorean liberation theology movement passed to his disciple Monsignor Victor Corral. Corral supported the right of indigenous people to oppose Ecuador's large landowners and their allies in the government and the military. He blamed Ecuador's rural problems on this powerful elite and worked with indigenous people in an effort to bring about change. Like his mentor, he embraced the liberation theology doctrine of "a preferencial option for the poor" and attacked those who described the progressive church as a foreign ideology that created only chaos and disorder. He answered critics by saying that liberation theologians were not tied to political parties or foreign ideologies but were concerned only with assisting the poor. He raised the ire of Chimborazo's landowners by defending a colleague, Pedro Torres, a Colombian working in Tixan, whom they had accused of making trouble and wanted to expel from the country. Corral told the landowners that Torres was respected by the indigenous people of Tixan and would not be removed. He condemned the landowners for using repressive tactics against indigenous organizations and stated that indigenous people could not do them any harm. He said there could be no social justice in Ecuador as long as indigenous people did not own land.[23]

Because of his intimate ties with the leaders of Ecuador's indigenous movement, Corral spoke for indigenous people in important forums; he became their voice within the Ecuadorean Episcopal Conference and with government officials. Corral hoped to establish a long-lasting dialogue on indigenous rights with the church and the national government. He advised the government that the indigenous movement, contrary to certain statements made by some politicians, operated independently of extremist political parties. He related that indigenous organizers were pained by the suggestion that they were incapable of organizing on their own. In a 1990 interview, in answer to a question on how the seeds planted by Proaño had continued to grow, Corral observed,

> This is a phrase that he (Proaño) often used. One day, while looking through the window of his study at the trees outside, he said that "he would go (someday), but the trees that he planted would remain."
>
> There was always great concern, both within and outside of the diocese of Riobamba, about how Proaño's work would be continued after he was gone. But the trees that were planted continue to grow. The entire pastoral staff of the diocese continues to cooperate as a community, in fact the diocese has grown. An indigenous vicarate has been created, the first of its kind in this country.
>
> There is more consciousness in the organizations and more organizations are present. Also, there is a feeling that a struggle for justice and social change is necessary, and there is hope for a transformation that would result in more justice and solidarity.[24]

Archbishop Proaño profoundly affected the Catholic-Protestant controversy in Ecuador. Through his work, progressive clergy realized that the Catholic church's failure to address the needs of the poor advanced the North American fundamentalist Protestant cause. This awakening led them to speak out against the church's lack of social concern and to recognize the need for a more profound evangelization. In search of a more democratic and egalitarian future for the poor, the Ecuadorean Catholic church challenged North American fundamentalist Protestantism by organizing groups that promoted the teachings and work of Archbishop Proaño. Of special importance were FEPP (Fondo Ecuatoriano Populorum Progressio; see chapter 6) and CEDHU, the Comisión Ecuménica de Derechos Humanos del Ecuador (Ecumenical Human Rights Commission of Ecuador). Of these two groups, CEDHU was the more ecumenical. It had strong ties to progressive Protestant and interdenominational groups as well as other Catholic organizations, believing that it could accept help from any group that promoted human rights in Latin America.

FEPP, created in 1970 under the auspices of the Ecuadorean Episcopal Conference, strove to follow the principle expressed by Pope Paul VI when he said, "To be authentic, development must be integral, that is, it must promote all men and all mankind."[25] Its prime objectives were to establish educational programs that would raise the social awareness of indigenous and campesino groups, to promote necessary financing for base community organization, and to counsel organizations that requested their assistance. FEPP also coordinated activities with national and international organizations that identified with its objectives; and it accepted donations and loans from public and private organizations.

FEPP recognized the serious problems of Ecuador's rural population. Since 1970, almost 4 million Ecuadoreans living in the countryside had undergone rapid change, primarily because of the country's petroleum boom (see chapters 3 and 5), and the organization was aware that the Andean campesino was losing his identity and cultural heritage, that he remained socially dominated and economically exploited within a modified but not improved social condition. FEPP emphasized the inequalities that existed between the urban and rural sectors of Ecuadorean society and within the rural sector itself. It believed the rural sector throughout Ecuador was rapidly declining. In the Sierra, the demise of the hacienda system brought about the fragmentation of indigenous communities and lands. Soil erosion and intense out-migration had further disastrous effects. On the Coast, the export-oriented plantation economy exploited workers and placed them in a precarious, never-ending struggle for survival. In the Oriente, environmental devastation, colonization, intensive logging, and petroleum exploitation all contributed to the destruction of the indigenous populations.[26]

From FEPP's point of view, the Ecuadorean government's responses to these problems were inadequate. To compensate for the government's indifference and inactivity, the agency provided technical training, advice,

and credit to campesino organizations. It helped support agricultural pro-
ducers, rural artisans, and coastal fisherman. As of 1985, FEPP had serviced
313 groups in sixteen of Ecuador's twenty provinces. These included freeholding communities, cooperatives, and work groups with or without legal
statutes. For the most part, they were CEBs that conformed in ethnic
makeup to the native communities in which they were located.[27]

CEDHU was founded in 1978 in the aftermath of dictatorial military
rule from 1972 to 1977 (see chapter 3). It was organized by Catholics, progressive Protestants, and labor organizations such as the Federación
Campesina y las Centrales Sindicales (Peasant Federation and Central Syndicates), the Unión Nacional de Periodistas (National Union of Journalists),
the Colegio de Médicos de Pichincha (Medical College of Pichincha), and
the Movimiento de Abogados Progresistas (Progressive Lawyers Movement). It was greatly influenced by Argentine, Chilean, and Uruguayan ex-
iles in Ecuador who believed the organization provided them some measure
of protection against the reaches of the military governments in their respective countries.[28]

The creation of CEDHU coincided with the beginning of the Roldos
Aguilera government and a favorable political climate. At that time the
Ecuadorean-based Asociación Latinoamericana de Derechos Humanos
(Latin American Human Rights Association) was founded to affirm Ecuador's stance against military dictatorship and in favor of human rights. In
1981 Elsie Monge, an Ecuadorean-born Maryknoll sister who had studied
in the United States, joined CEDHU to coordinate its activities. (The U.S.-
based Maryknoll order is strongly identified with liberation theology.) In
1975 Proaño brought Monge back to Ecuador after she had worked in
Guatemala and Panama. Initially she went to the Chota Valley in Imbabura,
an area referred to as the Africa of Ecuador because of its dry terrain and
black inhabitants. In Chota she labored in education and studied the local
people.

Under Monge, CEDHU published the bimonthly bulletin *Derechos del
Pueblo*, in which it listed violations of human rights in Ecuador. These
included accounts that did not get published in the general press. Each edition was a monograph concerned with a different problem such as health
care; housing; and the rights of women, children, and indigenous people.
CEDHU produced videos, radio programs, and cassettes to educate people
about their human rights and the need to respect and defend them. In 1986
Monge was named the Ecuadorean Woman of the Year for her leadership in

the defense of human rights. This honor had particular significance as it came during the repressive regime of León Febres Cordero.[29]

With Monge at the helm, CEDHU also worked hard to raise the consciousness of the more conservative elements within the church, though it believed that the church had become more concerned about human rights as a result of Archbishop Proaño's work. CEDHU understood that pockets of conservatism still existed and that a lack of support for human rights was endemic within the church in certain areas of the country. It cited as an example the city of Loja, in the southern Sierra, where the church hierarchy regarded the human rights organization as communistic. Ultimately, CEDHU was less concerned with what the conservative church thought and more intent on educating the poor to their basic human rights.[30]

CEDHU worked alongside both ecumenical progressive Protestant groups and interdenominational organizations, including CLAI (Consejo Latinamericana de Iglesias; see chapter 7) and SERPAJ, the Servicio Paz y Justicia (Latin American Peace and Justice Service). CLAI, which had come into existence as a result of a meeting of Latin American ecumenists in Oaxtepec, Mexico, in 1978, consisted of a hundred Protestant churches and organizations throughout Latin America. It practiced its own brand of liberation theology, denouncing United States intervention in Latin America, carrying out pastoral missions to refugees in areas ravaged by war, and intervening on behalf of disappeared persons or prisoners in countries where the military had installed repressive national security regimes.[31] SERPAJ, a nondenominational, nongovernmental ecumenical group, was founded by Adolfo Perez Esquivel, the 1980 Nobel Peace Prize winner from Argentina. It worked on behalf of indigenous groups in disputes with Latin American governments. During the 1970s and 1980s it was extremely active in Brazil.[32]

In principle, CEDHU believed it had a duty to work with any and all organizations that promoted basic human rights and attempted to satisfy the needs of poor people everywhere. It was mindful of the fact that there were vast differences between the North American fundamentalist Protestants and the more ecumenical national and Latin American churches. In addition to CLAI and SERPAJ, CEDHU worked with the Comisión Latinoamericana de Educación Cristiana (Latin American Christian Education Commission), the Acción Social Ecuménica Latinoamericana (Latin American Ecumenical Social Action), and the Unión Latinoamericana de

Juventudes Ecuménicas (Latin American Ecumenical Youth Union), all groups with similar objectives.[33]

As Ecuadorean liberation theologists and the agencies that espoused their principles worked in the areas of consciousness-raising, education, and community development, they learned to employ many of the techniques used by the foreign Protestants themselves, including radio, television, and the printed word. They understood that the outcome of their struggle would have long-term implications for the future of their country and of Latin America as a whole. In the final analysis, they came to the conclusion that it was important to hold the line in the religious field and not lose any more ground to their Protestant rivals from North America.

CHAPTER 9

The Protestant "Threat" and the Indigenous Response

We must respect the life, the purity, the sacredness,
which is water. We must respect the one God, the
heart of the sky, which is the sun. We must not do evil
while the sun shines upon his children. This is a
promise. Then we promise to respect the life of the
one creature, which is man. This is very important.
We say: "We cannot harm the life of one of your children. We cannot kill any of your creatures, neither
trees nor animals."
Rigoberta Menchu, I . . . Rigoberta Menchu:
An Indian Woman in Guatemala

SIMILAR IN TONE AND content to the Catholic church's response to North American fundamentalist Protestantism in the 1895–1990 period was the response of the indigenous people of Ecuador. Most of them viewed the proselytizing activities of Protestant groups as part of the most recent phase in a five-hundred-year conquest and the destruction of their way of life. Protestantism resembled traditional Catholicism to them and brought with it such disasters as the exploration and exploitation of mineral and agricultural resources; the colonization of indigenous territories; the ravaging of distinctive ecological zones, including the ruin of the rain forest and flora and fauna; and the eradication of native customs and religion.[1]

The indigenous people of Ecuador responded to this multifold threat in ways they believed would assure their cultural and physical survival. While a few accepted Protestantism and joined homegrown alliances such as

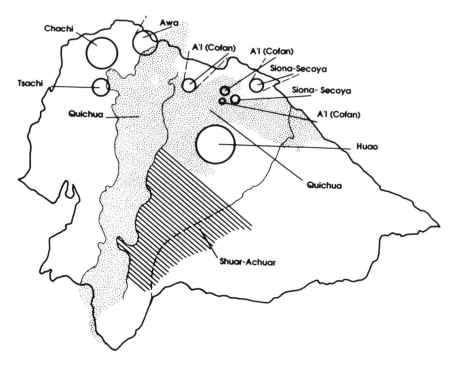

Map 3 *Indigenous Nationalities of Ecuador*

AIECH in Chimborazo, others responded by working with liberation theology groups like FEPP and CEDHU. Still others engaged in violence against Protestants—as, for example, in the 1980s when indigenous people took up arms against Protestants in Cotopaxi and the Huaorani declared their lands to be conflict zones prohibited to all missionaries, colonists, lumber and petroleum workers, and military personnel.[2]

By far the most important indigenous response in Ecuador during the 1895–1990 period was the consolidation of indigenous nationalities and their local organizations into one all-encompassing confederation. This body, known as the Confederación de Nacionalidades Indígenas del Ecuador (Confederation of Indigenous Nations of Ecuador) or CONAIE, came into existence when indigenous people from the Coast, the Sierra, and the Oriente met in Quito in November 1986. At that meeting they drew up CONAIE's statutes and outlined its objectives, which called for the defense of indigenous land, religion, and culture. Among the indigenous nationalities present were the Quichua, Shuar, Huaorani, Cofan, Siona, Secoya, Chachi, Tsachila, and Awa. Local organizations represented were FICI, the Federación Indígena y Campesina de Imbabura (Indigenous Peasant Federation of Imbabura); CONFENIAE, the Confederación de Nacionalidades Indígenas de la Amazonía Ecuatoriana (Confederation of Indigenous Nations of the Ecuadorean Amazon); the Federación de Centros Shuar (Shuar Federation); and UNAE, the Unión de Nativos de la Amazonía Ecuatoriana (Ecuadorean Amazon Native Union). Together these representatives of indigenous nationalities and local organizations produced a statement of principles asserting that the establishment of CONAIE represented the consolidation of the political presence of indigenous people at the national and international levels and the assumption of historic responsibilities in the political, economic, social, and cultural transformation of Ecuador. In essence, the indigenous groups created CONAIE to function as a parent organization for all the indigenous people of Ecuador. It would generate solidarity with similar organizations elsewhere in Latin America, safeguard indigenous culture, and elaborate an indigenous point of view on post-Colombian history.[3]

For the indigenous people of Ecuador, the founding of CONAIE began a new phase in the long, arduous history of indigenous response to foreign invasion in all of its manifestations, including that of North American fundamentalist Protestantism. In their view, CONAIE represented a modern-day outcry against the abuses, exploitation, extortion, and annihilation of indigenous people. In Ecuador, in the 1980s, most indigenous people understood that the colonial heritage persisted, that racial discrimination prevailed and bordered on ethnocide and genocide in some areas. They cited the fact that two groups—the Tetete and Zaparo—were already extinct and other groups—the Huaorani, Siona, Secoya, and Cofan in the province of Napo—were on the verge of extinction. The largest of these, the Huaorani, consisted of only 500 people. According to one source, extinction was the result of the historical process of conquest:

> The oppressive impact and the dependence that western civilization exercises, annuls the vital strength and pride of the free Indian and produces in him a psycho-biological, individual, and collective sadness of death. This biological-cultural liquidation is reinforced by external factors: the lack of vital space, the destruction and contamination of his environment, the rupture of his cosmological vision, and the presence of new diseases that were unknown to him

before. All this annihilates him physically, socially, spiritually, and culturally until it produces his disappearance.[4]

In the period from 1895 to 1990, for the indigenous people of Ecuador, the Spanish colonial institutions of the reducción and encomienda existed in their modern forms. With the assistance of fundamentalist Protestant and traditional Catholic missionaries, governments continued the economic integration of the resources of indigenous lands. As illustrated by the case of the SIL and the Huaorani, missionaries rounded up and forced indigenous people into prescribed territories. As it had done during the colonial period, the system operated on the pretense of transmitting civilization to the savages. The methods used to herd the indigenous people into reservations or missions were agrarian reform, programs of social and economic integration, and the creation of national parks.

With respect to the latter, the Yasuni National Park in the Oriente is a case in point. Founded in 1979, Yasuni contains 679,730 hectares of prime land, 4,000 to 5,000 species of flowers, over 600 species of birds (four times the number found in Ecuador's Galapagos Islands), 500 hundred different kinds of fish, 120 species of mammals, and more than 100 species of reptiles and amphibians. It is inhabited by harpy eagles, jaguars, manatees, freshwater dolphins, giant armadillos and otters, anteaters, and other endangered species of the tropical rain forest. Because of this diversity, UNESCO named Yasuni a biosphere reserve under its Man and Biosphere Program. The park also contains petroleum reserves in two blocks: a 200,000-hectare concession, Block 16, given to the Dupont affiliate CONOCO, extends into adjacent unprotected Huaorani lands; and a concession under consideration for CONOCO, Block 22, is entirely in Yasuni. The Huaorani lands can be taken over by the Ecuadorean government at any time for petroleum exploration and exploitation, even though it is widely known that collateral damage would occur to the indigenous people and the plants and animals of Yasuni.[5]

The Yasuni situation demonstrates the way the majority of governments in Ecuador between 1895 and 1990 looked at indigenous lands. These governments declared indigenous territories to be *tierras baldías,* unused common lands that had to be integrated into the national territory because of the riches they possessed, and they were eager to work with the new encomenderos, multinational corporations that exploited the mineral and agricultural resources of those lands. Rubber plantations, lumber mills, petroleum and mining companies, and agroindustrial conglomerates received the best and most extensive lands. During the 1970s and 1980s, this policy permitted the oil exploration activities of multinationals like CONOCO and the planting of the African palm, which is greatly prized for producing a cooking oil used throughout the world. (In the United States, palm oil is found in prepackaged and fast foods. It is highly dangerous, however, because it works within the human body to produce increased levels of cholesterol.[6])

The partition of lands of the indigenous people of Ecuador by multinational corporations with the assistance of national governments and missionaries from 1895 to 1990 was a new style in the five-hundred-year history of conquest. CONAIE pointed to the need for indigenous people to protect themselves against the grave economic, social, and racial inequalities inherent in the system of exploitation. The concept of *indio* as an inferior being, created in the colonial period, still dominated Ecuadorean and Latin American culture. The false idea that indigenous people would be redeemed through integration into national society lingered. CONAIE believed, on the contrary, that they should be viewed as distinct and that there should be alternatives for a new society. Toward that end, the agency formulated the idea of making Ecuador a plurinational state in which indigenous people would together constitute the important nucleus of society. In CONAIE's view, the plurinational state would be one that reflected the reality of the country and the continent, respected different national cultures, and supported social, political, and economic equality among all peoples.[7]

CONAIE believed that to resolve the problems of the indigenous people, all Ecuadoreans and Latin Americans must look to definitive alternatives to exploitation and oppression. As 1990 approached and CONAIE became a representative social organization and an important influence on the programs of the national government, the agency worked to define the historical and cultural identities of the diverse Ecuadorean ethnicities and to instill the idea of indigenous people as a people with a past, a present, and a future. It began to plan the 1992 celebration of the Quinto Centenario de la Invasión Española (the Fifth Centenary of the Spanish Invasion) in protest against the five hundred years of conquest. CONAIE claimed the right to act as the representative of Ecuador's indigenous people and to reject the officially announced concept of the national celebration as a celebration of the discovery of the Americas. Toward that end, CONAIE proposed the unification of diverse sectors of society in a massive political front, not only in Ecuador but also elsewhere in Latin America, with the fundamental objectives of restoring the dignity of indigenous people and repudiating all forms of subjugation and colonial and neocolonial practices.[8]

CONAIE devised as the basis for the countercelebration, a set of objectives centering around the indigenous response to the Conquest and calling for a massive indigenous people's campaign to refute the celebrations of that event and its part in shaping the history of Ecuador. The objectives demanded an analysis of the Conquest's effects on Indians, assurance that the people's campaign would be an effective political response to exploitation, the mobilization of indigenous peoples in defense of their right of self-determination, the development of political consciousness among the indigenous masses, wide participation by all popular organizations and solidarity among them, and the development of an ample program of study and scientific investigation of the situation of the indigenous population and other popular sectors in Ecuadorean society within the Latin American context.[9]

To achieve these objectives, CONAIE developed a plan of activities concerned with the organization of work groups, cultural promotion, and sociopolitical and historical research on subjects including oral history, indigenous art, music and dance, religion, questions of gender, language, law, medicine, ecology, education and literacy, community infrastructure, and literature. CONAIE determined that activities related to religion should center upon the compilation of documents on the treatment of indigenous people by both Catholic and Protestant missionaries and the study of indigenous religious alternatives in general. Though CONAIE acknowledged that its plan of activities would not reverse the past five hundred years of history, the agency believed that it might serve as a vehicle for bringing the problems of Ecuador's and Latin America's indigenous people to international attention.[10]

In late May and early June of 1990 CONAIE organized a mobilization of indigenous people throughout Ecuador. This move, which CONAIE hoped would not lead to violent confrontation, included boycotting marketplaces, blockading roads, seizing churches, and invading haciendas. It was intended to be a show of force and the first of its kind in Ecuador in size and scope. The indigenous people who supported it, some 150,000 strong, rallied behind the slogans "No more haciendas by 1992" and "Five hundred years of indigenous resistance."[11]

The CONAIE mobilization was suggested at a continental meeting of indigenous people at Bogotá, Colombia, in October 1989. It became a reality
after a CONAIE meeting in April 1990 at Pujilí, Ecuador. There CONAIE
determined that, as part of the mobilization, it would call for a dialogue
with the Ecuadorean government to discuss a sixteen-point program that
addressed the needs of indigenous people in education, taxation, credit and
debt, health care, religion, land and water rights, the environment and protection of archaeological sites, community development, political reform,
basic infrastructure, self-determination, and the cost of living (see appendix
2). At the same meeting CONAIE identified seventy existing land conflicts
in Ecuador that were held up in Ecuadorean courts and noted that litigation
had been hampered by delays, negligence, and an antiindigenous bias. Notably, as a response to North American fundamentalist Protestantism,
CONAIE called for the expulsion from Ecuador of all foreign religious sects
and development agencies including the SIL, which it believed had never left
the country after its official expulsion in 1981 and still operated under the
protection of World Vision.[12]

CONAIE's mobilization began in Pichincha on May 28; had spread to
Chimborazo, Cotopaxi, Tungurahua, Cañar, and Azuay by June 4; and
ended in Imbabura on June 11. The indigenous people of Chimborazo, with
its large number of Protestants, stood in the forefront of the movement.[13]

The first incident of the CONAIE mobilization set an undesired confron-
tational tone for the entire movement. On May 28, in Quito, 200 indigenous people under the leadership of CONAIE affiliate Runacunapac
Riccharimi (ECUARUNARI) seized the Santo Domingo Church in the colonial center of the city as a means of getting the government to listen to a
list of grievances. During the eight days they held the church, the Indians
slept and cooked on the church floor while police outside cordoned off the
area and used tear gas to disperse the crowds that had gathered. This led to
injuries and to the death, on May 31, of an infant girl less than two months
old. As a result, on June 4, eleven people inside the church—three women
and eight men—announced that they were on a hunger strike, an action
that caused more indigenous people to flock to the church and stopped all
activity in the center of Quito. Concerned government officials met with a
mediating commission made up of Monsignor Corral, Elsie Monge of
CEDHU, and Nelsa Curbelo of SERPAJ to work out an agreement to end
the takeover. As part of its terms, the government promised to listen to the

list of grievances if the indigenous people left the church. They did so on June 6 at 6:00 P.M., after Monsignor Corral offered a mass and prayers for the girl who had died.[14]

Elsewhere, because of the events in Quito, the CONAIE mobilization took on the appearance of warfare. On June 3, indigenous people from the community of Canguagua in Cayambe, north of Quito, blockaded all traffic on the Pan American Highway. The government responded by sending a military unit in an unsuccessful attempt to arrest some of the indigenous leaders. On June 6, the army and the indigenous people again confronted each other, this time in the neighboring community of Guachala, and indigenous leaders were beaten and arrested. On the same afternoon, indigenous people filled the central plaza of Canguagua, demanding the turnover of hacienda lands to them, cessation of the mistreatment of their leaders, payment of a fair price for their agricultural products, and an end to the high cost of living. In reaction, the military surrounded the central park, the county office building, the church, the telephone office, and the streets leading to the Pan American Highway. They failed to curtail the mobilization, however, and in the end the indigenous people in Cayambe declared that they had won a great victory.[15]

The CONAIE mobilization in Cotopaxi began on May 31 after a meeting of town council members from the different indigenous communities there. On June 2, it continued, with indigenous peoples blockading roads and seizing haciendas. On June 6, the mobilization took a dramatic turn when 30,000 Indians marched into silence in Latacunga, the provincial capital, and took over the central plaza. All along the route they were guarded by army airborne and special forces units. In a tension-filled atmosphere, under the guidance of the Movimiento Indígena de Cotopaxi (the Indigenous Movement of Cotopaxi, or MIC), the people presented their demands to Cotopaxi's governor, Latacunga's police chief, and government officials from the Instituto Ecuatoriano de Recurso Hidráulicos (Ecuadorean Department of Water Resources), the Instituto Ecuatoriano de Obras Sanitarios (Ecuadorean Department of Sanitary Works), the Instituto Ecuatoriano de Reforma Agraria (Ecuadorean Department of Agrarian Reform), and the Ministerio de Agricultura y Ganadería (Ministry of Agriculture and Livestock). They asked for a solution to the problems of land and credit, the enactment of CONAIE's sixteen-point program, a halt to inflation, a fair price for their products, a profit-sharing plan for MIC in the Cotopaxi cement factory, the expulsion of religious sects, the donation of land for MIC headquarters, and the respectful and fair treatment of indigenous people in public institutions. In the end, the officials all signed documents by which they promised to give a fair hearing to the demands.[16]

In the province of Chimborazo, the CONAIE mobilization began on June 4 when indigenous people invaded two haciendas. It continued on June 5 as 3,000 Indians from the community of La Moya engaged police and military in a confrontation in which the latter, using weapons and tear gas, inflicted injuries on the protesters. It ended when hundreds of Indian women surrounded the forces of public order and escorted them out of town. In Gatazo Grande, the mobilization took an ugly turn when the military shot and killed a twenty-three-year-old Indian man. On June 7, 30,000 indigenous people held a massive demonstration in Guamote, and the Protestant station "Radio Colta" was invaded after it warned Protestants not to join the mobilization. The invaders broadcast a new message, calling for the unification of all indigenous people.[17]

Throughout the Sierra, the events surrounding the CONAIE mobilization repeated themselves. In Tungurahua, on June 2, indigenous people blockaded roads; in Ambato, on June 5, they held a meeting with the provincial governor in which they stated that they wanted their culture, religion, and science recognized.[18] In Azuay, where the mobilization began on the morning of June 3, roads were blockaded, government offices including the Office of Indigenous Education in Cuenca were paralyzed, and a series of radio programs was broadcast to inform people of the CONAIE mobilization and its sixteen-point plan. In Cañar, indigenous people completely closed off the Pan American Highway.[19]

In Imbabura, indigenous people carrying little more than pickaxes and hoes faced off against a heavily armed military contingent. On June 4, they blockaded the Pan-American Highway at five different points; the following day they impeded the flow of traffic by throwing stones at cars; and on June 6 they completely paralyzed the highway by setting up a wall of 400 people. During the three key days of the mobilization in Imbabura, the army proved unable to control their actions.[20]

The CONAIE mobilization of 1990 appeared at first to sound the theme of victory throughout the Ecuadorean Sierra. Indigenous people were confident and hopeful as CONAIE officials met with the Ecuadorean government to ask for action on the sixteen-point plan. The government, however, due to pressure from landowners, cattle ranchers, and the military soon stalled on the dialogue. With that, CONAIE understood that the privileged classes in Ecuador, in reaction, would not accept the demands of indigenous people easily. It decided to retrench somewhat and wait for a more auspicious time to continue pressing its demands.

Despite this delay in getting its objectives met, the mobilization helped CONAIE by bringing international attention to its cause and led to its emergence as a leader in the greater indigenous struggle in the Americas. On July 17, 1990, CONAIE cohosted the First Continental Conference of Indigenous People with two other Latin American indigenous agencies: ONIC, the Organization of Indigenous Nationalities of Colombia; and SAIIC, the California-based South American and Meso-American Indian Information Center. This meeting began in the Senate Room of the National Congress but, because of government harrassment, was moved to a Baptist conference center thirty miles east of Quito. For the more than 300 Indian participants from North and South America, it was symbolically an encounter of the "Eagle of the North and the Condor of the South." Participants included Quichua, Shuar, Tsachila, Dine, Páez, Swinimish, Cree, Kuna, "Chicanos," Yaqui, Maya, Nahuatl, Zapoteca, Rapa Nui, Carib, Garifon, Aymara, Kolla, Mapuche, and Yanomami. Together these indigenous groups discussed such pertinant problems as the legacy of Columbus's "discovery," the devastation of their cultures, the destruction of their environment, and the struggle for human rights. They sang, danced, prayed, and visited the Ecuadorean countryside. Finally, despite some communication difficulties, they signed the Declaration of Quito, a document that called for the establishment of an indigenous leadership to help plan the 1992 countercelebration to the European discovery of the Americas.[21]

The CONAIE mobilization of 1990 was both a direct and an indirect response to Protestantism in Ecuador. The sixteen-point program unequivocally called for the expulsion of the SIL and other religious sects that threatened indigenous culture. On another level, the mobilization, through its call to communal action, impugned the fundamentalist Protestant tenets of individualism, discipline, and conformity. The movement upheld indigenous beliefs and showed them to be strong unifying influences. Implicit in it was the declaration that indigenous people had outgrown the missionary concept of them as ambivalent, childlike, sinful, and in need of salvation. Many indigenous people were helped by the movement to call upon their ancient gods, realizing that the religions of the Conquest could not resolve the great questions of cultural survival and self-determination.

By 1990 the indigenous peoples of Ecuador understood that in order to survive culturally and physically, they had to take matters into their own hands, and that this required educating themselves to national and international realities and organizing to become a viable political force. They believed they were important to Ecuadorean life and national sovereignty and that no national government or foreign religious mission could succeed unless it took them into account as equal partners in planning the future and eliminating the injustices and abuses of the past. They understood too that their struggle was the same one faced by indigenous people all over the Western Hemisphere. What had happened in Ecuador during the past five centuries had also happened in Mexico, Guatemala, Cuba, Brazil, Colombia, Chile, the United States, and Canada. In 1990, the indigenous of Ecuador had come together in a mass action that frightened the dominant elite and warned of more protest if changes were not made. Their actions were in keeping with the thoughts of Eduardo Galeano, who wrote that indigenous people, with their message, "offer all America, not just Latin America, basic keys of memory and prophecy: they bear witness to the past and at the same time shed light on the directions to be taken now."[22]

CONCLUSION

The white man hasn't triumphed. When the Indians vanish the rest will follow.

Pa'i Antonio Moreira, quoted by Alan Weisman and Sandy Tolan in Audobon, *November-December* 1992

What is the meaning of a faith that does not lead to serving the poor? What has Christian ministry done to awaken a sense of dignity among the poor and accompany them in searching for a way to overcome their poverty? How has Christian faith functioned? As an instrument for the recovery of the rights and the dignity of the poor, or as a tool for domesticating them and justifying their oppression? It appears to me that the pastoral practice of every Christian church in Latin America has been forced to respond to this challenge.

José Miguez Bonino, Latinamerica Press, *May* 28, 1987

DURING THE 1970S AND 1980S, in Latin America and the world, many religious and secular organizations called for social, political, and economic justice for indigenous people. In the forefront of that movement were the Program to Combat Racism, the Churches Commission on International Affairs of the WCC, and the Ethnology Department of the University of Berne in Switzerland. In January 1971 these institutions sponsored the Barbados Symposium on Inter-Ethnic Conflict in South America. At this meeting participants analyzed formal reports on the tribal populations of several South American countries and drafted a public statement called *The Declaration of Barbados—For the Liberation of the Indians.* They intended to define and clarify the problems of indigenous peoples and contribute to their struggle for liberation.[1]

The *Declaration of Barbados* was a demand for action to suspend multinational, religious, and governmental hostility against the indigenous people of the Americas. It contended that the root of the problem was the racism and aggression of governments that desired indigenous lands for the exploration and exploitation of their mineral and agricultural resources. It asked states, religious missions, and anthropologists to assume certain responsibilities to halt any action that harmed indigenous people. In its section on the responsibilities of religious missions, the *Declaration of Barbados* called missionaries to task and stated that the true way to help indigenous people was to cease all missionary activity. It termed the evangelization process inherently ethnocentric, a proponent of private ownership that exploited both land and labor, and a component of colonialism.[2]

The *Declaration of Barbados* offered measures that could be initiated immediately. It asked for a rational approach and a return to a true Christian ideology that respected the dignity of all groups and their right to self-determination. It spelled out the requirements that religious missions should follow in their actions toward indigenous people and warned that religious missions that failed to assume these minimal obligations would be held responsible by default for crimes of ethnocide and genocide (see appendix 3). It acknowledged, however, that some churches had already begun "a conscious and radical self-evaluation of the evangelical process."[3]

In the aftermath of the Barbados Symposium, other organizations held meetings and issued similar statements calling for the defense of indigenous people. Later, in 1971 the Catholic church expressed its agreement with the *Declaration of Barbados* at a meeting in Iquitos, Peru. There the church published the *Documento de Iquitos* (Document of Iquitos), which stated that the church could not complete its mission if it identified with only one people and one culture. At Iquitos the church expressed its solidarity with indigenous people and asserted that this implied their maximum respect for and acceptance of native culture. It also gave assurances that it would assist in protecting the biological and cultural survival of indigenous people by the constant revaluation of its missionary activities and by openly criticizing institutionalized injustice. In the conclusion of the *Document of Iquitos,* the church declared that it would help indigenous people to shape their own destiny.[4]

Elsewhere, in 1972 the ecumenical interdenominational church group UNELAM, the Movimiento Pro-Unidad Evangélica Latino-Americana (Latin American Evangelical Unity Movement), met in Asunción, Paraguay.

At this meeting UNELAM produced the *Documento de Asunción* (Document of Asunción), which declared that religious denominations must enter into frank discussions about the conditions of indigenous people. It especially called for assistance in the struggle against racism at the national and international levels, the unity of religious denominations in establishing a frank dialogue on the problems of indigenous people, and the provision of moral support to indigenous organizations.[5]

Foremost among meetings after the UNELAM conference were the 1974 Parlamento Indio Americano del Cono Sur (Southern Cone American Indian Parliament), also in Paraguay, and the February 1975 Native American Symposium at the University of Florida in Gainesville. The former conference, sponsored by the Catholic University of Asunción and the Indigenist Association of Paraguay with help from the Inter-American Foundation of the United States Congress and the Program to Combat Racism, concluded that the Indian was the owner of land it had inhabited for centuries with or without title and that respective governments must honor that idea. It maintained, furthermore, that the Indian had the right to receive a fair wage for his work and an education that respected and was related to indigenous teachings, culture, and language. The Native American Symposium lashed out against inferior education and its effects; the lack of respect for indigenous language; the failure of governments to bring about social, economic, and political justice; and the intrusion of groups that denigrated indigenous society. The participants in this conference made a list of recommendations that called for the institutionalization of bilingual educational programs, the restitution of indigenous lands, governmental help in improving the socioeconomic and political conditions of indigenous people, and the formation of an inter-American organization of indigenous people to coordinate activities of common interest.[6]

In the 1980s the United Nations demonstrated its concern for indigenous people. Beginning in 1982, the Work Group on Indigenous Populations of the Subcommission for the Prevention of Discrimination and the Protection of Minorities met annually, except for 1986. In 1988, at the public sessions of the Work Group, approximately 380 participants representing a number of countries and indigenous organizations discussed drafting a document entitled the "Universal Declaration of Indigenous Rights." In 1989 the United Nations again discussed this project in the hope that it would be approved by the General Assembly before the fateful quincentennial commemorations. When the new round of discussions ended, however, there were no guarantees that the document would be accepted without modifications before 1992.[7]

One important aspect of the "Universal Declaration of Indigenous Rights" was that it grew out of suggestions from indigenous people themselves. It contained six sections: 1) universal indigenous rights in general; 2) collective ethnic and cultural rights, including protection against ethnocide; 3) the rights of land and resources; 4) economic and social rights, including the maintenance of economic structures and traditional ways of life; 5) civil and political rights, including the respect for indigenous laws and customs and indigenous peoples' participation in decisions that affect their lives and destiny, such as the collective right of autonomy; and 6) recommendations for just procedures for resolving controversies between states and indigenous people.

The projected declaration made the link between the past, the present, and the future and stated that indigenous people of today are entitled to their ancestral lands and the right to pass them on to their descendants. Furthermore, it said that indigenous people could enjoy the use of their lands and benefit from what they produced. The drafters of the "Universal Declaration of Indigenous Rights" recognized that indigenous people had suffered grave damages as a result of infrastructure undertakings promoted by national governments. The document specifically mentioned hydroelectric projects and criticized the World Bank and other development agencies for providing funds without consideration for indigenous people. It criticized government programs that destroyed the ability of indigenous people to transmit their knowledge. It maintained that governments were wrong to try to eliminate indigenous language and that indigenous people must have the right to teach their own language and establish their own educational institutions. The document called for the right of indigenous people to participate in the political life of the states in which they resided, which would require the legal systems and political institutions of these states to recognize indigenous customs and laws. On religion, the projected declaration asserted that indigenous people had the right to observe, practice, and teach their own traditions as well as to maintain and have access to their sacred places.

As of the late 1980s, because of the projected "Universal Declaration of Indigenous Rights," indigenous people throughout the world had reason to believe that the United Nations had become aware of their problems and would act as an ally in guaranteeing their rights. They also thought the

U.N.'s discussions demonstrated their new-found international importance and reflected the acceptance of many of their demands. In Ecuador, as related by CONAIE, indigenous people had long believed that international organizations like the United Nations had the obligation to recognize and publicize their problems. In the past, indigenous groups in Ecuador had even spoken of wanting a fraternal indigenous organization within the framework of the United Nations to represent them.[8]

The meetings, discussions of solidarity, and projects of the 1970s and 1980s demonstrated that some people within the international community were concerned about the plight of indigenous people, not only because of their links to the past but also because they were necessary to the present and the future. Supporters expressed their belief that indigenous people were the guardians of the earth, the promoters of its biological diversity and keepers of its land, water, and resources. They believed that because indigenous people valued the land and were bound to it by necessity, they protected it better than developed countries and Third World states. In this environmentalist view, the survival of indigenous people in their natural surroundings was necessary to the well-being of the human race and the entire planet.[9]

The view of indigenous people as necessary for the protection of the environment was not shared by all. In Ecuador, North American fundamentalist Protestant missionaries took a position toward indigenous people that implied an alternative agenda, one that did not value their cultural and physical survival. In the minds of these Protestants, indigenous people existed only for their missionizing endeavors.

The fundamentalist Protestant vision, as exemplified by the Ecuadorean case, attempts to negate the reality that missionary activities are contributing to the disappearance of indigenous people all over the world. As mentioned previously, in Ecuador the Huaorani, Schuar, Achuar, Secoya and Siona, and Cofan are all threatened with extinction. The same is true of the Mapuche in Chile, the Lenca and Pupil in El Salvador, the Rama in Nicaragua, the Guaymi in Panama, and the Piaroa in Venezuela. In Brazil the Yanomami, Uru Eu Wau Wau, Waimiri-Atroari, Ka'por, Guaja, Kren-Ye Timbira, and Tembe are also threatened.[10] In no small measure, missionary activity has contributed to this alarming situation.

The question arises, why have so many within the Protestant missionary world not acted in concert with the international community in supporting the physical and cultural survival of indigenous people? That would be in the true Christian spirit of concern for one's fellow man. In substance, the answer is based on earthly considerations and has to do with the nature of evangelization itself. For many Protestant evangelical groups, there is no choice; their worldview is at stake. The promotion of the cultural and physical survival of indigenous people would be antithetical to the work they deem necessary. How could they strengthen what they consider a savage and heathen way of life without negating the validity of their own existence? From their perspective, there are too many innate contradictions between indigenous life, with its reverence for the earth, and the so-called civilized life characterized by progress, modernization, and mastery over the environment. In theological terms, the conflict of Protestant missionaries relates to the issue of what true Christian belief really means. Is Christianity committed to the values of individualism and profit or to a sense of community and sharing? Ultimately, the key question is, which message will emerge victorious?

Like traditional Catholicism, North American–based fundamentalist Protestantism offered salvation in a future life instead of relief from poverty and injustice in this one. Ecuadorean critics also claimed that it imposed ideas of individual initiative in a society made up of people who believed in and lived by cooperation and reciprocity; it naively and unconsciously contributed to ethnocidal and genocidal practices by failing to halt government and multinational removals of indigenous people from their lands; and it acted against the more progressive tenets of the Ecuadorean and Latin American ecumenical movements.

In 1900, the call of John R. Mott, executive director of the missionary Student Volunteer Movement (SVM), for "the evangelization of the world in this generation" was backed by a plan to send 50,000 missionaries into the world to convert all of its "unreached peoples."[11] Mott's call typified the approach of North American fundamentalist Protestantism toward "underdeveloped" countries like Ecuador throughout the 1895–1990 period. It presupposed that each generation would evangelize its own generation until the movement reached its goal. In recent decades, Billy Graham gave the plan of worldwide evangelization new impetus. At the International Congress for World Evangelization at Lausanne, Switzerland, in 1974, Graham concluded that the "World Church" was stronger than ever and ready to accept the challenge of world evangelization.[12] In 1984 he strengthened that conclusion in the following statement:

World evangelization is now a possibility before the end of this century. The world in which we live, however, is totally different from the world at the beginning of this century. The twentieth century was called the "Christian Century," but the dreams of . . . well-meaning theologians were shaken by World War I and shattered by World War II. But there is no variableness or shadow of turning with God. The gospel has not changed. Christ never changes, the power of the Spirit to transform lives never changes, and man's desperate need for God has not changed. The Great Commission from our Lord to go and preach the gospel to every person is unchanged. Christ's promise that he is with us to the end of the age never changes. Increasingly since the Lausanne Congress, evangelicals have been called upon to provide leadership in areas where they were either a small minority or almost did not exist before. Evangelism has taken on a new meaning. It is a time of great opportunity, but also a time of great responsibility. We are stewards of our evangelical heritage. We must evangelize at all costs while there is yet time. The night is coming when no one can work. We cannot look back. The world will not wait. World problems of poverty, overpopulation, and the threat of nuclear war are mounting by the hour. As someone has said, the world is changing, it is restless, and it seems to be dying. Now is the time to establish thousands of new beachheads around the world for the gospel.[13]

As Graham's statement affirmed, conservative and fundamentalist Protestants believed that the evangelization of the world was a necessary objective that had to be carried out as soon as possible. In Ecuador in the 1980s, the world evangelization crusade targeted indigenous people and mestizos who had migrated to the urban centers.[14] Similar targets were set for Chile, Mexico, Brazil, and Guatemala. This focus on the indigenous people and mestizos of Latin America's overpopulated cities demonstrated the Protestant understanding of the effects of rapid urbanization and the ready availability of potential converts. In the cities of Latin America, North American fundamentalist Protestantism found fertile ground for its world evangelization plan.

As of 1990, all indications pointed to the continued growth of Protestantism in Ecuador. In the principal cities of Guayaquil and Quito, Protestant churches already dominated portions of the landscape, a sign that as people migrated to the cities, as population increased, poverty-stricken Ecuadoreans continued to look to religion for solutions to their long-standing suffering. These poor posed a challenge to all religious institutions.

For North American Protestantism, it implied a choice to be made—whether to continue the old patterns of evangelization that harmed distinct cultures and ways of life or to endeavor to help create a more equitable and just society for all.

APPENDIX 1

NORTH AMERICAN PROTESTANT AGENCIES IN ECUADOR

"New" refers to the number of overseas personnel who arrived from North America between 1980 and 1983. "People groups" refers to the subgroups an agency has worked with. No date for "year began" means that the agency did not provide that information to the source.

Agency	Year Began	Personnel Now	New	Local Churches	People Groups
Assemblies of God	1962	14		40	
Back to the Bible	1970				
Baptist Bible Fellowship	1975	6			
Berean Mission	1959	20		3	2
Bretheren Assemblies		21			
Campus Crusade for Christ	1965				
Child Evangelism Fellowship	1952	2			
Christ Corps		1			
Christian and Missionary Alliance	1897	73		216	3
Christian Medical Society					
Christian Ref. World Relief	1983				
Christians in Action	1976	2		1	
Church of God (7th Day)	1970	1		8	
Church of God Prophecy Mission	1982			3	
Church of God World Missions	1971			15	
Church of the Nazarene (World Mission)	1972	8		12	
Churches of Christ		2		125	
Compassion International	1975	4	4	36	
Conservative Mennonite	1980	6		2	

Agency	Year Began	Personnel Now	New	Local Churches	People Groups
Disciples of Christ	1983	2			
Episcopal Church South American Missionary Society	1981		6		
Episcopal Church World Mission	1963	1			
Evangelical Covenant Church	1947	9		33	
Evangelical Mennonite Brethren	1951	6	1		
Fellowship of Independent Missions	1967	2			
Foursquare Missions International	1973	4		105	2
Free Methodist Church of North America	1982			1	
General Conference Seventh-Day Adventist	1905	4			
Gospel Missionary Union	1896	55	12	287	2
Gospel Outreach	1983	6		1	2
Icthus International	1983			2	
Independent Faith Mission	1982	2	2		
Latin American Mission	1975	3	1		
LOGOI	1984				
Luke Society	1981	2	2	200	1
Lutheran Church in America	1982	1	1		
Lutheran World Relief					
MAP International		3			
Maranatha Baptist Mission		2			
Mennonite Brethren Missions	1953	1			
Missionary Aviation Fellowship	1948	9			
Missionary Church Overseas	1945	22	3	10	1
OMS International	1952	34	6	22	2
Presbyterian Church in America	1975	11	5		
Slavic Gospel Association	1940	5	2		
Southern Baptist Convention	1950	41	25	68	
Technical Support Mission	1980	4	4	7	
Tele-Missions International	1977	2			

Agency	Year Began	Personnel		Local Churches	People Groups
		Now	New		
United Church Board (World Ministry)	1945	2			
United Methodist World Program					
United Pentecostal Church International	1959	5			
Word of Life Fellowship	1972	4			
World Baptist Fellowship	1972	12	2	8	
World Concern	1976	2	3		
World Literature Crusade	1975				
World Mission Prayer League	1951	20	5	14	
World Radio Missionary Fellowship	1931	222			
World Vision International	1975				
Wycliffe Associates	1979				
Wycliffe Bible Translators, International	1953	39	3		9
Youth for Christ/USA	1982	2	2		
Totals		699	89	1219	22

Source: Wilson, Samuel, and John Siewart, *Mission Handbook,* 13th edition, 1986.

APPENDIX 2

CONAIE'S SIXTEEN DEMANDS

1. Return of lands and territories taken from indigenous communities, without costly legal fees.

2. Sufficient water for human consumption and irrigation in indigenous communities, and a plan to prevent pollution of water supplies.

3. No municipal taxes on small properties owned by indigenous farmers.

4. Long-term financing for bilingual education programs in the communities.

5. Creation of provincial and regional credit agencies to be controlled by CONAIE.

6. Forgiveness of all debts to government ministries and banks incurred by indigenous communities.

7. Amendment of the first article of the constitution to proclaim Ecuador as a multi-national state.

8. Immediate delivery of funds and credits currently budgeted for indigenous nationalities.

9. Minimum two-year price freeze on all raw materials and manufactured goods used by the communities in agricultural production, and reasonable price increase on all agricultural goods sold by them, using free-market mechanisms.

10. Initiation and completion of all priority construction on basic infrastructure for indigenous communities.

11. Unrestricted import and export privileges for indigenous artisans and handicraft merchants.

12. National legislation and enforcement to provide for strict protection and controlled exploration of archaeological sites, under the supervision of CONAIE.

13. Expulsion of the Summer Institute of Linguistics, in accordance with Executive Decree 1159 of 1981.

14. Respect for the rights of children and greater government awareness of their current plight.
15. National support for indigenous medicine.
16. Immediate dismantling of political party organizations that parallel government institutions at the municipal and provincial levels, and which manipulate political consciousness and elections in indigenous communities.

Source: Les Field, "Ecuador's Pan-Indian Uprising," *NACLA Report on the Americas* 25, no. 3 (December 1991).

APPENDIX 3

DECLARATION OF BARBADOS:
ON THE RESPONSIBILITY OF RELIGIOUS MISSIONS

1. Overcome the intrinsic Herodianism of the evangelical process, itself a mechanism of colonization, Europeanization, and alienation of Indian society.

2. Assume a position of true respect for Indian culture ending a long and shameful history of despotism and intolerance characteristic of missionary work, which rarely manifests sensitivity to aboriginal religious sentiments and values.

3. Halt the theft of Indian property by religious missionaries who appropriate labor, lands, and natural resources as their own, and the indifference in the face of Indian expropriation by third parties.

4. Extinguish the sumptuous and lavish spirit of the missions themselves, expressed in various forms, but all too often based on exploitation of Indian labor.

5. Stop the competition among religious groups and confessions for Indian souls— a common occurrence leading to the buying and selling of believers and internal strife provoked by conflicting religious loyalties.

6. Suppress the secular practice of removing Indian children from their families for long periods in boarding schools where they are imbued with values not their own, converting them in this way into marginal individuals, incapable of living either in the larger national society or their native communities.

7. Break with pseudo-moralist isolation which imposes a false puritanical ethic, incapacitating the Indian for coping with the national society—an ethic which the churches have been unable to impose on that same national society.

8. Abandon those blackmail procedures implicit in the offering of goods and services to Indian society in return for total submission.

9. Suspend immediately all practices of population displacement or concentration in order to evangelize and assimilate more effectively, a process that often pro-

vokes an increase in morbidity, mortality, and family disorganization among Indian communities.

10. End the criminal practice of serving as intermediaries for the exploitation of Indian labor.

NOTES

INTRODUCTION

1. Patricio Pazmino, " 'Médicos' y Evangelistas Extranjeros Envenenan a Co-munidades," *Punta de Vista* 430 (August 13, 1990): 12.

2. Ibid.

3. John McCoy, "Robbing Peter to Pay Paul: The Evangelical Tide," *Latinamerica Press,* June 29, 1989, 2.

4. For data on Catholic Pentecostalism or the "Catholic Charismatic Renewal," see Thomas J. Chordas, "Catholic Pentecostalism: A New Word in the New World," in *Perspectives on Pentecostalism: Case Studies from the Caribbean and Latin America,* ed. Stephen D. Glazier (Washington, D.C.: University Press of America, 1980), 143.

5. Tomás Bamat, *¿Salvación o Dominación? Las Sectas Religiosas en el Ecuador* (Quito: Editorial El Conejo, 1986), 32. See appendix 1 for a list of all Protestant agencies in Ecuador as of 1986.

6. David Stoll, *Is Latin America Turning Protestant? The Politics of Evangelical Growth* (Berkeley & Los Angeles: University of California Press, 1990), 337.

7. Anthropologist José L. Pereira, interview by author, June 27, 1988, Quito, Catholic University of Ecuador.

8. See Nelson A. Rockefeller, *The Rockefeller Report on the Americas* (Chicago: Quadrangle Books, 1969), 68, 80.

9. "Oil on Troubled Waters," *NACLA's Latin America and Empire Report* 9, no. 8 (November 1975): 30.

10. "Galo Plaza: The Politics of Prosperity," *NACLA's Latin America and Empire Report* 9, no. 8 (November 1975): 11.

11. For the "Conspiracy Theory" view of Protestant intrusion in Ecuador, see David Stoll, *Fishers of Men or Founders of Empire? The Wycliffe Bible Translators in Latin America* (London: Zed Press, 1982), 211–19; and María Albán Estrada and Juan Pablo Muñoz, *Con Dios Todo Se Puede: La Invasión de las Sectas al Ecuador* (Quito: Editorial Planeta, 1987), 31.

12. Washington Padilla, interview by author, July 25, 1988, Quito. See also Washington Padilla, *La Iglesia y los Dioses Modernos: Historia del Protestantismo en el Ecuador* (Quito: Corporación Editorial Nacional, 1989).

CHAPTER 1: THE HISTORICAL SETTING

1. Edwin E. Erikson et al., *Area Handbook for Ecuador* (Washington, D.C.: U.S. Government Printing Office, 1966), 28.

2. Gerald Clark, *The Coming Explosion in Latin America* (New York: David McKay, 1963), 152.

3. Aurelio Espinosa Polit, "Catholicism and National Tradition," in *The Conflict between Church and State in Latin America*, ed. Frederick B. Pike (New York: Knopf, 1964), 103.

4. Marie-Danielle Demelas and Yves Saint-Geours, *Jerusalen y Babilonia: Religión y Politica en el Ecuador, 1780–1880* (Quito: Corporación Editorial Nacional, 1988), 14–15.

5. Erikson, et al., *Area Handbook*, 29–30.

6. For an account of Orellana's discovery of the Amazon, see Miguel Albornoz, *Orellana: El Caballero de las Amazonas* (Quito: Ediciones del Banco Central del Ecuador, 1987).

7. Enrique M. Villasis Teran, *Historia de la Evangelización del Quito* (Quito: Gráficas Iberia, 1987), 1–3.

8. For important studies of the Catholic mission system in the Audiencia of Quito, see Francisco Miranda Rivadeneira, *Crisis en las Misiones y Mutilación Territorial* (Quito: Banco Central del Ecuador, 1986); and P. Lorenzo García, *Historia de las Misiones en la Amazonía Ecuatoriana* (Quito: Ediciones Abya-Yala, 1985).

9. Oscar Efren Reyes, *Breve Historia General del Ecuador* (Quito: Ministerio de Gobierno, 1988), 1:253.

10. See Steve J. Stern, *Peru's Indian Peoples and the Challenge of Spanish Conquest: Huamanga to 1640* (Madison: University of Wisconsin Press, 1982), 51–80.

11. E. Bradford Burns, *Latin America: A Concise Interpretative History,* 5th ed. (Englewood Cliffs, N.J.: Prentice-Hall, 1990), 32.

12. Reyes, *Breve Historia* 1:259.

13. Ibid., 260.

14. Oswaldo Hurtado, *Political Power in Ecuador,* trans. Nick D. Mills, Jr. (Boulder, Colo.: Westview, 1985), 32–33.

15. See Segundo E. Moreno Yañez, *Sublevaciones Indígenas en la Audiencia de Quito* (Quito: Ediciones de la Universidad Católica, 1976), 29–332.

16. Hurtado, *Political Power,* 33.

17. E. Bradford Burns, *The Poverty of Progress: Latin America in the Nineteenth Century* (Berkeley & Los Angeles: University of California Press, 1980), 113–14.

18. José Carlos Mariátegui, *Seven Interpretive Essays on Peruvian Reality,* trans. Marjory Urquidi (Austin: University of Texas Press, 1971), 21, 31.

19. For an extensive appraisal of the *Patronato Real,* see J. Lloyd Mecham, *Church and State in Latin America* (Chapel Hill: University of North Carolina Press, 1966), chapter 1.

20. Ibid., 13, 14, 16.

21. Filoteo Samaniego Salazar, "Colonial Art of Ecuador," in *The Roman Catholic Church in Colonial Latin America,* ed. Richard E. Greenleaf (New York: Knopf, 1971), 251, 253. For further discussion of Ecuadorean colonial painting and sculpture, see José Gabriel Navarro, *Artes Plasticas Ecuatorianos* (Mexico, D.F.: Fondo de Cultura Económica, 1945), vol. 4.

22. Reyes, *Breve Historia* 1:262.

23. Padilla, *La Iglesia y los Dioses,* 57.

24. Hurtado, *Political Power,* 30–31.

25. Ibid., 31–32.

26. Espinosa Polit, "Catholicism," 106.

27. Marie-Danielle Demelas and Yves Saint-Geours, "Una Revolución Conservadora de Fundamento Religioso: El Ecuador (1809–1875)," in *Estados y Naciones en los Andes,* ed. J. P. Deler and Yves Saint-Geours (Lima: Instituto de Estudios Peruanos, 1986), 440.

28. Hurtado, *Political Power,* 149–60.

29. For an understanding of García Moreno's relationship to the Jesuits, see Francisco Miranda Rivadeneira, *García Moreno y la Compañía de Jesús* (Quito: Imprenta y Ediciones Lexigrama, 1976).

30. For more on García Moreno and Eloy Alfaro, see Reyes, *Breve Historia* 2–3:132–59, 197–247. For García Moreno, see Benjamin Carrión, *García Moreno: El Santo del Patíbulo* (Buenos Aires: Fondo de Cultura Económica, 1959); and Hon. Mary Monica Maxwell-Scott, *Gabriel García Moreno: Regenerator of Ecuador* (London: R. & T. Washbourne, 1914). For Eloy Alfaro, see Alfredo Pareja y Diez-Canseco, *La Hoguera Bárbara: Vida de Eloy Alfaro* (Mexico City: Compañía General Editoral; 1944); and Wilfredo Loor, *Eloy Alfaro* (Quito: Talleres Gráficos "Minerva," 1981).

31. Frank MacDonald Spindler, *Nineteenth-Century Ecuador: A Historical Introduction* (Fairfax, Va.: George Mason University Press, 1987), 59.

32. Mecham, *Church and State,* 143–48.

33. Reyes, *Breve Historia* 2–3: 144.

34. Spindler, *Nineteenth-Century Ecuador,* 82.

35. Juan Montalvo's writings are included in Frank MacDonald Spindler and Nancy Cook Brooks, eds., *Selections from Juan Montalvo Translated from the Spanish* (Tempe, Ariz.: Center for Latin American Studies, Arizona State University, 1984).

36. Spindler, *Nineteenth-Century Ecuador,* 84.
37. Ibid., 88.
38. James D. Cockcroft, *Neighbors in Turmoil: Latin America* (New York: Harper & Row, 1989), 377.
39. Hurtado, *Political Power,* 111–12.
40. Ibid., 118.
41. Spindler, *Nineteenth-Century Ecuador,* 171.
42. Reyes, *Breve Historia* 2–3: 220.
43. Ibid., 230.
44. Ibid., 231.
45. Hurtado, *Political Power,* 59.
46. Spindler, *Nineteenth-Century Ecuador,* 199.
47. *Historia de las Luchas Populares: De la Revolución Liberal a la Masacre de 1922* (Quito: Centro de Estudios y Difusión Social, 1985), 19.
48. Reyes, *Breve Historia* 2–3:246.
49. *Historia de las Luchas,* 19.

CHAPTER 2: EARLY PROTESTANT GROUPS, 1896–1931

1. For a history of the work of the Bible societies in Ecuador during the nineteenth century, see Padilla, *La Iglesia y los Dioses,* 53–157.
2. Ibid., 142–43.
3. Ronn F. Pineo, "Misery and Death in the Pearl of the Pacific: Health Care in Guayaquil, Ecuador, 1870–1925," *Hispanic American Historical Review* 70, no. 4 (November 1990): 621–22.
4. For the history of the fundamentalist movement in the United States, see James Barr, *Fundamentalism* (London: SCM Press, 1977); and George M. Marsden, *Fundamentalism and American Culture* (New York: Oxford University Press, 1980).
5. Bamat, *¿Salvación o Dominación?* 102. See also Prudencio Damboriena, *El Protestantismo en América Latina* (Fribourg, Switzerland: Oficina International de Investigaciones Sociales de FERES, 1962), 241–42.
6. Scott S. Robinson, "Fulfilling the Mission: North American Evangelism in Ecuador," in *Is God an American,* ed. Soren Hvalkof and Peter Aaby (Copenhagen: International Work Group for Indigenous Affairs, 1981), 42.
7. José Eduardo Vergara de la Torre, "La Juliana: Revolución y Modernización," *La Liebre Illustrada,* July 10, 1982, 2. Hurtado, *Political Power,* 255–56.
8. Reyes, *Breve Historia* 2–3:268–74.
9. Paul E. Kuhl, "Protestant Missionary Activity and Freedom of Religion in Ecuador, Peru, and Bolivia" (Ph.D diss., Southern Illinois University, 1982), 398–400.

10. Padilla, *La Iglesia y los Dioses*, 251–53.

11. Kuhl, "Protestant Missionary Activity," 401.

12. Padilla, *La Iglesia y los Dioses*, 255–60.

13. Ibid., 291–92.

14. Kuhl, "Protestant Missionary Activity," 387–88.

15. Padilla, *La Iglesia y los Dioses*, 196.

16. Ibid., 198.

17. Ibid., 200–201.

18. Robinson, "Fulfilling the Mission," 44.

19. Padilla, *La Iglesia y los Dioses*, 205.

20. Ibid., 207–9.

21. Ibid., 218. This phrase appeared in a letter from Federico Antay, a Peruvian Bible salesman, to Thomas Wood on December 13, 1897.

22. Loor, *Eloy Alfaro*, 446.

23. Padilla, *La Iglesia y los Dioses*, 226.

24. Ibid., 231.

25. Marsden, *Fundamentalism*, 83, 128.

26. Kuhl, "Protestant Missionary Activity," 396–97.

27. Padilla, *La Iglesia y los Dioses*, 265.

28. "Pioneer Years," *Ecuadorian* (Summer-Fall 1987): 5.

29. "The Blind Man of Junín," *Ecuadorian* (Summer-Fall 1987): 11–13.

30. "Pioneer Years," 6.

31. "Two Strong Pillars," *Ecuadorian* (Summer-Fall 1987): 18.

32. Bamat, *¿Salvación o Dominación?* 107.

33. David Martin, *Tongues of Fire: The Explosion of Protestantism in Latin America* (Cambridge: Basil Blackwell, 1990), 80–81.

34. Throughout Ecuadorean history, the Shuar have been the target of missionaries. They were pursued by the Jesuits in the colonial period and in the twentieth century by the CMA and Catholic Salesian Order. For a history of relations between the Shuar and Christian missions from the sixteenth century to the 1980s, see Juan Bottasso, *Los Shuar y las Misiones: Entre la Hostilidad y el Dialogo* (Quito: Mundo Shuar, 1982).

35. "Pioneer Years," 7.

36. The writings of Ellen G. White include *The Great Controversy, Patriarchs and Prophets, Prophets and Kings, Desire of Ages,* and *The Act of Apostles.* These and other works can be found in various editions.

37. Stoll, *Is Latin America?* 103. Stoll's figures come from P. J. Johnstone, *Operation World*, 3d ed. (Bromley, Kent, England: Send the Light Books, 1982); and George Colvin, "Adventists Balance Gains Challenges," *Christian Century*, August 14, 1985, 738–39.

38. Martin, *Tongues of Fire*, 86.

39. *Seventh-Day Adventist Encyclopedia*, rev. ed. (Washington, D.C.: Review and Herald, 1976), 408.

40. Padilla, *La Iglesia y los Dioses*, 292.

41. *Seventh-Day Adventist Encyclopedia*, 409.

42. Bamat, *¿Salvación o Dominación?* 104.

43. *Seventh-Day Adventist Encyclopedia*, 409.

44. Padilla, *La Iglesia y los Dioses*, 276 (author's translation).

45. Ibid., 294.

46. *Seventh-Day Adventist Encyclopedia*, 409.

47. For the work of the Fords in Chimborazo, see Mrs. Orley Ford, *In the High Andes* (Nashville: Southern Publishing Association, 1932).

48. *Seventh-Day Adventist Encyclopedia*, 409.

49. Deborah J. Baldwin, *Protestants and the Mexican Revolution: Missionaries, Ministers, and Social Change* (Chicago: University of Chicago Press, 1990), 48–49. Baldwin demonstrates the truth of this statement for Mexico. It was equally true, however, for other countries. In Ecuador, the prime example was the city of Ambato.

CHAPTER 3: HCJB RADIO, "THE VOICE OF THE ANDES," 1931–1990

1. Bamat, *¿Salvación o Dominación?* 150.

2. Padilla, *La Iglesia y los Dioses*, 354–55.

3. Erickson, et al., *Area Handbook*, 55.

4. Padilla, *La Iglesia y los Dioses*, 360–61.

5. Ibid.

6. "Oil on Troubled Waters," 29–31.

7. Reyes, *Breve Historia* 2–3:301.

8. Cockcroft, *Neighbors in Turmoil*, 380. For a view of Plaza Lasso's ties to the United Fruit Company, see "Galo Plaza: The Politics of Prosperity," 11.

9. Reyes, *Breve Historia* 2–3:326.

10. Cockcroft, *Neighbors in Turmoil*, 380.

11. "Boom or Bust," 12–13.

12. For a view of the political career of Velasco Ibarra, see Agustín Cueva, *The Process of Political Domination in Ecuador*, trans. Danielle Salti (New Brunswick, N.J.: Transaction Books, 1982), 63–96.

13. Cockcroft, *Neighbors in Turmoil*, 382.

14. Ibid., 383.

15. Reyes, *Breve Historia* 2–3:329.

16. Judith Kimerling, S. Jacob Scherr, and J. Eugene Gibson, *Amazon Crude* (Washington, D.C.: National Resources Defense Council, 1991), 46.

17. Lois Neely, *Come Up to This Mountain: The Miracle of Clarence W. Jones* (Wheaton, Ill.: Tyndale House, 1982), 81.

18. Clarence W. Jones, *Radio: The New Missionary* (Chicago: Moody, 1946), 25–33.

19. Ibid., 43–46.

20. Ibid., 37.

21. Padilla, *La Iglesia y los Dioses,* 357.

22. Cook, *Seeds in the Wind,* 46.

23. "A Stronger Voice to the World" (Opa Locka, Fla.: World Radio Missionary Fellowship, [1988?]), 3. "Heralding Christ Jesus' Blessings: Technical Services" (Opa Locka, Fla.: World Radio Missionary Fellowship, [1986?]), 2.

24. Cook, *Seeds in the Wind,* 68.

25. Padilla, *La Iglesia y los Dioses,* 364.

26. *HCJB World Radio: The Challenge of Missions* (Quito: Imprenta Vozandes, 1986), 10–11. See "Heralding Christ Jesus' Blessings: Broadcasting," 5 (statistical chart). The term *nordic* is used by HCJB to refer to the languages of Scandinavia.

27. Cook, *Seeds in the Wind,* 159–65.

28. "Heralding Christ Jesus' Blessings: Spanish Ministries," 2–6.

29. Bamat, *¿Salvación o Dominación?* 153. For a complete view of religious-right television programming in Latin America, see Hugo Assmann, *La Iglesia Electrónica y su Impacto en América Latina: Invitación a un Estudio* (San José, Costa Rica: DEI, 1987); "Iglesia Electrónica y Marketing, *Chasqui* 21 (January-March 1987): 6; and "La Iglesia Electrónica en América Latina, *Chasqui* 22 (April-June 1987): 48.

30. *HCJB World Radio,* 29–30.

31. Cook, *Seeds in the Wind,* 129; Jones, *Radio,* 73–74.

32. Cook, *Seeds in the Wind,* 129.

33. Ibid., 129–33.

34. For a view of the work of Nate Saint, see Russell T. Hitt, *Jungle Pilot: The Life and Witness of Nate Saint* (New York: Harper, 1954).

35. Cook, *Seeds in the Wind,* 134.

36. Also see Elisabeth Elliot, *Through Gates of Splendor* (New York: Harper, 1957).

37. Cook, *Seeds in the Wind,* 136.

38. Ibid., 139.

39. Bamat, *¿Salvación o Dominación?* 152.

40. *Papers from Two Periods in the History of the Evangelical Church in Ecuador* (Quito: Centro Cristiano de Recursos Educativos, [1978?]).

41. Cook, *Seeds in the Wind,* 8–12.

42. "Informe a la Tercera Asamblea de la Confraternidad Evangelica Ecuatoriana," in *Papers from Two Periods,* 1–9.

43. Cook to Padilla, in *Papers from Two Periods,* 10.

44. Padilla to Cook, in *Papers from Two Periods,* 1–5.

45. Ibid., 1.
46. Ibid., 2.
47. Ibid., 3.
48. Heralding Christ Jesus' Blessings: Spanish Ministries," 4.
49. Richard D. Jacquin, interview with author, Opa Locka, Florida, February 10, 1992, World Radio Missionary Fellowship.
50. Bamat, *¿Salvación o Dominación?* 152.

CHAPTER 4: THE SUMMER INSTITUTE OF LINGUISTICS, 1952–1981

1. Samuel Wilson and John Siewart, eds., *Mission Handbook: North American Protestant Missionaries Overseas,* 13th ed. (Monrovia, Calif.: Marc, 1986), 601, 603.
2. Robinson, "Fulfilling the Mission," 46.
3. Jones, *Radio,* 119–20.
4. Robinson, "Fulfilling the Mission," 46.
5. "The World of Wycliffe" (Wycliffe Bible Translators, Huntington Beach, Calif.: [1987?]), 2.
6. Summer Institute of Linguistics/Wycliffe Bible Translators, "General Statistics," 1987.
7. Wycliffe Bible Translators, "Help Wanted," 1986.
8. Virginia Garrard Burnett, "A History of Protestantism in Guatemala" (Ph.D diss., Tulane University, 1986), 81.
9. Billy Graham with Philip Yancey, "Unforgettable Uncle Cam," *Reader's Digest,* September 1986 (reprint, Wycliffe Bible Translators, 1986), 3.
10. Eunice V. Pike, "Historical Sketch," in *The Summer Institute of Linguistics: Its Works and Contributions,* ed. Ruth M. Brend and Kenneth L. Pike (Paris: Mouton 1977), 1.
11. Ibid., 2.
12. See W. Cameron Townsend, *Lázaro Cárdenas, Mexican Democrat* (Ann Arbor, Mich.: George Wahr, 1952).
13. W. Cameron Townsend, *They Found a Common Language* (New York: Harper & Row, 1971), viii.
14. Pike, "Historical Sketch," 3.
15. Ibid., 4.
16. Wallis and Bennett, *Two Thousand Tongues to Go,* 155, 157–58.
17. Stoll, *Fishers of Men,* 84, 85, 88.
18. The name Auca in Quechua means "killers" or "savages." Huaorani simply means "the people"; it is the name the indigenous people prefer to use.
19. Jerry Bledsoe, "Saint," *Esquire* (July 1972): 130.
20. Bamat, *¿Salvación o Dominación?* 157–58.

21. David Stoll, "Words Can Be Used in So Many Ways," in Hvalkof and Aaby, *Is God an American?* 23.

22. Wallis and Bennett, *Two Thousand Tongues to Go,* 216.

23. Bamat, *¿Salvación o Dominación?* 158. For a view of the SIL's activities among the Siona-Secoya that compares the SIL to the Jesuits of the eighteenth century, see William T. Vickers, "The Jesuits and the SIL: External Policies for Ecuador's Tucanoans through Three Centuries," in *Is God an American?* 51–61.

24. For the actual expulsion decree, see Ginette Cano et al., *Los Nuevos Conquistadores: El Instituto Lingüístico de Verano en América Latina* (Quito: CEDIS y FENOC, 1979), 363–69; or Jorge Trujillo, *Los Obscuros Designios del Dios y del Imperio: El Instituto Lingüístico de Verano en el Ecuador* (Quito: Centro de Investigaciones y Estudios Socioeconómicos, 1981), 135–38.

25. Ethel Emily Wallis, *The Dayuma Story: Life under Auca Spears* (New York: Harper, 1960), 23–29.

26. Bledsoe, "Saint," 132.

27. Stoll, *Fishers of Men,* 284.

28. Ibid.

29. "Go Ye and Preach the Gospel: Five Do and Die," *Life,* January 30, 1956, 14–15.

30. Bledsoe, "Saint," 132.

31. "Go Ye and Preach," 15.

32. "A Tale That Was Told," *Newsweek,* January 23, 1956, 58–59.

33. "Go Ye and Preach," 16–17.

34. Ibid., 18.

35. For a view of the work of Bishop Labaca among the Huaorani, see Alejandro Labaca Ugarte, *Crónica Huaorani* (Quito: Ediciones CICAME, 1988).

36. In 1977 Petroecuador was called the Corporación Estatal Petrolera Ecuatoriana or CEPE.

37. For an account of the first attack, see *El Comercio* (Quito), May 11, 1977. For the second attack and a description of the Red Feet, see "Alejandro e Inés, Dos Signos de Dios para Nuestro Tiempo" (Quito: Fondo Ecuatoriano Populorum Progressio, 1988), 6.

38. Andres Oppenheimer, "Killer Indians Resist Advance of Civilization," *Miami Herald,* August 23, 1987, 1.

39. Ibid.

CHAPTER 5: THE SUMMER INSTITUTE OF LINGUISTICS—SALVATION OR GENOCIDE?

1. Bledsoe, "Saint," 127.

2. Ibid., 145.

3. According to Andres Oppenheimer in "Killer Indians," the Huaorani attackers were the Red Feet.

4. Bledsoe, "Saint," 145.

5. Stoll, *Fishers of Men*, 306–7.

6. Bledsoe, "Saint," 145.

7. Stoll, *Fishers of Men*, 287. For the story of Chief Tariri, see Ethel Emily Wallis, *Tariri, My Story* (New York: Harper & Row, 1965). For a pictorial account of the SIL's work in Peru, see Matthew Huxley and Cornell Capa, *Farewell to Eden* (London: Chatto & Windus, 1965).

8. Stoll, *Fishers of Men*, 309–12.

9. Bledsoe, "Saint," 145.

10. Ibid., 146. The cultural survival adaptations described here have been forced upon the Huaorani by scarcity of food and land.

11. Stoll, *Fishers of Men*, 289.

12. David W. Schodt, *Ecuador: An Andean Enigma* (Boulder, Colo.: Westview, 1987), 99, 106.

13. Ibid., 106.

14. Bledsoe, "Saint," 146.

15. Ibid., 147.

16. Ibid.

17. Catherine Peeke, quoted in Stoll, *Fishers of Men*, 296–97.

18. Bledsoe, "Saint," 152.

19. Stoll, *Fishers of Men*, 300.

20. Ibid., 301.

21. For the work of Jim Yost at the Tiwaeno mission, see "Jungle Identity Crisis: Auca Country Revisited," *Christianity Today* (January 1980): 48–50.

22. Stoll, *Fishers of Men*, 303–4.

23. Ibid., 305.

24. Ibid., 307–8, 312.

25. Stoll, "Words Can Be Used," 35.

26. Cano, *Los Nuevos Conquistadores*, 364. Trujillo, *Los Obscuros Designios*, 136.

27. Estrada and Munoz, *Con Dios Todo Se Puede*, 49, 52.

28. Ibid., 52.

29. Ibid., 196.

30. "Organizaciones: CONFENAIE Denuncia Que el Gobierno Prepara Nueva Intromisión del Instituto Lingüístico de Verano al Pais." *Acción* (August 1986): 56–58.

CHAPTER 6: WORLD VISION, 1975–1990

1. For a complete view of freeholding communities, see P. R. Odell and D. A. Preston, *Economies and Societies in Latin America: A Geographical Interpretation* (New York: John Wiley, 1978), 34–39.

2. Reyes, *Breve Historia* 1:128–29.

3. *La Bocina* (January 1984): 12.

4. Estrada and Munoz, *Con Dios Todo,* 41.

5. Leonidas E. Proaño, "La Organización Campesina en El Centro del Pais" (Quito, FEPP, [1988?]), 10–11.

6. "Evaluación y Seguimiento De Visión Mundial En Algunas Comunidades Indígenas de la Sierra Ecuatoriana" (Quito, Centro de Planificación y Estudios Sociales [CEPLAES], 1984), 51.

7. Wilson and Siewart, *Mission Handbook,* 307–8.

8. World Vision International, *People and Projects* (Monrovia, Calif.: 1985), 3–4, 120–21.

9. Wilson and Siewart, *Mission Handbook,* 308, 603.

10. "Evaluación y Seguimiento," 19.

11. Norman B. Rohrer, *Open Arms* (Wheaton, Ill.: Tyndale House, 1987), 43.

12. Ibid., 56–57.

13. *Moody Monthly* (September 1958): 53. Rohrer, *Open Arms,* 223–30.

14. Rohrer, *Open Arms,* 223–30.

15. Bamat, *¿Salvación o Dominación?* 160.

16. W. Stanley Mooneyham, *What Do You Say to a Hungry World?* (Waco, Tex.: Word Books, 1975), 12.

17. Ibid., 13.

18. "World Vision: The Pull to the Right," *NACLA Report on the Americas* 23 (January-February 1984): 21.

19. Stoll, *Is Latin America?* 288.

20. "Visión Mundial, ¿Qué Es y Como Trabaja?" (Quito: Ediciones Abya-Yala, 1984), 1.

21. *People and Projects,* 105.

22. Ibid., 106.

23. "Pueblos Del Ecuador" (Quito: Ediciones Abya-Yala, 1986), 10.

24. "Evaluación y Seguimiento," 173.

25. For a view of the exploitation and degradation of huasipungo life in Ecuador, see Jorge Icaza, *Huasipungo* (Buenos Aires: Editorial Losada), 1953.

26. Francisco Gangotena, "Diversity: An Indian Strategy for Survival, in Crisis," paper presented at the 40th Annual Conference on Latin America, Andean Crisis: Traditional Dilemmas and Contemporary Challenges, the Center for Latin American Studies, University of Florida, Gainesville, Fla., March 26–29, 1991.

27. Blanca Muratorio, "Protestantism, Ethnicity, and Class in Chimborazo," in *Cultural Transformations and Ethnicity in Modern Ecuador,* ed. Norman E. Whitten, Jr. (Urbana: University of Illinois Press, 1981), 506, 514.

28. Ibid., 515.

29. Ibid., 516, 517.

30. "Evaluación y Seguimiento," 176.
31. Ibid., 176–78.
32. Ibid., 178–84.
33. "Vision Mundial, ¿Qué es?" 3–4.
34. "Evaluación y Seguimiento," 184.
35. Ibid., 185.
36. Ibid., 186, 187.
37. The following statements of Padilla, Teran, and Proaño were quoted in Estrada and Muñoz, *Con Dios Todo,* 43–45 (author's translation).
38. Rohrer, *Open Arms,* 142.

CHAPTER 7: THE PENTECOSTALS AND THE INDEPENDENTS, 1950–1990

1. Prudencio Damboriena, *Tongues as of Fire* (Washington: Corpus Books, 1969), 1, 86.
2. Milton V. Backman, Jr., *Christian Churches of America: Origin and Beliefs* (Provo, Utah: Brigham Young University Press, 1976), 194–96.
3. Damboriena, *Tongues as of Fire,* 15.
4. Vinson Synan, *The Holiness-Pentecostal Movement in the United States* (Grand Rapids, Mich.: Eerdmans, 1971), 61–62.
5. Marsden, *Fundamentalism,* 93.
6. Synan, *Holiness-Pentecostal Movement,* 95–116.
7. Stanley M. Burgess and Gary B. McGee, eds., *Dictionary of Pentecostal and Charismatic Movements* (Grand Rapids, Mich.: Zondervan, 1988), 3.
8. Jean Pierre Bastian, *Breve Historia del Protestantismo en América Latina* (Mexico, D.F.: Casa Unida de Publicaciones, 1986), 130–31.
9. William R. Read, Victor M. Monterroso, and Harmon A. Johnson, *Latin American Church Growth* (Grand Rapids, Mich.: Eerdmans, 1969), 137, 165.
10. C. Peter Wagner, *Look Out! The Pentecostals Are Coming* (Carol Stream, Ill.: Creation House, 1973), 18–27. For a Spanish translation, see Pedro Wagner, *Avance del Pentecostalismo en Latinoamerica* (Miami: Editorial Vida, 1987), 9–19.
11. Christian Lalive d'Epinay, *Haven of the Masses* (London: Lutterworth Press, 1969), 7–14.
12. Wagner, *Avance,* 14–16.
13. Ibid., 11–12, 14, 17. In 1979 the Pentecostal movement in Argentina eventually came under the leadership of Omar Cabrera and his Visión del Futuro (Future Vision) movement. In 1984 Visión del Futuro had more than 135,000 members dispersed in thirty-five centers around the country. For studies on Protestantism in Argentina, see Alfredo Silletta, *La Secta Moon: Como Destruir la Democracia* (Buenos Aires: El Cid Editor, 1985); *Las Sectas Invaden la Argentina* (Buenos Aires: Edito-

rial Contrapunto, 1987; and *Multinacionales de la Fe: Religión, Sectas, e Iglesia Electrónica* (Buenos Aires: Editorial Contrapunto, 1988).

14. Burgess and McGee, eds., *Dictionary of Pentecostal and Charismatic Movements*, 390.

15. Stoll, *Is Latin America?* 225–26.

16. Ibid., 228–29. For work on Nicaragua, see David Haslam, *Faith in Struggle: The Protestant Churches in Nicaragua and Their Response to the Revolution* (London: Epworth, 1987).

17. Read, Monterroso, and Johnson, *Latin American Church,* 313.

18. Bamat, ¿Salvación o Dominación? 125.

19. Wagner, *Look Out!* 60; *Avance,* 41–42.

20. Kenneth L. Woodward, Penny Lernoux, and Mac Margolis, "The Protestant Push," *Newsweek,* September 1, 1989, 63.

21. "The Rise of the Religious Right in Central America," *The Inter-Hemispheric Education Resource Center Bulletin* 10 (Summer-Fall 1987): 4.

22. Deborah Huntington, "God's Saving Plan," in Enrique Dominguez and Deborah Huntington, "The Salvation Brokers: Conservative Evangelicals in Central America," *NACLA Report on the Americas* 17, no. 1 (January-February 1984): 26.

23. Stoll, *Is Latin America?* 200.

24. Burnett, "A History of Protestantism," 238.

25. Ibid., 240.

26. Ibid., 248.

27. Sara Diamond, "Holy Warriors," *NACLA Report on the Americas* 22, no. 5 (September-October 1988): 35.

28. David Stoll, "Guatemala Elects a Born-Again President," *Christian Century* 108, no. 6 (February 1991): 189–90.

29. Bamat, ¿Salvación o Dominación? 126.

30. Padilla, *Los Dioses Modernos,* 400.

31. Read, Monterroso, and Johnson, *Latin American Church,* 122.

32. Wagner, *Look Out!* 53–56; *Avance,* 35.

33. Padilla, *Los Dioses Modernos,* 400.

34. Hurtado, *Political Power,* 264.

35. Read, Monterroso, and Johnson, *Latin American Church,* 95–99, 10–12.

36. Pentecostalism was third behind a generalized "others" classification of 29 percent and the GMU/AIECH with 25 percent. See the *Directorio de la Iglesia Evangélica del Ecuador* (Quito: Comite Interdenominacional Pro-Directorio, 1985), 375–405.

37. Bamat, ¿Salvación o Dominación? 90.

38. Estrada and Muñoz, *Con Dios Todo,* 66–67 (author's translation).

39. Burgess and McGee, *Dictionary of Pentecostal and Charismatic Movements,* 395–96. For an article that deals with recent trends in Hispanic Protestantism in the

United States, see Andres Tapia, "Viva Los Evangélicos!" *Christianity Today* (October 28, 1991): 17–22.

40. Moises Ramos, "Clamor a Dios: Entre la Protesta Legítima y la Inquisición Religiosa (parte 1)," *Claridad*, September 16–22, 1988, 12, 29.

41. "Sectas y Desmovilización Campesina: Lectura de un Caso Concreto, Tolontag y El Marco," *Opciones y Experiencias* (1987): 6.

42. Ibid.

43. Ibid., 16.

44. Estrada y Muñoz, *Con Dios Todo,* 78–80.

45. Ibid., 83–84 (author's translation).

46. Ibid., 86 (author's translation).

47. Bamat, *¿Salvación o Dominación?* 130–31 (author's translation).

48. Ibid. (author's translation).

49. Silletta, *Multinacionales de la Fe,* 147–48; Stoll, *Is Latin America?* 320; Haslam, *Faith in Struggle,* 57–62.

50. George Sullivan-Davis, "Chile: Evangelicals Step Up Criticism of Pinochet Regime," *Latinamerica Press,* June 4, 1987, 6–7.

CHAPTER 8: THE PROTESTANT "THREAT" AND THE CATHOLIC RESPONSE

1. Kuhl, "Protestant Missionary Activity," 393.

2. "Tres Leccioncillas de Doctrina Cristiana Sobre El Protestantismo" (Quito: Imprenta de Clero, 1900), 13. Carlos María de la Torre, "Tercera Carta Pastoral" (Riobamba: Imprenta "La Moderna," 1922), 2. The above are but two examples of catechisms. Other literature appeared bearing such intriguing titles as "El Protestantismo de Donde Viene y a Donde Va" (Where Protestantism comes from and where it is going, 1898) and "El Protestantismo Condenado por si Mismo o Sea Historia de la Reforma Protestante en Inglaterra e Irlanda: En la Cual Se Demuestra que Dicha Reforma Ha Emprobecido y Degradado la Masa del Pueblo en Ambos Paises" (Protestantism condemned by itself, or, in other words, the history of the Protestant Reformation in England and Ireland: Which demonstrates that said reform has impoverished and degraded the masses in both countries, 1913).

3. Aurelio Espinosa Polit, "El Laicismo, la Herejía del Día" (Quito: Biblioteca Aurelio Espinosa Polit, 1960), see p. 314.

4. Padilla, *Los Dioses Modernos,* 361–62.

5. Tomás Bamat, "Ecuador: Bishops Lament Recent Election's Demogogic Use of Religious Language," *Latinamerica Press,* June 30, 1988, 5.

6. Penny Lernoux, *Cry of the People* (London: Penguin, 1980), 31, 37–47, 413–48.

7. Ibid., 32.

8. John Alvarez García and Christian Restrepo Calle, eds., *Camilo Torres: His Life and Message*, trans. Virginia M. O'Grady (Springfield, Ill.: Templegate, 1968), 126–27.

9. For an account of Carney's life up to his disappearance, see J. Guadalupe Carney, *To Be a Revolutionary: An Autobiography* (San Francisco: Harper & Row, 1985). For a list of those martyred in Latin America from 1964 to 1978, see Lernoux, *Cry of the People*, 463–70.

10. For Gutiérrez's theology, see Gustavo Gutiérrez, *A Theology of Liberation* (Maryknoll, N.Y.: Orbis Books, 1972).

11. Philip Berryman, *Liberation Theology* (Oak Park, Ill.: Meyer Stone, 1987), 26.

12. Gustavo Gutiérrez, "Liberation Theology: Gutiérrez Reflects on 20 Years Urging Option for the Poor," interview by Mario Campos, *Latinamerica Press*, July 14, 1988, 5.

13. Stoll, *Is Latin America?* 138.

14. Leonidas E. Proaño, *Concientización, Evangelización, Política* (Salamanca, Spain: Ediciones Sígueme, 1987), 103–4 (author's translation).

15. Ibid., 105 (author's translation).

16. Hurtado, *Political Power*, 269–70.

17. Quoted in Lernoux, *Cry of the People*, 138.

18. Ibid., 139.

19. Ibid., 141.

20. Comisión Ecuménica De Derechos Humanos, *Derechos del Pueblo* 32 (March 1986): 4, 5 (author's translation).

21. Ibid.

22. *Hoy*, September 5, 1988, 5A.

23. "La Iglesia Responde a Los Terratenientes," *Punta de Vista* special edition, June 11, 1990, 11–12.

24. Victor Corral, "We Want to Build an Indigenous Church," interview by Leslie Wirpsa, *Latinamerica Press*, November 15, 1990, 5.

25. Fondo Ecuatoriano Populorum Progressio, "Breve Presentacion," 3.

26. Ibid., 3–4.

27. Ibid., 6–10.

28. Simón Espinosa, "Elsie Monge: La Mujer de los Derechos," *Revista Diners* (July 1988): 57.

29. Ibid., 54. For documentation on the human rights abuses of the Febres Cordero government, see Americas Watch and the Andean Commission of Jurists, *Human Rights in Ecuador* (New York: Americas Watch, 1988).

30. For a view of CEDHU's work in the cause of human rights, see *Human Rights in Ecuador*, 68.

31. Simón Espinosa, interview by author, July 13, 1988, CLAI Office, Quito.

32. Jaime Wright, "In Brazil, SERPAJ Focuses on Land Rights of Indigenous," interview by Dafne Plou, *Latinamerica Press*, April 20, 1989, 6.

33. Washington Padilla, "Las Iglesias Protestantes y Los Derechos Humanos," *Derechos del Pueblos,* no. 32 (March 1986): 9.

CHAPTER 9: THE PROTESTANT "THREAT" AND THE INDIGENOUS RESPONSE

1. In Ecuador, the nonprofit Fundación Natura (Nature Foundation) strives to protect the environment. In the past it has worked with CEDHU and indigenous groups to prevent environmental damage. It publishes *Colibrí,* a journal financed with the help of the Inter-American Foundation.

2. Estrada and Muñoz, *Con Dios Todo,* 38. Patricio Torres, "Los Aucas 'en guerra'," *Kipu* 9 (July-December 1987): 225.

3. Confederación de Nacionalidades Indígenas de la Amazonía Ecuatoriana, *Amanecer Indio* (December 1986): 7–8.

4. Unión de Nativos de la Amazonía Ecuatoriana, "Problematica Indígena y Colonización en el Oriente Ecuatoriano" (Quito, [1985?]): 7, 8, 9 (author's translation).

5. For a complete picture of the role of Yasuni National Park in petroleum production in Ecuador, see Kimerling, *Amazon Crude,* 85–92.

6. John M. Ashley, "African Palm Oil: Impacts in Equador's Amazon," *Cultural Survival Quarterly* 11 (1986): 55–60. This is a thorough study on African palm oil production in Ecuador.

7. Confederación de Nacionalidades Indígenas del Ecuador, *500 Años De Resistencia India* (Quito, 1988), 10–11.

8. Ibid., 12.

9. Ibid., 13–14.

10. Ibid., 20.

11. "Despierta El Gigante," *Vistazo,* July 19, 1990, 4–10.

12. "Levantamiento Indígena Prepara CONAIE," *Punta de Vista* 418 (May 21, 1990): 5.

13. For a firsthand view of the 1990 CONAIE mobilization see the 30-minute videocassette *El Levantimiento Indígena,* produced and directed by CEDIS-CONAIE, and "Despierta El Gigante," 4–10.

14. "Ni Una Hacienda en el 92," *Punta de Vista* 421 (June 11, 1990): 4–5.

15. "Indios de Cayambe Defendieron Con Valor Sus Derechos," *Punta de Vista* 421 (June 11, 1990): 4.

16. "La Sublevación de los Cabildos," *Punta de Vista* 421 (June 11, 1990): 6.

17. "Despierta El Gigante," 6–7.

18. "Amplia Solidaridad," *Punta de Vista* 421 (June 11, 1990): 10.

19. "Sin Pan, Tierra y Libertad No Hay Democracia," *Punta de Vista* 421 (June 11, 1990): 10.

20. "Nosotros Hemos Ganado Esta Guerra," *Punta de Vista* 421 (June 11, 1990): 3.

21. For an account of the indigenous conference in Quito, see Elizabeth Bobsy Draper, "Minga In Ecuador," *Z Magazine*, December 1990, pp. 33–38. See also *Columbus Didn't Discover Us*, a 24-minute videocassette produced by Robbie Leppzer and directed by Wil Echevarria, Erik van Lennap, and Pedro Rivera, Turning Tide Productions, 1992.

22. Eduardo Galeano, "1492 Reconsidered," *Latinamerica Press*, January 28, 1988, 3.

CONCLUSION

1. World Council of Churches (Rooseveltown, N.Y.: White Roots for Peace [1971?]), 1–5.

2. Ibid., 3–4.

3. Ibid., 4.

4. Federacion de Centros Shuar, *Solución Original a un Problema Actual* (Sucua, Ecuador, 1976), 39–40.

5. Ibid., 40–41.

6. Ibid., 41–43.

7. Rudolpho Stavenhagen, "Los Derechos Indígenas: Nuevo Enfoque Del Sistema Internacional," paper presented at the 15th International Congress of the Latin American Studies Association, Miami, Fla., December 4–6, 1989, 3–4.

8. *Solución Original*, 28.

9. Chris Wille, "The World According to Nietschmann," *Audobon* (November-December 1992): 73. Bernard Nietschmann is a geographer and environmentalist from the University of California. He has studied the Miskito Indians of Nicaragua. His books include *Between Land and Water: The Subsistence Ecology of the Miskito Indians, Eastern Nicaragua* (New York: Seminar Press, 1973); and *The Unknown War: The Miskito Nation, Nicaragua and the United States* (New York: Freedom House, 1989).

10. Alan Weisman and Sandy Tolan, "Out of Time," *Audubon* (November-December 1992): 72–73.

11. Robert T. Coote, "Taking Aim on 2000 A.D.," in Wilson and Siewart, *Mission Handbook*, 36.

12. Edward R. Dayton and Samuel Wilson, eds. *The Future of World Evangelization: Unreached Peoples '84* (Monrovia, Calif.: Missions Advanced Research and Communication Center, 1984), 7.

13. Ibid., 8–9.

14. Ibid., 605. According to World Vision's Registry of the Unreached.

BIBLIOGRAPHY

PRIMARY SOURCES

General

Americas Watch and the Andean Commission of Jurists. *Human Rights in Ecuador.* New York: Americas Watch, 1988.

Brend, Ruth M., and Kenneth L. Pike., eds. *The Summer Institute of Linguistics: Its Works and Contributions.* Paris: Mouton, 1977.

Conferencia General del Episcopado Latinoamericano. *Puebla: La Evangelización en el Presente y en el Futuro de América Latina.* Caracas: Ediciones Tripode, 1979.

Dayton, Edward R., and David A. Fraser. *Planning Strategies for World Evangelization.* Grand Rapids, Mich.: Eerdmans, 1980.

Dayton, Edward R., and Samuel Wilson., eds. *The Future of World Evangelization: Unreached Peoples '84.* Monrovia, Calif.: Missions Advanced Research and Communication Center, 1984.

Declaración de la Conferencia Episcopal Ecuatoriana sobre la Promoción de la Justicia Social. Quito, 1977.

Declaración de la Conferencia Episcopal Ecuatoriana. Quito: Ediciones "Justicia Y Paz," 1985.

Declaración Universal de los Derechos de los Pueblos. Quito: Fondo Ecuatoriano Populorum Progressio, [1988?].

Holland, Clifton L., ed. *World Christianity: Central America and the Caribbean.* Monrovia, Calif.: Missions Advanced Research and Communication Center, 1981.

John Paul II. "La Evangelización de la Cultura." *Cultura* 8, no. 22 (May-August 1985): 23–28.

Leon, Lydia. trans. "CONFENIAE Denounces Agribusiness in Eastern Ecuador— An Open Letter." *Cultural Survival Quarterly* 10, no. 1 (1986): 33–37.

Montalvo, Juan. *Las Catilinarias y Otros Textos.* Caracas: Biblioteca Ayacucho, 1977.

Oaxtepec 1978: Unidad y Misión en América Latina. San José, Costa Rica: Comite Editorial del CLAI, 1980.

Papers from Two Periods in the History of the Evangelical Church in Ecuador. Quito: Centro Cristiano de Recursos Educativos, [1978?].

People and Projects. Monrovia, Calif.: World Vision International, 1985.

Segunda Consulta Ecuménica de Pastoral Indígena. *Aporte de los Indígenas de América Latina a la Teología Cristiana.* Quito: Ediciones Abya-Yala, 1986.

World Council of Churches. *Declaration of Barbados—For the Liberation of the Indians.* Rooseveltown, N.Y.: White Roots for Peace, [1971?].

Missionary Accounts

Bottasso B., Juan. *Los Shuar y Las Misiones.* Quito: Mundo Shuar, 1982.

Carney, J. Guadalupe. *To Be a Revolutionary: An Autobiography.* San Francisco: Harper & Row, 1985.

Coleman, Robert E. *Plan Supremo de Evangelización.* El Paso, Tex.: Casa Bautista de Publicaciones, 1983.

Cook, Frank S. *Seeds in the Wind.* Opa Locka, Fla.: World Radio Missionary Fellowship, 1982.

Dayton, Edward R. *Faith That Goes Farther: Facing the Contradictions of Life.* Portland, Oreg.: Multnomah Press, 1984.

Elliot, Elisabeth. *No Graven Image.* New York: Harper & Row, 1966.

———. *Through Gates of Splendor.* New York: Harper, 1957.

Ford, Orley. *In the High Andes.* Nashville: Southern Publishing Association, 1932.

Graham, Franklin, with Jeanette Lockerbie. *Bob Pierce: This One Thing I Do.* Waco, Tex.: Word Books, 1983.

Hitt, Russell T. *Jungle Pilot: The Life and Witness of Nate Saint.* New York: Harper, 1954.

Howard, George P. *Religious Liberty in Latin America?* Philadelphia: Westminster Press, 1945.

Huxley, Matthew, and Cornell Capa. *Farewell to Eden.* London: Chatto & Windus, 1965.

Jones, Clarence W. *Radio: The New Missionary.* Chicago: Moody, 1946.

Labaca Ugarte, Alejandro. *Crónica Huaorani.* Quito: Ediciones CICAME, 1988.

Mackay, John A. *Christianity on the Frontier.* New York: Macmillan, 1950.

———. *The Other Spanish Christ.* New York: Macmillan, 1933.

Mooneyham, W. Stanley. *What Do You Say to a Hungry World?* Waco, Tex.: Word Books, 1975.

Neely, Lois. *Come Up to This Mountain: The Miracle of Clarence W. Jones.* Wheaton, Ill.: Tyndale House, 1982.

Nida, Eugene A. *Communication of the Gospel in Latin America*. Cuernavaca, México: SONDEOS, 1969.

———. *Customs and Cultures: Anthropology for Christian Missions*. New York: Harper, 1954.

Palau, Luis. *El Climax de la Historia*. Miami: Editorial Unilit, 1986.

———. *Mi Respuesta*. Miami: Editorial Unilit, 1986.

Parham, Sarah E. *The Life of Charles F. Parham*. New York: Garland, 1985.

Pierce, Bob. *Big Day at Da Me*. Waco, Tex.: Word Books, 1968.

Rohrer, Norman B. *Open Arms*. Wheaton, Ill.: Tyndale House, 1987.

Rycroft, W. Stanley. *On This Foundation: The Evangelical Witness in Latin America*. New York: Friendship Press, 1942.

———. *Religion and Faith in Latin America*. Philadelphia: Westminster, 1958.

Simpson, A. B. *Mensajes Misioneros*. Barcelona: Libros CLIE, 1985.

Spain, Mildred. *And in Samaria: A Story of Fifty Years' Missionary Witness in Central America, 1890–1940*. Dallas: Central American Mission, 1940.

Wagner, C. Peter. *Look Out! The Pentecostals are Coming*. Carol Stream, Ill.: Creation House, 1973.

Wallis, Ethel Emily, and Maria Angela Bennett. *The Dayuma Story: Life under Auca Spears*. New York: Harper, 1960.

———. *Tariri: My Story*. New York: Harper, 1965.

———. *Two Thousand Tongues to Go: The Story of the Wycliffe Bible Translators*. New York: Harper, 1959.

Religious Pamphlets

Archdiocese of Quito. "Tres Leccioncillas de Doctrina Cristiana sobre El Protestantismo." Quito: Imprenta del Clero, 1900.

De la Torre, Carlos María. "Carta Pastoral: Trata Del Protestantismo." Riobamba: Imprenta la Moderna, 1922.

Fondo Ecuatoriano Populorum Progressio. "Breve Presentacion." Quito, [1988?].

Jungle Aviation and Radio Services. "Speeding Bible Translation." Waxhaw, N.C., 1987.

Missions International 4. "How to Form an Evangelism and World/Missions Ministries Leadership Team." Los Angeles, California, [1987?].

Polit, Aurelio Espinosa. "El Laicismo, la Herejía del Día." Quito: Biblioteca Aurelio Espinosa Polit, 1960.

Proaño, Leonidas E. "La Organización Campesina en el Centro del Pais." Quito: Fondo Ecuatoriano Populorum Progressio, [1988?].

World Radio Missionary Fellowship. "HCJB World Radio: The Challenge of Mission." Quito: Imprenta Vozandes, 1988.

Wycliffe Bible Translators. "The World of Wycliffe." Huntington Beach, Calif., [1987?].

Bibliography

Indigenous Pamphlets

Confederación de Nacionalidades Indígenas de la Amazonía Ecuatoriana. "Palma Africana y Ethnocidio." Quito: CEDIS, 1985.

Confederación de Nacionalidades Indígenas del Ecuador. "500 Años De Resistencia India." Quito: 1988.

Federación de Centros Shuar. "Solución Original a un Problema Actual." Sucua, Ecuador: 1976.

"Pueblos Del Ecuador." Quito: Ediciones Abya-Yala, 1986.

Unión de Nativos de la Amazonía Ecuatoriana. "Problematica Indígena y Colonización en el Oriente Ecuatoriano." Quito: [1985?].

SECONDARY SOURCES

Books

Agee, Philip. *Inside the Company: CIA Diary*. New York: Stonehill, 1975.

Albornoz, Miguel. *Orellana: El Caballero de las Amazonas*. Quito: Ediciones del Banco Central del Ecuador, 1987.

Alvarez García, John, and Christian Restrepo Calle, eds., *Camilo Torres: His Life and Message*. Springfield, Ill.: Templegate, 1968.

Assmann, Hugo. *La Iglesia Electrónica y Su Impacto en América Latina: Invitación a un Estudio*. San José, Costa Rica: DEI, 1987.

Backman, Milton Vaughn. *Christian Churches of America: Origins and Beliefs*. Provo, Utah: Brigham Young University, 1976.

Baldwin, Deborah J. *Protestants and the Mexican Revolution: Missionaries, Ministers, and Social Change*. Chicago: University of Chicago Press, 1990.

Bamat, Tomás. *¿Salvación o Dominación? Las Sectas Religiosas en el Ecuador*. Quito: Editorial El Conejo, 1986.

Barr, James. *Fundamentalism*. London: SCM Press, 1977.

Bastian, Jean-Pierre. *Breve Historia del Protestantismo en América Latina*. México City: Casa Unida de Publicaciones, 1986.

———. *Los Disidentes: Sociedades Protestantes y Revolución en México, 1872–1911*. Mexico City: El Colegio de México, 1989.

———. *Protestantismo y Sociedad en México*. Mexico City: Casa Unida de Publicaciones, 1983.

Benitez, Lilyan, and Alicia Garces. *Culturas Ecuatorianas: Ayer y Hoy*. Quito: Ediciones Abya Yala, 1987.

Berryman, Philip. *Liberation Theology*. Oak Park, Ill.: Meyer Stone, 1987.

———. *The Religious Roots of Rebellion*. Maryknoll, N.Y.: Orbis Books, 1984.

Brown, Lyle C., and William F. Cooper, eds. *Religion in Latin American Life and Literature*. Waco, Tex.: Markham Press & Fund, 1980.

Burns, E. Bradford. *Latin America: A Concise Interpretive History*. 5th ed. Englewood Cliffs, N.J.: Prentice-Hall, 1990.

———. *The Poverty of Progress: Latin America in the Nineteenth Century*. Berkeley & Los Angeles: University of California Press, 1980.

Caedin, Alberto. *Movimientos Religiosos Modernos*. Madrid: Salvat Editores, 1982.

Cano, Ginette, et al. *Los Nuevos Conquistadores: El Instituto Lingüístico de Verano en América Latina*. Quito: CEDIS & FENOC, 1979.

Carletti, P. Antonio. *Recuerdos de un Misionero*. Ambato: Editorial "Pio XII," 1977.

Carpenter, Joel A., ed. *Missionary Innovation and Expansion*. New York: Garland, 1988.

Carrión, Benjamin. *García Moreno: El Santo del Patíbulo*. Buenos Aires: Fondo de Cultura Económica, 1959.

Clark, Gerald. *The Coming Explosion in Latin America*. New York: David McKay, 1963.

Cockcroft, James D. *Neighbors in Turmoil: Latin America*. New York: Harper & Row, 1989.

Cueva, Agustín. *The Process of Political Domination in Ecuador*. Translated by Danielle Salti. New Brunswick, N.Y.: Transaction Books, 1982.

Damboriena, Prudencio. *El Protestantismo en América Latina*. Fribourg, Switzerland: Oficina Internacional de Investigaciones Sociales de FERES, 1962.

———. *Tongues as of Fire*. Washington: Corpus Books, 1969.

Deler, J. P., and Yves Saint-Geours, eds. *Estados y Naciones en los Andes*. 2 vols. Lima: Instituto de Estudios Peruanos, 1986.

Demelas, Marie-Danielle, and Yves Saint-Geours, eds. *Jerusalen y Babilonia: Religión y Política en el Ecuador, 1780–1880*. Quito: Corporación Editorial Nacional, 1988.

De Soto, Hernando. *El Otro Sendero*. Bogota: Editorial Oveja Negra, 1987.

Diamond, Sara. *Spiritual Warfare: The Politics of the Christian Right*. Boston: South End Press, 1989.

Díaz del Castillo, Bernal. *Historia Verdadera de la Conquista de la Nueva España*. Madrid: Editorial Espasa-Calpe, 1968.

Dussel, Enrique D. *History and the Theology of Liberation*. Maryknoll, N.Y.: Orbis Books, 1976.

———. *A History of the Church in Latin America*. Grand Rapids, Mich.: Eerdmans, 1981.

Escobar, Samuel, ed. *Precursores Evangélicos: Diego Thomson y Francisco Penzotti*. Lima: Ediciones Presencia, 1984.

Estrada, María Albán, and Juan Pablo Muñoz. *Con Dios Todo Se Puede: La Invasión de las Sectas al Ecuador*. Quito: Editorial Planeta, 1987.

Bibliography

García, John Alvarez, and Christian Restrepo Calle. *Camilo Torres: His Life and Message.* Translated by Virginia M. O'Grady. Springfield, Ill.: Templegate, 1968.

García, P. Lorenzo. *Historia de las Misiones en la Amazonía Ecuatoriana.* Quito: Ediciones Abya-Yala, 1985.

Gaver, Jessyca Russell. *Pentecostalism.* New York: Award Books, 1971.

Geffre, Claude, and Gustavo Gutiérrez, eds. *The Mystical and Political Dimensions of the Christian Faith.* New York: Herder & Herder, 1974.

Glazier, Stephen D., ed. *Perspectives on Pentecostalism: Case Studies from the Caribbean and Latin America.* Washington, D.C.: University Press of America, 1980.

Goff, James R., Jr. *Fields White unto Harvest: Charles F. Parham and the Missionary Origins of Pentecostalism.* Fayetteville: University of Arkansas Press, 1988.

Greenleaf, Richard E., ed. *The Roman Catholic Church in Colonial Latin America.* New York: Knopf, 1971.

Grubb, Kenneth. *Religion in Central America.* London: World Dominion Press, 1937.

Gutiérrez, Gustavo. *A Theology of Liberation.* Maryknoll, N.Y.: Orbis Books, 1972.

———. *We Drink from Our Own Wells.* Maryknoll, N.Y.: Orbis Books, 1984.

Haslam, David. *Faith in Struggle: The Protestant Churches in Nicaragua and Their Response to the Revolution.* London: Epworth, 1987.

Hurtado, Oswaldo. *Political Power in Ecuador.* Translated by Nick D. Mills, Jr. Boulder, Colo.: Westview, 1985.

Hvalkof, Soren, and Peter Aaby, eds. *Is God an American? An Anthropological Perspective on the Summer Institute of Linguistics.* Copenhagen: International Work Group for Indigenous Affairs, 1981.

Ibarra, Alicia. *Los Indígenas y El Estado en el Ecuador.* Quito: Ediciones Abya-Yala, 1987.

Icaza, Jorge. *Huasipungo.* Buenos Aires: Editorial Losada, 1953.

Kimerling, Judith, et al. *Amazon Crude.* Washington, D.C.: National Resources Defense Council, 1991.

Lalive d'Epinay, Christian. *Haven of the Masses.* London: Lutterworth, 1969.

Land, Gary, ed. *Adventism in America.* Grand Rapids, Mich.: Eerdmans, 1986.

Landsberger, Henry A., ed. *The Church and Social Change in Latin America.* Notre Dame: University of Notre Dame Press, 1970.

Lange, Martin, and Reinhold Iblacker. *Witness of Hope: The Persecutions of Christians in Latin America.* Maryknoll, N.Y.: Orbis Books, 1980.

Larrea, Fernando, ed. *La Amazonía Presente Y. . . . ?* Quito: Ed. Abya-Yala, Ildis, Tierra Viva, [1988?].

Lernoux, Penny. *Cry of the People.* London: Penguin, 1980.

Levine, Daniel H., ed. *Religion and Political Conflict in Latin America.* Chapel Hill & London: University of North Carolina Press, 1986.

Loor, Wilfredo. *Eloy Alfaro.* Quito: Talleres Gráficos "Minerva," 1981.

Lopez Trujillo, Alfonso. *De Medellín a Puebla.* Madrid: Biblioteca de Autores Cristianos, 1980.

Mariátegui, José Carlos. *Seven Interpretive Essays on Peruvian Reality.* Translated by Marjory Urquidi. Austin: University of Texas Press, 1971.

Marsden, George M. *Fundamentalism and American Culture.* New York: Oxford University Press, 1980.

Martin, David. *Tongues of Fire: The Explosion of Protestantism in Latin America.* Cambridge: Basil Blackwell, 1990.

Martz, John D. *Politics and Petroleum in Ecuador.* New Brunswick, N.J.: Transaction Books, 1987.

Maxwell-Scott, Mrs. *Gabriel García Moreno: Regenerator of Ecuador.* London: R. & T. Washbourne, 1914.

McGavran, Donald Anderson, ed. *Church Growth and Christian Mission.* New York: Harper & Row, 1965.

Mecham, J. Lloyd. *Church and State in Latin America: A History of Politico-Ecclesiastic Relations.* Chapel Hill: University of North Carolina Press, 1966.

Menchu, Rigoberta. *I . . . Rigoberta Menchu: An Indian Woman in Guatemala.* Translated by Ann Wright and edited by Elisabeth Burgos-Debray. London: Verso, 1984.

Moreno Yañez, Segundo E., *Sublevaciones Indígenas en la Audiencia de Quito.* Quito: Ediciones de la Universidad Católica, 1985.

Muratorio, Blanca. *Etnicidad, Evangelización y Protesta en el Ecuador.* Quito: Centro de Investigaciones y Estudios Socio-Economicos, 1982.

———. *Rucuyaya Alonso y la Historia Social y Economica del Alto Napo, 1850–1959.* Quito: Ediciones Abya-Yala, 1987.

Naranjo, Marcelo F., José L. Pereira, and Norman E. Whitten, Jr., eds. *Temas sobre la Continuidad y Adaptación Cultural Ecuatoriana.* Quito: Ediciones de la Universidad Católica, 1977.

Navarro, José Gabriel. *Artes plásticas ecuatorianos.* Vol 4. *Collección Tierra Firme.* Mexico City: Fondo de Cultura Económica, 1945.

Neill, Stephen. *Colonialism and Christian Missions.* New York: McGraw-Hill, 1966.

Nelson, Wilton M. *Protestantism in Central America.* Grand Rapids, Mich.: Eerdmans, 1984.

Nietschmann, Bernard. *Between Land and Water: The Subsistence Ecology of the Miskito Indians, Eastern Nicaragua.* New York: Seminar Press, 1973.

———. *The Unknown War: The Miskito Nation, Nicaragua and the United States.* New York: Freedom House, 1989.

Odell, P. R., and D. A. Preston. *Economies and Societies in Latin America: A Geographical Interpretation*. New York: Wiley, 1978.

Padilla, Washington. *La Iglesia y los Dioses Modernos: Historia del Protestantismo en el Ecuador*. Quito: Corporación Editorial Nacional, 1989.

Palomino, Cebero. *El Instituto Lingüístico de Verano: Un Fraude*. Lima: Ediciones Rupa Rupa, 1980.

Pareja y Diez-Canseco, Alfredo. *La Hoguera Bárbara: Vida de Eloy Alfaro*. Mexico City: Compañnía General Editora, 1944.

Phelan, John Leddy. *The Kingdom of Quito in the Seventeenth Century*. Madison: University of Wisconsin Press, 1967.

Pike, Frederick B., ed. *The Conflict between Church and State in Latin America*. New York: Knopf, 1964.

Prescott, William H. *History of the Conquest of Mexico and History of the Conquest of Peru*. New York, 1931.

Prien, Hans-Jurgen. *Historia del Cristianismo en América Latina*. Salamanca, Spain: Ediciones Sígueme, 1985.

Proaño, Leonidas E. *Concientización, Evangelización, Política*. Salamanca, Spain: Ediciones Sígueme, 1987.

Quarraciono, Antonio, ed. *Sectas en América Latina*. Guatemala City: Consejo Episcopal Latinoamericana, 1981.

Read, William R., Victor M. Monterroso, and Harmon A. Johnson. *Latin American Church Growth*. Grand Rapids, Mich.: William B. Eerdmans, 1969.

Reyes, Oscar Efren. *Breve Historia General del Ecuador*. 15th edition. 3 vols. Quito: Ministerio de Gobierno, 1988.

Rivadeneira, Francisco Miranda. *Crisis en las Misiones y Mutilación Territorial*. Quito: Banco Central del Ecuador, 1986.

———. *García Moreno y la Compañía de Jesús*. Quito: Imprenta y Ediciones Lexigrama, 1976.

Ruiz, Jaime N. *Del Vaticano al Ecuador*. Quito: Fundación "Luis Chusig," 1984.

Schodt, David W. *Ecuador: An Andean Enigma*. Boulder, Colo.: Westview, 1987.

Silletta, Alfredo. *Multinacionales de la Fe: Religión, Sectas, e Iglesia Electrónica*. Buenos Aires: Editorial Contrapunto, 1988.

———. *Las Sectas Invaden la Argentina*. Buenos Aires: Editorial Contrapunto, 1987.

———. *La Secta Moon: Como Destruir la Democracia*. Buenos Aires: El Cid Editor, 1985.

Spindler, Frank MacDonald. *Nineteenth-Century Ecuador: A Historical Introduction*. Fairfax, Va.: George Mason University Press, 1987.

———, and Nancy Cook Brooks. *Selections from Juan Montalvo Translated from the Spanish*. Tempe, Ariz.: Center for Latin American Studies, Arizona State University, 1984.

Stern, Steve J. *Peru's Indian Peoples and the Challenge of Spanish Conquest: Huamanga to 1640.* Madison: University of Wisconsin Press, 1982.

Stoll, David L. *Fishers of Men or Founders of Empire? The Wycliffe Bible Translators in Latin America.* London: Zed Press, 1982.

———. *Is Latin America Turning Protestant?* Berkeley & Los Angeles: University of California Press, 1990.

Suárez, Luis, and Mario García. *Extinción de Animales en el Ecuador.* Quito: Fundación Natura, 1986.

Synan, Vinson. *The Holiness-Pentecostal Movement in the United States.* Grand Rapids, Mich.: William B. Eerdmans, 1971.

Townsend, W. Cameron. *Lázaro Cárdenas, Mexican Democrat.* Ann Arbor, Mich.: George Wahr, 1952.

———. *They Found a Common Language.* New York: Harper & Row, 1971.

Trujillo, Jorge. *Los Obscuros Designios del Dios y del Imperio: El Instituto Lingüístico de Verano en el Ecuador.* Quito: Centro de Investigaciones y Estudios Socioeconómicos, 1981.

Villacis Teran, Enrique María. *Historia de la Evangelización del Quito.* Quito: Gráficas Iberia 1987.

Whitten, Norman E., Jr., ed. *Cultural Transformations and Ethnicity in Modern Ecuador.* Urbana: University of Illinois Press, 1981.

———. *Sacha Runa: Ethnicity and Adaptation of Ecuadorian Jungle Quichua.* Chicago: University of Illinois Press, 1976.

———. *Sicuanga Runa: The Other Side of Development in Amazonian Ecuador.* Chicago: University of Illinois Press, 1985.

Zinn, Howard. *A People's History of the United States.* New York: Harper & Row, 1980.

Encyclopedias, Dictionaries, Handbooks, and Reports

Barrett, David., ed., *World Christian Encyclopedia.* Cambridge: Oxford University Press, 1982.

———. Gerald H. Anderson, and John Goodwin, eds. *Concise Dictionary of the Christian World Mission.* New York: Abingdon Press, 1971.

Burgess, Stanley M., and Gary B. McGee, eds. *Dictionary of Pentecostal and Charismatic Movements.* Grand Rapids, Mich.: Zondervan, 1988.

"Ecuador: Oil Up for Grabs," *NACLA's Latin America and Empire Report* 9, no. 8 (November 1975): 1–38.

Encyclopedia of Missions: Descriptive, Historical, Biographical, Statistical. 2d edition. New York: Funk & Wagnals, 1904.

Erickson, Edwin E., et al. *Area Handbook for Ecuador.* Washington, D.C.: U.S. Government Printing Office, 1966.

Bibliography

Goddard, Burton L., ed. *The Encyclopedia of Modern Christian Missions.* Camden, N.J.: Thomas Nelson, 1967.

Historia de Las Luchas Populares: De La Revolución Liberal a la Masacre de 1922. Quito: Centro de Estudios y Difusión Social, 1982.

Rockefeller, Nelson A. *The Rockefeller Report on the Americas.* New York Times Edition. Chicago: Quadrangle Books, 1969.

Seventh-Day Adventist Encyclopedia. Rev. edition. Washington, D.C.: Review and Herald, 1976.

Visión Mundial en el Ecuador. Serie Educacion Popular, Cuaderno no. 2. Quito: CEPLAES, 1984.

Visión Mundial: Evaluación y Seguimiento en Algunas Comunidades de la Sierra Ecuatoriana. Quito: Centro de Planificación y Estudios Sociales, 1984.

Wilson, Samuel, and John Siewart. *Mission Handbook.* 13th edition. Monrovia, Calif.: Missions Advanced Research and Communication Center, 1986.

Articles

Ashley, John M. "African Palm Oil: Impacts in Equador's Amazon." *Cultural Survival Quarterly* 11 (1986): 55–60.

Assman, Hugo. "Iglesia Electrónica y Marketing." *Chasqui* 21 (January-March 1987): 6–13.

———. "La Iglesia Electrónica en América Latina." *Chasqui* 22 (April-May 1987): 48–57.

Bamat, Tomás. "Ecuador: Bishops Lament Recent Election's Demagogic Use of Religious Language." *Latinamerica Press,* June 30, 1988, 5.

Bledsoe, Jerry. "Saint." *Esquire* (July 1972): 127–54.

Burnett, Virginia Garrard. "Protestantism in Latin America." *Latin American Research Review* 27, no. 1 (1992): 218–30.

———. "Protestantism in Rural Guatemala, 1872–1954." *Latin American Research Review* 24, no. 2 (1989): 127–42.

Chordas, Thomas J., "Catholic Pentecostalism: A New Word in the New World." In *Perspectives on Pentecostalism: Case Studies from the Caribbean and Latin America,* edited by Stephen D. Glazier, 143–75. Washington, D.C.: University Press of America, 1980.

Conaghan, Catherine M. "Ecuador Swings toward Social Democracy." *Current History* (March 1989): 137.

Corral, Victor. "We Want to Build an Indigenous Church." Interview by Leslie Wirpsa. *Latinamerica Press,* November 15, 1990, 5.

Council of CONFENIAE. "CONFENIAE—An Indian Confederation in Eastern Ecuador." *Cultural Survival Quarterly* (December 1984): 18–19.

Diamond, Sara. "Holy Warriors." *NACLA Report on the Americas* 22, no. 5 (September-October 1988): 28–37.

Bibliography

Domínguez, Enrique, and Deborah Huntington. "The Salvation Brokers: Conservative Evangelicals in Central America." *NACLA Report on the Americas* 17, no. 1 (January-February 1984): 2–36.

Draper, Elizabeth Bobsy. "Minga in Ecuador." *Z Magazine* (December 1990): 33–38.

Espinosa, Simón. "Elsie Monge: La Mujer de los Derechos." *Revista Diners* (July 1988): 54–59.

Field, Les. "Ecuador's Pan-Indian Uprising." *NACLA Report on the Americas* 25, no. 3 (December 1991): 39–44.

Galeano, Eduardo. "1492 Reconsidered." *Latinamerica Press*, January 28, 1988, 3.

Graham, Billy, with Philip Yancey. "Unforgettable Uncle Cam." *Reader's Digest*, September, 1986. Reprint, Wycliffe Bible Translators, 1986.

Gutiérrez, Gustavo. "Liberation Theology: Gutiérrez Reflects on 20 Years Urging Option For the Poor." Interview by Mario Campos. *Latinamerica Press*, July 14, 1988, 5.

———. "¿Quién es el Indio? La Perspectiva Teologica de Bartolomé de las Casas." *Iglesia, Pueblos y Culturas* 9 (April-June 1988): 5–22.

Kemper, Vicki, with Larry Engel. "A Prophet's Vision and Grace: The Life of Dom Helder Camara." *Sojourners* (December 1987): 12–15.

Jijón, Carolina. "Palma Africana Deterioro Ecologico o Social?" *Colibrí* 1 (September-December 1986): 37–44.

Lernoux, Penny. "Casting Out the People's Church." *Nation*, August 27-September 3, 1988, 161–65.

MacDonald, Theodore, Jr. "Shuar Children: Bilingual-Bicultural Education." *Cultural Survival Quarterly* 10, no. 4 (1986): 18–20.

Maust, John. "Jungle Identity Crisis: Auca Country Revisited." *Christianity Today* (January 1980): 48–50.

McCoy, John. "Robbing Peter to Pay Paul: The Evangelical Tide." *Latinamerica Press*, June 29, 1989, 2.

McIntyre, Loren. "Ecuador: Low and Lofty Astride the Equator." *National Geographic* (February 1968): 259–98.

"Miguez Bonino: Faith Must Yield Concern, Responsibility, and Political Action." Interview by Luis Gallegos. *Latinamerica Press*, May 28, 1987, 5.

Pereira V., José L. "Multilinguismo y Educación Bilingue en el Oriente Ecuatoriano." *Cultura* 2, no. 4 (1979): 241–55.

Pineo, Ronn F. "Misery and Death in the Pearl of the Pacific: Health Care in Guayaquil, Ecuador, 1870–1925." *Hispanic American Historical Review* 70, no. 4 (November 1990): 621–22.

Ramos, Moises. "Clamor a Dios: Entre la Protesta Legítima y la Inquisición Religiosa (parte 1)." *Claridad*, September 16–22, 1988.

Rose, Susan D., and Steve Brouwer. "The Export of Fundamentalist Americanism: U.S. Evangelical Education in Guatemala." *Latin American Perspectives* 17, no. 4 (Fall 1989): 42–56.

Schwartz, Norman. "Ethnicity, Politics, and Cultural Survival." *Cultural Survival Quarterly* 7, no. 1 (Spring 1983): 20–22.

Stoll, David. "Antropólogos versus evangelistas: Las controversias del Instituto de Verano y las nuevas tribus misioneras en América Latina." *Iglesia, Pueblos y Culturas* 8 (January–March 1988): 149–98.

———. "Guatemala Elects a Born-Again President." *Christian Century* 108, no. 6 (February 1991): 189–90.

———. "Guatemala: Why They Like Ríos Montt." *NACLA* 24, no. 4 (December–January 1990–91): 4–7.

———. "The New Jerusalem of the Americas?" *Cultural Survival Quarterly* 7, no. 1 (Spring 1983): 28–31.

Sullivan-Davis, George. "Chile: Evangelicals Step Up Criticism of Pinochet Regime." *Latinamerica Press*, June 4, 1987, 6–7.

Tapia, Andrés. "Viva los evangélicos!" *Christianity Today*, October 28, 1991, 17–22.

Weisman, Alan, and Sandy Tolan. "Out of Time." *Audubon* (November–December 1992): 68–73.

Wille, Chris. "The World According to Nietschmann," *Audubon* (November–December 1992): 73.

Wright, Jaime. "In Brazil, SERPAJ Focuses on Land Rights of Indigenous." Interview by Dafne Plou. *Latinamerica Press*, April 20, 1989, 6.

Dissertations, Theses, and Unpublished Papers

Burnett, Virginia Garrard. "A History of Protestantism in Guatemala." Ph.D diss., Tulane University, 1986.

Gangotena, Francisco, "Diversity, an Indian Strategy for Survival, in Crisis." Paper presented at the 40th Annual Conference on Latin America, Andean Crisis: Traditional Dilemmas and Contemporary Challenges, the Center for Latin American Studies, University of Florida, Gainesville, Fla., March 26–29, 1991.

Kuhl, Paul E. "Protestant Missionary Activity and Freedom of Religion in Ecuador, Peru, and Bolivia." Ph.D diss., Southern Illinois University, 1982.

Parr, Jaye Stover. "A Study of a Religious Speech Variety." Tesis de Licenciatura, Pontificia Universidad Católica del Ecuador, 1977.

Reed, Jerold Franklyn. "A Componential Analysis of the Ecuadorian Protestant Church." Ph.D diss., Fuller Theological Seminary, School of World Missions, 1974.

Bibliography

Stavenhagen, Rudolpho. "Los Derechos Indígenas: Nuevo Enfoque del Sistema Internacional." Paper presented at the 15th International Congress of the Latin American Studies Association, Miami, Fla., December 4–6, 1989.

Videorecordings

Columbus Didn't Discover Us. Produced by Robbie Leppzer. Directed by Wil Echevarria, Erik van Lennap, and Pedro Rivera. 24 min., 1992. Turning Tide Productions.

El Levantimiento Indígena. Produced and directed by CEDIS-CONAIE. 30 min., 1990.

INDEX